A Standing Ovation
for
THE LAST LAUGH

"Fascinating . . . from Milton Berle and pie-in-the-face to the legendary Lord Buckley to the spaced-out antics of Cheech and Chong . . . jokes . . . glimpses into not-so-private lives . . . material . . . about their work, about agents, rooms, other comics, how they get their routines, how they steal them . . . Berger is a man who thoroughly understands his subject!"
—*Chicago Tribune Book World*

"The first genuinely realistic book I can recall which takes the reader behind the scenes in nightclubs, saloons, tank-towns, and one-night stands of all kinds to demonstrate what it takes for a stand-up comic to make it into the big time . . . more stand-up routines . . . more jokes in these pages than you have heard in years!"
—*John Barkham Reviews*

"For those who like a laugh, this book is loaded with them!"
—*San Francisco Examiner*

and the cheers
go on...

and on ...

"Undoubtedly the best book yet written about the atmosphere and dynamics of stand-up comedy; the world's most peculiar profession. It is a virtual chronological history of the art. Phil Berger is a terrifically talented writer, though not that exciting in person."

—*Robert Klein*

"Most authors, even some good ones, miss by a mile when they try to recreate the world of the professional comedian. Not Phil Berger. His book is utterly authentic, a fascinating account of what life is like in an important area of American humor."

—*Steve Allen*

"A searing ride into a nether world like the fun house crazy mirror room . . . hugely interesting . . . for anyone who has ever laughed at any comic on any platform."

—*Los Angeles Times*

By Phil Berger

THE LAST LAUGH
MIRACLE ON 33RD STREET

The
Last Laugh

The World of the
Stand-Up Comics

BY PHIL BERGER

BALLANTINE BOOKS • NEW YORK

ACKNOWLEDGMENTS

Albert Brooks' "Famous School for Comedians" is reprinted by permission of *Esquire*. © 1971 by Esquire Inc.

Lord Buckley comedy material is used by permission of James T. Dickson.

Dick Davy comedy routines by permission of Columbia Records.

Will Jordan comedy routines by special permission of Suellen Productions. All rights reserved.

Portions of material on Dick Gregory are from the book *Nigger: An Autobiography* by Dick Gregory with Robert Lipsyte. Copyright © 1964 by Dick Gregory Enterprises, Inc. Published by E. P. Dutton and Co., Inc., and used with their permission.

Lenny Bruce comedy routines by permission of the estate of Lenny Bruce.

Richard Pryor comedy routines from the album *Craps*. By permission of Laff Records.

Special thanks to Ms. Alice Reville.

Library of Congress Catalog Card Number: 74-20690

ISBN 0-345-24856-2-195

This edition published by arrangement with William Morrow & Company, Inc.

Printed in Canada.

First Ballantine Books Edition: March, 1976

TO LESLIE
with love

The Last Laugh

Part One

Words came in nervous pats for the agent Friar. When he did business, it sounded like espionage or infidelity.

With him, something was always going. In Sunnyside, the Bronx, Brooklyn, New York, New Jersey and Staten Island, the bars all ran amateur nights. Friar got fifty dollars each joint he put the talent in.

In 1944 he sent the comic Keefe, a thin sharp-featured kid of fifteen with a bogus ID for places that disdained ordinary amusements. As Friar liked to say, "Frank Sinatra, Frank Sinatra, n-never won a prize. He never won a prize," a notion he was not above repeating.

It was that way with the agent—the same cautions and bad jokes and stammered regrets. "You d-d-disappointed me, you d-d-disappointed me," he was always saying to no-shows. In truth, he had acts to spare, many of the sort to excite Mr. Ripley's interest.

Like Suicide Kelly, who jumped headfirst from chairs stacked to the ceiling and got up with vertebrae somehow still intact. Or the pretend Cagney, who strutted through doors, thumbs hooked under his belt, asking,

"Aww-ull raaaght, when do I get on?" He was always in black and white outfits, face powdered to the precise pallor Cagney had before the world went to technicolor. His act was a number of death scenes as Cagney.

They were very big in places like the Horseshoe, the Merry-Go-Round, the Lighthouse, working-class bars that liked the odd spark in their entertainment. To a point, of course. There were some Friar sent that got the dander up.

Madame Butterfly was one. She was a fat old woman with a red cosmetic dot on each cheek that made her look more like a clown than the coloratura she pretended to be. Against a nightly ruckus, she did her double-talk opera, tuneless trills of the moment's origin. She was never flustered by the jeers. Neither was the grandiose figure in tux and homburg and walking stick who did an eye-rolling Jolson as an escapee from an asylum might.

Even Madame Pumpernickel, who accompanied other acts on the piano, was a bit daft. She had the gossamer air of Blanche DuBois and a farfetched sense of future. She'd eye the trade tabloids up and down, as if tomorrow she'd be in Carnegie Hall, not the Sunnyside Cafe. She was one of a cast of thousands in those war years. There were whistlers, fire eaters, stand-up crazies of every denomination. The last vaudeville, it was.

Friar booked it out of the old Roseland Building in an office whose walls were covered with stock photos of entertainers, a gallery of bad acts. One shot showed him as a boy soprano. That was long ago. For now, he sat at back of the room, set off by wood railing. On the wall was a phone. When it rang, he would jog the receiver so it'd fly off the hook. Grabbing it one-handed, he'd croak into the mouthpiece, "You're looking good," a line he'd heard when he was back in knickers.

There were prizes in the "amateurs"—five dollars, three dollars and two dollars—and they were fought for with elaborate strategies. The chances of a kid like Keefe winning were slim. It took more than an act in the amateurs. Blarney and bazazz were essential.

A past master of it was Pop Kennedy, *aka* Piccolo Pete. He was a short codger with thinning hair and a mousey aspect that reminded movie buffs in the bars of the actor Charley Grapewin. Old Pop was always in a beat-up World War I uniform, the fat wife with him in her babushka. She sat in a corner while he went around the bar with a story he told in a whimper. *My-wife-and-I . . . no-place-to-stay . . . I'm-a-veteran.*

And then Pop was up there in the uniform with the ocarina he played, blowing star-spangled beauties out of it—"Semper Fidelis"/"Anchors Aweigh"/"The Caissons Go Rolling Along." He took no chances either. If it figured to be close, he'd work a blood capsule up a nostril and give a whack so he'd be hemorrhaging at the "God Bless America" finish. A real heavyweight, Pop—and one of Friar's regulars.

With good attendance, Keefe soon was too. For Friar did not like to be d-d-disappointed. A regular got subway fare, typewritten directions and a guaranteed two dollars for each bar he played. He also got to hear what was on Friar's mind. "Kiss-me-I'm-coming, fuck-me-I'm-going," he liked to say, squinting out of a face that was the image of Harry Truman.

Sometimes, Friar turned up in the bars to introduce his acts and queue them up after for the crowd's decision. There were nights the outcome was disputed, usually when locals thought their choice was "jobbed." Those nights had a pattern. A cry of "fix" was raised and then the furniture. Keefe never was around at the end, the conclusion forgone for him. He'd move on to another bar to make the guarantee.

Two, three places he did in a night, a boney quiet kid who was transformed up on the boards. He'd get a glow as he did a fast echo of bigtime mimics like Arthur Blake and Larry Storch, moving with the quick of a dancer. It was secret heart: around the neighborhood, no one heard boo from Keefe. The first time his parents saw him perform, they conceded they hadn't a clue.

The amateurs were not really for comics, though. Keefe, Will Jordan, Lenny Bruce, Bobby Shields all came through there, none of them ever getting the giggles the irregulars did. It took a certain fine lunacy to cut it in the saloons, a spirit so misbegotten as to be useless anywhere else. An act was made for the beer pits the way Christians were for the lions.

Not the bars but Broadway was where a comic wanted to be in the last days of World War II.

And some of them were—in presentation houses that ran stage shows with a feature film. They were movie theaters, each one committed to the films of a particular studio. The Roxy played 20th Century-Fox's, the Strand had Warner Bros.', the Capitol MGM's.

The comic was always part of the live bill. Indeed on V-E day/1945, Dean Murphy was at the Paramount in Times Square, across the street from where a replica of Lady Liberty soared high above the sidewalk. Murphy was another of the impressionists the kid Keefe was raised on, smiley jacks that trotted out Bogey and Walter Brennan and Cooper and Grant as predictably as the priest did Amen.

For GIs in that city that day, the uniform was a free pass to get into the Polo Ground ("use entrance on Eighth Avenue and 159th St.") to see the Giants and the Reds baseball teams. Those who wanted to stay downtown could have a few laughs for nothing too. At the Roxy on 7th Avenue and 50th Street was Jerry Lester (the movie was *Diamond Horseshoe* with Betty Grable). Willie Howard was at the Capitol on Broadway at 51st (*The Clock* starred Judy Garland and Robert Walker).

If civilian Keefe was there in the days after the war, it was as a paying customer, one who'd get his money's worth by seeing the same show more than once—always to hear the comics. Morey Amsterdam would be up there, or Jan Murray, some pro with the quick delivery and the timing to whisk the laughs out of a line. On nights when the comic was right it was one gag on top of another, the laughs like a rolling ball of sound.

Most of them worked fast, and had to. It was the quicktoc that made so-so gags run. Even the name

4

guys did it. Youngman at the Roxy would walk out, wring a few bars from the fiddle and

> My wife has an even disposition—miserable all the time.

> A friend in Texas was so rich he bought his dog a boy to play with.

bup bup bup.

Henny did to the performing minute what Ringling Brothers did to the coupe. He got it full up. In random fashion the jokes came. No comedic paragraphs for Youngman. He just hit the joke and waited, moving into the breach to crank the next, treating them all with a curious neutrality.

But the thing moved. He knew the secrets of his own comic rattle and made it work. What jokes he had, he added to all the time. *King of the one-liners* was what his answering service would say years later for openers.

What Youngman was to the quick-hit straight delivery, Milton Berle was to the mugging antic way. Unlike a "line comic," Berle offered wrinkles beyond what a gag could. There were jokes, but with Berle it was often the outsized expression (the "take") he got the laugh on. It was buffoonery that risked an occasional gibe. Berle's act encouraged it. Here and there were gags so bad they had to fail. And when they did, Milton was ready.

> You heckled me twenty years ago. I never forget a suit.

He was resourceful in tight corners. If a line got but a single laugh, he'd quip, "Thanks, Mom," and add when that got a response from the other side of the room, "Oh, you moved," with timing no Benrus could keep.

It was gag-premise comedy, a style built on one-liners, short jokes delivered in punchy salvos. It was the way Berle and most of the comics worked. What Milton also shared with them was some of the same material. In the cities he played, he often looked in on other comics, sometimes, it was said, in the company of a girl versed in shorthand. It kept him in material.

Berle was notorious for stealing acts. Fred Allen once sent him a bundle of pictures and this note— "You're using my act. You might as well put my photographs in the lobby too." If Milton was, as he was called, "The Thief of Badgag," he was not the first. The gag heist was as old as vaudeville. In those times, magazines like *Whiz Bang* and *College Humor* were to the comic what the "pony" is to the student of Latin.

Of the comics that took from the man, few considered the source, and then only in phrases like "as that merry wag so and so says." More often they did not, though Berle was buccaneer enough to do what comics will—make a joke of it.

> This is not my act. I have no act. I have everybody's act,

he'd quip with a sly bucked grin when a joked failed. At twenty-three thousand dollars for seven days at the Roxy, it made the crime pay.

For a Berle, it was beside the point. A gag was a neuter until tutored by Milton's particular comedic "english," rationale in keeping with a comic ego that could covet the very gags it purported not to need.

From where Keefe sat, hegelian twists ran poor second to the curves the boys put to their lines. If the jokes were often lame, they were never so bad a Morey or Milton was at a loss. Not with the beat they put on them. It did to gags what the hare did to the hound—made the muthas run.

No such luck in Friar's case.
He'd say,

> Half a brain more, you'd be a half wit

and if Keefe laughed, it was in looking back. By 1946, he was.

Out of the amateurs, he was into wages, making them in the very places Friar booked. With the war over, some of them had regular shows on weekends.

Comics just out of the armed services came back to a lively scene. The late '40s and early '50s were boom times for night spots. In Brooklyn alone were so many clubs a guy could work all year and never have to leave the borough. The Jinx. The Bali. The Pink Elephant. Any number of quasi-Copas with fake palm trees and mirrored walls and maître d's who kept the help moving with the puckered sounds of street romeos.

In those places, a comic wore a tux and max-factored smile and worked to the dress-up trade with boozing jokes like

HE: I say, Grace. Are you having another?

SHE: Oh no, it's just the way me coat hangs

—nothing rougher if he wanted to stay on the good side of the bosses, often pinky-ringed galentos who kept a sharp eye on the chorus line and the coffers. Their comics they wanted funny, cut-rate (one hundred and fifty dollars a week) and clean. If one did a line considered too "blue," he was told not to, by fellows who inspired easy listening.

The strip joints were not nearly so fussy over the king's English. In there, a joke like

Was at a hotel. Called the clerk. Told him I had a leak in the sink. He said, "Go ahead, the customer's always right"

would do—if a comic could get a word in. It was hard to. Ladies were what customers were buying. It led to a variety of approaches. Comics came out with toilet seats around their necks and did the lines out of them. Or they made friends with the patrons while the strips were on, and worked their names into the gags. Others just talked into the din and scrammed. And nobody much cared.

There were comics who worked the strips for what

they could take out in flesh. The money was never great—one hundred and twenty-five dollars or so a week—but the wages of sin held their horny souls together. Others would have booked the infernal circles as soon as do another strip.

In the chaos, comics could say anything—and did. Keefe's introductions—

> Here she is, direct from prom night at Dracula's castle, a young lady who studied dancing with St. Vitus

—were often the only words an audience listened to. Strippers did too, and once in a while they didn't like what they heard. It happened to a comic named Bobby Baxter, a quick-talking fellow with a torso built up with weights, brute strength that was no edge against a tiny stripper who took exception to what he said about her. "I'm not cute and effervescent!" she snapped. "I'm beautiful and don't you forget that, Mister!"

Baxter, who'd been around strippers on and off since the late '30s, was used to their moods. He'd had girls with a gripe against him show themselves off-stage too. "Show you their jugs," he said, "and the more you ignored them, the more they'd show you. They'd drop something and pick it up and show you their ass."

If comics got shown a hard time in the Catskills, it was never quite so fancy. In the '30s, this resort area, ninety miles from Manhattan, prospered, aided by its overworked comics, the one diversion the tightfisted innkeepers sprang for. They were East European Jews, ex-farmers who insisted on a full dollar's return.

They got it vit de comics, who worked long hours under the bosses' watchful eyes. *Nu? Don't sit around. Be funny.* Comics that tried to keep Broadway hours found the owners at their door early in the A.M. with a glass orange juice in hand.

The Catskill comic went all day long. He jumped fully-clothed into swimming pools, kibbitzed card games, led social nights and occasionally did jokes.

Toomling, it was called—from the English "tumulting."

For this, he got two hundred and fifty dollars for the summer, sweatshop wages that kept old pros from working there. Mostly they were comic beginners, New York kids with the cardboard suitcase and the proverbial song in their heart. They arrived with names like Aaron Chwatt, Murray Janofsky, Philip Feldman, Joseph Abramowitz, and when next heard from they'd be Red Buttons, Jan Murray, Phil Foster and Joey Adams. The Catskills of the '30s were a training ground. After World War II, though, many of the places there booked comics for one-nighters or weekends rather than the whole season.

The pay varied. In the same Catskills were posh resorts like Grossinger's and the Nevele, and budget-minded bungalow colonies called *kuchalanes,* meaning roughly, "cook for yourself." The fun came when the comic was mismatched to the place. One time Jack E. Leonard, the insult comedian, was sent to a *kuchalane* where mostly old Orthodox Jews went. Leonard came out, saw an audience of yarmulke-clad elders and quipped,

Welcome Legionnaires.

In the late '40s, agents like Charlie Rapp used comics by the dozens on summer weekends in the Catskills. They went in carloads to defray expenses, divvying gas money on the trip up Route 17. Some of them began to do it regularly. Comics like Jack Roy, Georgie Starr and Buddy Hackett would stop by the Brooklyn flat Lenny Bruce shared with his mom, Sally Marr. Sally, a working comic herself, knew the times to be had on Catskill weekends when the girls came up. She'd see them off with an admonition—"Make sure my kid gets some!"

Working around, guys got to know each other.

In the case of Bruce's crowd, they had a nodding acquaintance going back.

Georgie Starr met Lenny in the Bali on Ocean Parkway just after the war. Bruce was a bright-eyed kid with the butterfat face, soft lines not yet turned angular. Then, and for some time after, he was the kind of man words like "sweet" and "warm" were applied to—by comics not given to using them.

A note of wry mockery was their custom. Starr, some twenty-five years later, would write his sons while on a European holiday:

> Camp is sure great. I'm not even home-sick. My counselors are great guys. Tomorrow I take my Dolphin test. . . .

the echo of their correspondence to him in years past.

Back then, though, Starr had the boy-face with pomaded rows of curls that rose up into a wave—a look of the lost. In fact, when Jack Roy saw him for the first time sitting outside an agent's office, he thought, "What is this *nebicle?*"

The sight so moved Roy, he took him by the office of Sam Gold, an agent specializing in low-priced gigs. Gold was legend for the tight operation he ran. Each morning, arriving at his office, he'd order a Danish and beat the price of coffee by heating up his own on the electric coil he kept there. As he himself confessed to comics, "I can't help being cheap."

And he couldn't. He took his end, however small. He cut in for spare change other agents might not. Where Gold's boys went, adversity followed. Acts often were fired without wages, leaving them stranded in distant places with only Sam to bail them out. He was good as Godot to wait for.

Jack Roy was no stranger to the clubs and strip joints Gold booked. He'd worked them for years, a big man with a clipped street-tough sound and a hounded appearance. He was Jack-be-nimble at doubt and woe, a master at its bilious rhetoric. Eh-this. Eh-that. Nada dada it was, the pessimist's dark freight. Roy was its living look: an eye that had the worried premonition in it and hyperactive sweat glands that made the visage a theater.

Afternoons he wound up at Georgie Starr's apartment in Brooklyn, he was in the comic minority. Where Starr or Lenny Bruce had the sprightly air that acts did then, Roy did not. When he got up to amuse the crew in that flat on Avenue N and East 5th Street, it was with every fidget showing. He'd hanky down a brow, fuss with his collar. He had the nerve ends of a hack comic. Years later, he'd use the chaotic metabolism to mobilize his comic, one he renamed Rodney Dangerfield. But on '40s afternoons in Brooklyn, it betrayed Jack Roy. As a comic, he didn't look the part.

The one in that bunch that did was Buddy Hackett, a roly-poly with an elfin face and a squeegeed sound. In his mouth, New Yaawk tawk had a merry ring. With Hackett, it was as if he'd walked off the drawing board at Looney Tunes studios. He was to the manner born.

In Starr's place, or other walk-ups in Brooklyn, the lot of them took turns being funny, and were invariably upstaged by the nonpro among them, a tall hot-eyed kid who, having broken up corner boys at a candy store on Bay Parkway and 86th Street, graduated to the lounge at Brooklyn College. Joe Ancis was his name.

Here was a wound-tight school-bright crash talker, who used words in blasts of wild and surreal fancy to introduce the id to the Ancis. His far-out comic configurations were of a submerged soul he dared not try, out of fear drummed in him by love oppressed, the beware weird Jewish kind. It made his hot flashes S-O-S from the deep. It was ouch that crouched back of the routines he did.

When Ancis transferred from Brooklyn College to St. John's, he began to pop in at Broadway hangouts of comics. He'd come around to the Brill Building with Whitey Martin, who did a pantomime record act and later was an agent. Through Martin, Ancis met other comics, and soon he was doing his stuff for them.

It wasn't what they were used to. Ancis' material came not from easy gag formulas but from the boiler room. It was what de Sade might have done had he knocked around Bensonhurst, a strange three-reeler of Japanese cunnilinguists, malarial marines, nympho nurses, stereotypical Jews, gay gym teachers—routines that wound to bizarre conclusions, many of which he created on the fly. None of the others worked in so original a way.

When Bruce won the "Talent Scouts" on TV and a week's work at the Strand, it was with impressions he did as a Bavarian emcee—"Aw-right Louie, drop the oogen ge shplugen/ein shvei you dirty rat." He worked in a new straw hat and was so hard up for minutes he stooped to jokes Joe Miller would have passed on.

Starr was, by his own admission, an eclectic creation. He had the "Babalu" chunk Alan King did and the "Melody in 4-F" that was Danny Kaye's. A little this. A little that. He got by.

Hackett was not the comic who'd require an *Adults Only* sign when he'd work in Las Vegas in the '60s. Bawdy Buddy was spiritual light years away.

And Roy was—well—black Jack, a glum figure who missed the cheerio quality. What he had even then, though, was a knack for thinking up material. He'd be around Kellogg's Cafeteria on 49th Street, off 7th Avenue, just after the war, trying gags out on other comics. *Whaddaya think, man? Whaddaya think?* He had a bit where people applauded in ways that revealed their callings. The barber's was like the sharpening of a razor on a strap. The secretary's was with the fingers moving. The farmer's like milking a cow. *It's all right, Jack. All right.*

Ancis was not made for clubs. The Brill Building— any place there were comics/hipsters/wise guys around —was perfect. He couldn't have played to commercial audiences in the late '40s—the material was too outrageous. It had the twisted insignia of the man on it, a personal touch not often seen back then. The long, lean, dark-haired Ancis worked out of a head full up with fear and confusions.

Joe was raised in a home where watch-out was the word. "My whole scene," he said, "was a fantasy world. My parents were oppressive, dig? Both of them were the same two of the *zelba*, reinforcing each other. 'Don't eat chopped meat in restaurants.' That kind of thing. Friends of mine had the same kind of mother, but the father was a card player. Something like that, dig?"

Though he was always advising cronies to strike out on their own, Joe himself lived at home until he was thirty-five, taking his indoctrination with him whenever he strayed out of the neighborhood. Perils everywhere: mayonnaise jars/pool halls/*shicksas*.

Ancis' greatest fear was public toilets, no seat of which was good enough for his bottom. To those stools he brought a strategist's wit that would have done Clausewitz proud. He lined the seat with toilet tissue and then undressed to his shoes. Near naked, he crouched atop the seat like a great prehistoric bird.

It worked, except for the time he forgot to latch the door to the stall. On that day, another man happened by, opened the door and found Ancis looming obscenely. The poor bastard fled with a shout.

As a comic, it was Ancis who was the fugitive. "I couldn't," he said, "blow in front of just anybody." Even when told he was the funniest cat around, he sensed he was a limited edition. A parlor dynamo. He lacked—and knew it—the shine-on to stand among imperfect strangers, and make them laugh. It took resiliency his upbringing denied him. It was why years later, when Ancis heard his parents lurked around corners to see his kids made it home safely from school, he warned them off.

Only in places where he had familiar faces was Ancis right. But at those times he could, as he put it, "cripple the motherfuckers." The sentences came with a mad mix of alliteration, Yiddishisms, fantasies, word pictures and erudition, a cargo that made new rhymes and rhythms. In source and sorcery, Ancis—a B.B.A. in accounting—was an original.

There were other guys like Ancis around, street-corner wits who worked best around comics.

They'd come by Hanson's, a luncheonette in the same building—1650 Broadway—where many of the agents had offices.

It was a hangout not only for comics and entertainers but for fringe wisecrackers too. Ancis was there. So were jokers whose idea of laughs was more low-brow than his.

Izzy the loan shark was that type. Izzy would see

13

some rube out-of-towner wander in off the avenue and before the startled fellow knew-what, Izzy was on his knees before him. Upside the guy's fly he'd jack a thumb that he'd suck on, just as the whipped cream he had in his mouth came spilling out.

With Izzy, it was dead-end. He hadn't the look or twinkle of a real comic. A guy who did was Jackie Lord, a kinetic hip-talking character. Lord would be around Hanson's, flicking his hair back from his forehead, saying in that nasal rabbity way—"Gheez, man. I gotta get with the jokes. Gotta get with the jokes."

At the tables at the rear of Hanson's, where comics encamped with quarter-minimum items, Jackie was always there, a thin little man whose words came out in bursts like telegram transmissions. He reminded Keefe of Edward Brophy, quintessential hang-around guy in the movies. Lord had a way about him that comics found funny. And he had a weird story or two of his own.

Bouncing into Hanson's, past drug and cosmetic concessions, on by the lunch counter and into the back, Jackie brimmed with the comic fevers. *Gheez, man. Gotta get with the jokes.* But invited onstage in clubs that comic cronies of his played, Lord proved no favorite with the customers. It kept him to his day job.

He sold siding, same racket Joe Ancis wound up in. It was perfect for the both of them. They could keep the late hours comics did and, with their glow-eyed persuasion, make a sum fast. With Jackie, it was always on the chance something would turn out for him. It didn't, back then. One time in an audition at a place Keefe was working, it ended with the chill silence again and Lord muttering comedic kaddish. "Oh, maaa-n, I'm in trouble. I'm in trouble. Hey, Keefe, I'm in trouble."

A whole other thing to be funny for real. In Hanson's, Lenny Gaines was another who'd leave them laughing. He was a whiz at table bits. Lenny would palm a salt shaker and invert it smack up against his face so it'd spill.

Nurse, nurse. Nosebleed,

he'd scream, and swing to another bit while he had them laughing. As a friend of pop singer Eddie Fisher, Gaines made the rounds of Hollywood parties, and was considered a funny guy out there.

Once he was down in New Orleans, hanging out in the French Quarter. At night, the bus tours rolled in, bringing schoolmarms to night spots like Stormy's Casino Royale, where a comic name of Frankie Ray was playing. Gaines liked to divert them, *Right this way, please,* take them through the Quarter's darker passages in circuitous routes that wound back to the bus.

A singer who caught Gaines in Hanson's figured he'd be perfect to team up with. Martin and Lewis were hot then, provoking imitators. Up to Canada the two of them trekked for a date. But when the spotlight went on, Lenny didn't. Deep freeze up north.

A comic who cut it both ways—on the cafe circuit and in Broadway hangouts—was Will Jordan. Of the working pros, he regularly cracked them up in Hanson's. Jordan was a mimic by trade, a man who could rearrange his tidy features to resemble others'. As just Will, he had the high forehead and wide grin that gave his face a slightly Oriental cast when he smiled.

In the early '50s in Hanson's it was not with his act he got laughs but with material he made up on the spot, riffs that packed the tables at the back of the place. Jordan got crowds—comics like Orson Bean, Milt Kamen, Jackie Gayle, Keefe. Even the guys who used a safety pin and wire to make free calls on Hanson's toll phones came over to have a listen. Will didn't disappoint them.

He was, in the comic term, a good "table man." Like Lenny Gaines, Jordan could work from the objects around him. He'd fold a napkin so it resembled the kind of quill the American colonials had. With it, he began a routine on the Declaration of Independence, using a glass of water for ink and salt for blotting powder. In his version, it ended with John Adams unable to find space to sign—after Mr. Hancock had put his signature to the document.

Anything within his reach Jordan put to use. He made the napkin dispenser a camera. It wasn't by accident that more than twenty years later Jerry Lewis as a TV talk show host enlivened a dull passage with an actress when he took a box of Kleenex and began "snapping" photos of her. Lewis had often stopped by Hanson's.

No shame in that. Part of the game was memory. All the great comics—and Lewis, in his way, was one—drew on their experiences. In his time, Joe Smith, of the vaudevillian Smith and Dale, had been in a stage production that called for him to fire a gun. One night he did and the weapon made no sound. In spite of it, the actor he aimed at "died" on the spot. Ad-libbed Smith: "He died of fright." Years later a similar situation arose and Smith used the line again.

In the '50s, Jordan rarely repeated himself. In a blink, he was out of one character and into another, most of them strange fellows whose normal appearance was a cover. Here he was the German language teacher as the closet Nazi.

> All right, student. Goot nabbin, oogen ge shplugen, ge shpliggen iggen, ga shplaigin haig n haig, haig & haig, students. Now, you'll be here for six months. We are going to learn a little German. Know what I mean? Ve're gonna really pick up on German. And we'll learn all the umlauts and all that jazz. Ve're gonna pick up on all this stuff, you know. Now students, there has been in the past very unhappy relationship between the students and the teacher. Students are afraid of their teachers. That shouldn't be that way. Let us be friendly, students. Friendly. In fact, during these next few months, I don't even want you to think of me as a teacher. I would rather you thought of me AS . . . YOURR LEADER! VE VILL MAKE AN ARMY AND . . .

There he was a rabbinical smoothie, turning words into polysyllabic taffy, stretching an "Is-roy-a-el" to its tensile limit and ending off-pulpit with the diction of Pitkin Avenue.

It was with malice aforethought Will worked, a change from the goody two-shoes that comics—including Jordan in clubs—did. When just winging it, he swung his weight around. The humor had a "bite" and a nice pathological lunacy. And it used the hipster idiom of jazz, often incongruously. For the comics at Hanson's, it had a radically different feel. They loved it.

Most of what Will tried was "inside" material, a spoof of show biz subjects that Jordan was sure the public didn't want to hear. He did it as a comic bulletin for the boys at Hanson's, content to leave the laughs there. For a living, he stuck to the standard mimicry.

At Hanson's, even the impressions varied. Will did the actor James Mason before others tried him. The timbre of Mason's speaking voice was similar to Jordan's, but Will made it serve for more than the Britisher. One instant, he was a wind-him-up Georgie Jessel with words on a reel-to-reel tape recorder implanted on his person. The next he was Sammy Davis and Paul Muni just after exchanging glass eyes. Years later he did Ralph Bellamy too—announcing the settlement of an actors strike in the voice of a stage character he'd played. As FDR, Bellamy concluded, "We have nothing to fe-ah . . . except David Merrick itself."

Occasionally, Jordan drew on his own experiences in the business. He told of the time he'd hired a fast-talking press agent at a hundred dollars a week to get the name "Will Jordan" around:

> So I go to him, a hundred dollars the first week. Nothing. Not even the Brooklyn *Eagle*. Forget about it. Zero. I said, "What happened?"

PRESS AGENT: They're talking about you, baby. They are talking about you.

And so it went. The hundred-dollar payment every week. No word of him anywhere. And the press agent's insistence they were talking about him.

> At the end of the fifth week, forget about it, right? That's it. Five hundred dollars. A life's savings. Nothing. I come in. I'm angry. I'm mortified. I'm embarrassed. I mean, I said, "What does this mean? My five hundred dollars. Nothing."

PRESS
AGENT: They're talking about—

JORDAN: They're talking about me? What are they saying?

PRESS   They're saying, "Whatever happened to
AGENT: Will . . . We don't hear about . . . "

With Will it always wound back to doing to stars with voice and a dash venom what David Levine later did to political figures. He made fun of them by pointed distortion. He had George DeWitt knit his own toupee. The Frankenstein monster came up from the table with a voice like Liberace's. Later, he was to have Sammy Davis and May Britt going over wedding plans, settling on smorgasbord and watermelon for the feed.

Comics crowded around Jordan at Hanson's. Some afternoons the commotion led Hans Hanson to shoo the bunch of them out of his place and into the B&G coffee shop next door. "Qvit hangin' around here. Vy do you hang around here? Qvit hangin' around," Hanson said, words that were bounced back at him. For with the comics in there, an impression of Hans was as requisite as one of Cagney.

Hanson was a Dane who'd suffer only countryman Victor Borge among the comics. Borge did an act in which the standard punctuations —!?/ were executed with sound equivalents, the model for which, it was rumored, was in an act back home. In Hanson's, Victor had the run of the place—and sometimes took change at the cash register.

The other comics, Hans could have done without. But chase one, another came in. And all the time foolin' around. "Qvit foolin' around, vil ya?" No way. Anything went within those four walls. Sometimes the phone rang and it was Sally Marr, Lenny's mom, calling the Hanson's crazy who fancied himself a crooner and was indulged in it by Bruce's crowd. The call was always from a place like "Honolulu" with an offer that required him to fly out at his own expense.

Bruce once managed to get him a job at a synagogue social. For laughs, a bunch of them turned out to cheer their man on. It ended with a premature last hurrah and all of them scurrying out of there with enraged congregants screaming Yiddish epithets after them.

There were other characters that came around. One was an entertainer who'd arrive with his dog and chat up the comics on the sidewalks outside the place. In the course of conversation, he'd say the name *Adolf Hitler*. At its mention, the dog would raise a leg and pee.

"The Doctor" was renowned too. He was a comic/emcee who carried a satchel with assorted erotic props. Joe Ancis referred to him as "the Olsen and Johnson of sex." The Doctor was always ready for it. Georgie Starr would be driving down Broadway with the Doctor and a lady in the backseat. He'd glance out the window a second, and next time he'd check the rearview mirror the couple was out of sight. *And I'd turn around . . . down on the floor sucking . . . right on the floor.*

The Doctor once was in Buffalo, New York, with Starr and another comic in a hotel room when he got the urge. With no girl there, he did what he had to. He asked Starr to lend him his pomade, and proceeded to whack off. Twenty minutes later, he wanted the pomade again. *Man, my pomade. It was expensive for those times. We were all poor.*

The satchel was what intrigued other comics. The Doctor was far in advance of his times, the sexually repressed '50s. The first time Starr saw it, Georgie was with a Spanish dancer he had very large eyes for. The Doc invited them by a Broadway hotel for a party.

Once there, he got things going. Out came the satchel. He had insulation he put around the door-jambs. There were extension cords and vibrators and dildoes and appurtenances to elongate the phallus.

Vrrrmmm. The vibrator hummed as the Doctor gave her his technological best. The Doctor used every trick in his bag. Jellies and flavored douches and mufflers to quiet the vibrators. Olsen and Johnson indeed. Starr found the laughter welling up. *It was hilarious. I had to go into the bathroom. I didn't want to blow the thing. I was laughing hysterically.*

Women and wages ran one-two with comics working their way up in the business in the '50s. It was an open market both ways. A comic named Lee Tully walked into a club in Montreal on a late afternoon to rehearse his music and found a waiter pointing to the bar. "Your girl's here," he said.

A quick glance to the bar—Tully saw a beauty sitting there. He idled by and greeted the girl, who wondered how long was he in town. Tully figured she was the singer on the bill and chatted amiably awhile. Then she asked where he was staying. And off they went.

When she got undressed and showered soon as they got to his room, Tully knew he was on to something. *And she didn't leave my room for three weeks.*

For guys who grew up horny in the '40s, the business was a revelation. It threw them into contact with (ooo-ooo-ooo) "fast women," the dream of every American male of that era. Strippers were often good that way. Bobby Baxter saw a comic balling one over a barrel while the boss upstairs shouted down it was show time. There was one stripper who'd screw comics and then wash and towel down assiduously after to keep her boyfriend from figuring. She told them he was on to her and, when she'd walk in, he'd kiss her and reach down to see if she was wet. Hello, boom, right to the snapper.

Occasionally comics who worked out of New York returned to the city with a girl in tow. "We called them road broads," said Georgie Starr, "and we'd talk a girl into coming back to New York. But once you got back to New York, you didn't want to support them, right? Money was tight and everything. Also, you're not going to just dump them out. It would be cruel, you know. So you'd have a girl to screw on the way home and we all used to leave them at a wild theatrical hotel years ago on Forty-sixth Street with Al the Baker.

"There are certain people in life . . . certain guys who the day they got laid it ruined their lives. They found out getting fucked is good and it ruins their whole fucking life. Ever know a guy like that? It's all they're into . . . well this guy Al was a little Jewish guy, sort of short arms, little beady eyes . . . very horny guy.

"What happened was his father left him a very successful bakery. But to bake you have to be up at like four or five in the morning to make the rolls and all. So we'd pull into town, say from Cleveland or someplace with a road broad, right? And take them over to Al the Baker's.

"He's very horny. He'd see us walking in with the girl. *Oooh, she's nice. Fix me up.* Those little short arms would try to touch the ass. And on the way, we'd tell her, 'Oh, we know a wonderful man who will take care of you. You can stay with him for a while.' And leave her with Al the Baker, right? The guy could never get up to go make the *chalehs*. So he blew the business. The bakery store went. All for sex. I mean, he'd fall madly in love with every girl we'd bring, madly in love. And he'd buy them clothes and take care of them. Of course, once they got on their feet and got money, they'd fly the coop. The man was a grotesque idiot, you know."

If comics went for the odd licks a Will Jordan or Joe Ancis did, they considered them impractical for cash gigs.

At the tables in Hanson's, they talked gags or stories to each other. That was what the agents were buying. Jokes jokes jokes, or record synchs (Jerry

Lewis started that way) or mimicry. The line there was, "When in trouble, do Cagney."

They did dirty for their own kicks.

> This girl comes in the stable. Guy sees her that's never been laid. "Wanna f-f-fuck her," he says.

> His friend says, "The trouble with you is you frighten women away. You don't know how to talk. You gotta romance, you gotta ease into it."

> He says, "Well, h-h-how do you do that?" Friend says, "Well, you gotta get in a conversation with her." Guy wants to know how.

> Friend says, "Well, go and paint one leg on the horse green and then when she comes in, she'll see that the horse's leg is green, she'll ask what happened to the horse. That way, you'll get into a conversation. And one thing leads to another."

> He paints the leg green and the girl comes in. She gets on the horse and she rides off. Goes back to his friend. Says, "I painted the leg green but n-n-nothing happened."

> Friend tells him to paint the other three legs green. So he paints the other three legs green. The next day, she comes in, she gets on the horse and she rides off. Goes back to his friend, says, "N-n-nothing happened."

> Friend tells him to paint the whole horse green. He does. The girl comes in, she looks, she says, "What happened? The horse is green."

> The guy says, "Wanna fuck?"

It was a story to suit the times. Women were dandy goods but so mysterious and inaccessible as to make the whole m/f thing damnably hard.

In Hans' place, comics came on to girls that wandered in, some of them copping a feel or better in the back. Sex was a caper; the intrigue that surrounded it was often greater than the gism hit.

At the Latin Casino in Philadelphia, comics took inferior dressing quarters to get the knothole view of the chorus girls. Not the only place either. At a Chinese-run club in Brooklyn were apertures too—and they required none of the rubbernecking it took at the Latin Casino. Any time a fellow looked, the girl was perfectly framed. The reason was simple. In the cubicle where the girls dressed, the chairs were nailed to the floor.

Bobby Baxter worked there once, and thought he did well enough to be invited back. To his surprise, he wasn't. Short time after, he met a comic friend of his who'd been booked in there. Every so often after that Baxter would see him and discover he was still working the place.

One day Baxter confessed he couldn't figure why *he* wasn't asked back. He was told it was probably because he didn't wear his tuxedo to work. The dressing room, it turned out, was for the boss and his waiters to cop looks. Comics not hipped to it didn't last.

In that spirit, the primal comedy scream was the one emitted when a comic dropped his trousers in a public place. Jack Roy did it in the Confucius on 52nd Street. A Hanson's comic went him one better. He ran bare-ass naked into the streets, leaving Hans to mutter, "Comics. Vat do I need vit' comics. Qvit hangin' around."

Not unusual. Among comics it was tribal rite, freudian whisper of what the gig came to. It was not just the knock-around comics that did it. Even among the Lindy's bunch it was common. Berle was renowned for what he showed. At a stag party prior to his second marriage, Milton had to ask the comics there not to refer to the size of his apparatus again—his future father-in-law was in the audience. To which Youngman quipped, "Let's see his."

It kept the gears turning. Henny in his sixties came into rooms with the same katzenjammer crazy he'd had at Lindy's where with Berle and Fat Jack Leonard he'd ruled the room years before. He had pockets full of foole's gold—buzzers that went off when he goosed a passing waiter, stickers he slapped on girls' drinks ("Warning: The contents of this drink may cause intercourse"). He had lines too:

> Hey, waiter. Wave your white napkin at me. That's right, all Italians surrender.

> I said, "Sammy, you're a Jew. How come you dance like a colored guy?"

Bup bup bup—Youngman in a pasta joint or up at the Roxy was the same.

Back in the late '40s/early '50s, lines went like carom shots at Lindy's, a Broadway restaurant. Berle was the honcho in there. When he came in, the first table up front was given him. On his entry, he never sat down, prefering to kibitz first with those he knew, or just stand with the Bugs Bunny orthodontic grin and eye around. Once, while he was doing that, he noticed a man at his table. He asked how he was and continued to smile and look over the room. Not hearing the man say his mother had just died, Berle said absently, "Oh, that's nice."

If Berle was the big man in Lindy's, it did not keep him from being the butt of an occasional practical joke. One time, he saw a hundred-dollar bill under his table. As he surreptitiously reached for it, the bill flew off, at the end of a manipulated thread.

In those days, Berle had a standing offer to pay five to ten dollars on the spot to comics who gave him jokes he could use. One fellow began to hit him up regularly with one-liners Milton liked the sound of. He was so prolific that Berle began to wonder. Then he figured it out. The jokes came from Milton's own file, a treasury Berle allowed gag-starved comics to use. He was buying jokes he already owned.

Fat Jack was often at Berle's table, a moon-faced man whose words conveyed the swagger of insult.

Errh, errh, little cocher. The *errh errh* was what Fat Jack used to say when the boys in the Chicago pool halls razzed him. Unable to frame a quick retort, he quacked back the rhythm of their insults *errh errh errh errh.* Later, when he played the Oriental Theater in Chicago, they came to watch him, and every time he tried to do a line, they drowned it out *errh errh errh errh.*

In those days, Leonard was a 360-pound lifeguard, doing his eight minutes at the Oriental and State theaters at night, the same act, word-for-word, with the same hat-spinning exit. Gone to New York, he soon needed more material. All he had, though, were bits like

> Went with a girl reminded me of "Melancholy Baby." Had a shape like a melon and a face like *chaleh,*

lines that left audiences cold. Out of desperation Jack E. began to insult them,

> Errh errh . . . I just want to say . . . if you had lived, you would have been a very sick man,

and found a style in it.

"The shpritz," it was called—a cross fire of insults fashioned in Fat Jack's stumbling away. It suited the head table at Lindy's.

The shpritz was what corner boys did to knock wits, lines that went to the nexus plexus and left the quick talker standing tall. Basic lookit-me.

Whatever ego was in it, some of it was ego-to-please. Will Jordan caught it in a masterly bit in which Sir Ralph Richardson, weary of his crowd's quoting Shakespeare and talking of Sacco and Vanzetti, hies to Lindy's where, by god, the comics are. Taken in to their charmed circle, they give him what he wants, the energy of their fine vulgar style. Soon, he, Sir Ralph, is talking on their terms:

> Fat Jack, do some more of those uh . . . shtichloch. Yes, I love those table shtich-

> loch. You're a great table man. What
> happens to you on the floor? Offstage,
> you're a dynamo. What is it when you
> get in front of people, you fall apart?
> What is it with you? And Henny . . .
> Henny . . . you're so magnificent. But
> must you do those old one-liners . . . why
> don't you hip up your act, get with it,
> you know?

Sir Ralph becomes one of them, and welcomes the
give and take. When Fat Jack says, "Hello, you British idiot. I just want to say, Ralph, you ought to stick
your monocle in your nose. You got no talent, kid.
You ought to walk backwards. I saw Laurence Olivier
and I think you're imitating him and he's imitating
you sideways." Richardson is in heaven.

> Shpritz me again, Fat Jack. I love to hear
> . . . in your terms, "put me down." I like
> to be put down. I love that talk . . . it's
> wonderful. Everybody tells me how great
> I am. Put me down. Shpritz me, by all
> means.

It wasn't confined to Lindy's either with that crew.
Once in a while Berle came by Hanson's to toomle
the merchandise. "I call de po-lice, I call de po-lice,"
Hanson vowed, as Berle sped off in a waiting limousine, unable to resist a parting cry of "Nazi."

Years later, Berle still had the rascally drive. And
it looked good on him. A case could be made for the
gig's being better than lamb glands or Geritol. Berle
and his kind hustled time the way they did an audience: they kept on the move. No social security for
them. They worked. They didn't let the legend die.
It kept the kiddo in them. Not so long ago the great
George Burns made a record company re-shoot an
album cover so his young lady would be shown to
better advantage on it.

Agents occasionally stopped in Hanson's on their
way to and from their offices. Sometimes it was like

the Keystone Kops with comics chasing after them to ask about jobs jobs jobs and the agents muttering anything to get off the hook.

The feeling about agents was best expressed by a comic named Jack Zero who, when asked how he got the gout in his toe, replied, "I kicked an agent in the heart."

Of course, the agents had their own problems. "I remember Sam Gold," said Georgie Starr, "one time had a guy who was a bad act in his office. An old timer, and he was bad, rarely worked. He wasn't good. But New Year's Eve, everybody works . . . every guy breathing, every act, 'cause everyone needs a show on New Year's Eve.

"Well, Sam Gold had a big book. He'd have the clubs, he'd write in each block who's working where. So he's looking at this big book . . . looking at the clock. Ten o'clock at night already. Looking at this comic who's standing there with a cane and bow tie, you know.

"Sam's quiet. Looking, waiting for the phone to ring. Maybe there'll be a comedian he can use. Looks at the clock. Sees it's a quarter to eleven already. He's got to send somebody. New Year's Eve. Doesn't have a comedian. Looks at the guy and back at the book. Looks at the clock. This is going on. Finally, he writes out a contract, signals him over, says, 'Here. Go make trouble.'"

Trouble there was. They were tough places, and not a few were run by strongarms of varied dissuasions. A joke like

> You hear Italians are gangsters, right?
> Me, I say they're lovers. Take Al Capone.
> You think he ever forgot Valentine's Day?

could bring a mug with the Yogi Berra diction to the door to ask that it be bumped from the act. It gave a comic a clue to the owner's origins.

Those owners were not always susceptible to reasoning. Many of them had managed nicely without socratic precepts. A barrel-chested comic name of Shecky Greene discovered it when he informed the boss of a place he worked that he'd be moving on. "We'll tell you when," the owner said. "And that'll cost you ten dollars for bothering us."

There was never any question they could back their words. It was why when an early comic partner of Greene's, Sammy Shore, asked for his check and had the owner stick a gun to his head, he acquired religion. It turned out to be the man's idea of a joke, but it was odds-on next time he'd mean it.

Racketeeer humor tended to go that way. They were Runyonesque characters, many of them, and they liked the prank that made a fellow squirm. In one club in whose upstairs the acts boarded, two lugs ran through a room a comic was sleeping in, firing guns and shouting, FOOL WITH MY WIFE, YOU SON OF A BITCH!!?! That the bullets turned out to be blanks was not much relief to the bleary-eyed act.

Georgie Starr worked a club in Brooklyn that racketeers came to after hours for a command performance. They got it, and gave each act a healthy tip. Afterward, Starr saw them in the streets, stripping a car of its hubcaps. Odd boys. They had their code. Conversation with them on women ended if the subject turned to cunnilingus. *PTOO*, they'd go. *You fuckin' degenerate*. And they'd walk.

There were places—called "bust-out" joints—where customers were charged for drinks according to how well-off they looked. Comics had to watch it too. Bar tabs were monkeyed with. By-the-drink was the way to pay. Salary—a hundred and fifty to two hundred dollars a week—did not go far. Out of it came the hotel bill, meals and incidental expenses. It was why a former hoofer-turned-comic, Leonard Barr, picked up a stripper's clothes for an extra seven dollars a week.

To hang on to what loose change they had, comics schemed. Bobby Baxter remembered: "In those days, I was always just about broke. So whenever I'd go into a high-class joint to eat, first thing I'd do is check the toilet in there—make sure there was a window to an alley or street. See, you'd eat the big meal, then just before the bill came, you'd pay a visit to the men's room and bolt out the window.

"Was with another guy one time. Working in Chicago at a place called the Hi Hat. Went into a classy restaurant. Ate. The two of us saunter to the head. The window's high up, so the guy boosts me. I'm out the window. And as I'm coming down, someone gives me a hand. I don't think anything of it at first. Somehow, I had it in my mind it was my pal out there helping me. Of course it wasn't. It was the boss and some colored buck with a meat cleaver in his hand. I had no money. Lucky for us, the other guy did. He had some bills concealed in his shoes."

With money tight, only a few invested in material, maybe with the old vaudevillian Billy Glason, who lived in an apartment over the Stage Deli and wrote and/or compiled jokes.

> This is without a doubt the last word in PROFESSIONAL COMEDY MATE-RIAL. This is a COMEDY BIBLE . . . and ENCYCLOPEDIA . . . a MASTER-PIECE of COMPILATION and CLAS-SIFICATION. It is the most fabulous compilation ever assembled and put between covers LAFF-A-BETICALLY arranged to cover every conceivable subject from A to Z,

Glason said in his circulars.

For a price, a comic could pick up one of Glason's volumes in the memorabilia-filled outer office of his apartment where Billy sat in baggy trousers and T-shirt brimming with paunch, carrying on about the old vaud-e-ville.

Right up on the wall was a photo of a marquee with Glason's name top of the bill and the boyo himself standing outside with a grin. From his voluminous files, he could (and would) drag out reprint accounts of a boffo night in 1922.

Most comics didn't bother with Glason. The material was taken from higher-ups in the business, acts who could afford to buy jokes. Backstage at the Paramount or Roxy were gagwriters like Gary Belkin or

Neil (Doc) Simon, looking to peddle some "special material"—the phrase for pay-for-play jokes.

The comic working in Jersey City or Steubenville used whatever he could, and scruples be damned. No great pains were made to camouflage either. A British comic who got hold of Bob Orben's one-liners from the States was known to deliver them in England precisely the way they were written—even leaving references like Brooklyn and Jackson Heights in.

Whatever lines a comic had, he needed a few in the pinch, moments when insults flew. He had to hit quick and still keep the favor of the crowd.

It took a complete arsenal to operate in some rooms. Comics had to be ready for

man,
>   Get back in the woodwork with the rest
            of the worms

woman,
            Now you know why they find women
            cut up in trunks

or wit,
            His ad libs aren't worth the paper they're
            written on.

Done with the right mix of ginger and bounce, it was case closed.

Name comics could tinker with crowds in the places they played. Joe E. Lewis might say,

            You'll notice that I'm doing a very fast
            show. I'm cutting out all the laughs.
            These jokes may not sound like much
            to you, but your laughs don't sound like
            much to me either

and get away with it. In a dive it was riskier. To answer the cry "Bring on the broads" with, as Lenny Bruce did,

            I'd like to but then you wouldn't have
            any company at the bar

could stir up rooms where *shtarke* boys sat with their ladies. It was not by Marquis of Queensberry they proceeded. Jack Roy was worked over in an alley for remarks he made onstage—two guys held him in a chair while a third let him have it.

Don Rickles was an economy-sized Fat Jack. He had the round face and bouncy step that Leonard did, and a snap-quack voice that delineated his invective. Leonard's was sound and fury that literally might signify nothing. With Rickles, it was more to the point. He had his troubles when he first tried the insult style.

Another comic who didn't kowtow was the colorful Lord Buckley, an American who affected the manners of British aristocracy. Buckley had been around awhile, going back to the '30s. In the clubs, he was known to say or do anything that came to mind. At a Clark Street bust-out in Chicago, he cut men's ties or sprayed seltzer into ladies' cleavage. There were joints where he got away with it, protected by racket guys who got a kick out of him.

In Chicago's Ball of Fire, Buckley hadn't the muscle behind him. And one night when a heckler got on him, the Lord—standing ramrod straight, head erect—ahsked the gentleman to step outside. Buckley was a big-chested six-footer but the heckler was built bigger. For several minutes, the customers sat and waited. Then Buckley came in, bloody, beat-up and disheveled. He took a cigarette out and resumed, as though nothing had occurred. The other gent came in unmarked a few moments after.

Keefe was put upon too in the gin mills and joints —the "toilets" as they were known. The worst was in York, Pennsylvania, not far from a local barbell company.

"Downstairs," he said, "they had what they called a nightclub, which was a combination bar and luncheonette. Linoleum floors—like real luncheonette thing. Chrome-plated tables and chairs, formica tops. And everybody that came in there . . . like Marlon Brando was the big thing in that town, I guess. I don't know if they were all weight lifters but they certainly seemed like the type. The girls too. They dressed the same as the men. Everybody showed up in white T-shirts and dungarees.

"It was like . . . the first show I walked out and there's this crowd there, and I got on my tuxedo with the butterfly tie. And right in front, ringside, there's this girl with the T-shirt and the levis on and one leg up on the table. One leg up on the table, one on the floor. With a bottle of beer in her hand. And then she says, 'You look like a goil.'

"And they all laugh and I lean over and say,

'Don't you wish you did?'

Well, at this, the whole audience practically got to their feet. They started to get out of their chairs like they're gonna attack me. *Rrrr.* And in back of me I hear the same. *Rrr. Rrr.* It's the band. Like the band is in with this crowd. I'm surrounded.

"For a week, I'd go out there three times a night and talk to myself because they would just go, 'Get off, you bum, you fruit, you stink.' A big drag. If I had had the money I would have gotten on the bus and gone right back. But I had to wait the week out to get paid so I could leave the place. So I worked every night—and pretty much to the same bunch."

The death a comic died in the dives was nothing like the one Frank D'Amore risked. When the North Koreans struck across the 38th parallel in June of 1950, it set off a chain of events that put reservist D'Amore at the front lines in 1952 doing jokes.

He was with the Tenth Special Service Company, the first outfit to do an army show in Korea, which put it under the scrutiny of the Generals. "The army was paying money for it and General Matthew Ridgway wanted to see what he was getting for his money. So we went to the Eighth Army Headquarters. And just like you see in the movies—a bombed-out church in Taegu with the roof gone, and the poster 'Beware of the Enemy' and all that shit. And we did the show up on the altar—like opening night of a Broadway show. It got written up in *The New York Times*.

"The troops came in and then the generals from the Eighth Army sat in the front row. And finally

Ridgway came in with his polished grenade that he wore on his chest. I don't know what the fuck he was going to blow up with that grenade. It was a thing with him. Like the other guy with the two pistols, Patton.

"And we were told backstage not to talk to the officers, just do the show. We did. If Ridgway laughed, we knew we were going to do a tour. Otherwise, we would have canceled and broken the whole company up. Well, he did laugh, and when he laughed, the staff laughed. When he didn't laugh, the staff didn't laugh."

D'Amore went where Bob Hope didn't—the thick of the action—continuing a tradition dating back to the Civil War when George L. Fox, a white-face clown and pantomimist performed for the troops. "We looked," D'Amore said, "like regular army— with three trucks and a jeep. Many times we'd just clean some dirt, put the tarp down, the scenery up and do the show. For backstage, we had a truck we used as a dressing room."

In a period of a year, D'Amore did a show every other day. The Tenth Special Service Company went everywhere—from Taegu to Pusan and Chonju and back up to Seoul for the evacuation. D'Amore was close enough to the action to get military decorations during that time.

It wasn't easy. For, as D'Amore remembered, "We had a chickenshit captain. He was worried that this would turn into one of the Second World War outfits. A lot of them became very gay. You know, one guy would bring his friend in. Before you know it, the whole outfit was flying around the place. So the captain ran it tight."

Out in the fields it was tight too. During one show, artillery troopers had to get up to fire a mission. Another time, reconnaissance planes landing on an airstrip near the performing area kept coming in lower and lower for a look until one of them piled up, sending three thousand marines to their feet to turn the plane over. The pilot came out ok—a couple of scratches, no more.

When not doing the shows, D'Amore sometimes

33

was sent to medevac centers where wounded soldiers were. "We were there all the time, talking to guys. Go into the tent, break out the banjos and guitars. I'd jump around and scream and do some imitations. Like Jerry Lewis, 'cause Jerry was very big then. And the kids would all laugh at him.

"One time I did a show to one guy in a hospital in Japan. That's where they sent our wounded GIs. He was all in traction. Somebody asked me. Said he hadn't smiled in a long time. Go in, see if you can make him smile. Said fuck, yeah. Was young then. I ran in and, man, I told him jokes, I did imitations, I jumped, I climbed the walls. And this guy just looked at me with the tiniest smile 'cause he couldn't laugh. He was all busted up."

As a staff sergeant/comic, D'Amore often worked in rice paddies where human excrement was used for manure. The irony of it he saw a few years later as a civilian gigging at the Calgary Stampede Grounds. There, he had a bag of horse shit thrown at him. It was, it sometimes seemed, the element comics worked in.

A tough nut it was.

The things a comic went through often made him want out of the business.

It was that way with Shecky Greene. For a while, he made more money playing semipro softball against the likes of Bill Skowron and Goose Tatum than he did telling jokes.

One week, he was up in Wisconsin doing a double with Sammy Shore, the next week he was enrolling at the University of Illinois to get a degree in phys. ed. Then he'd say what the hell and off he'd go with a comic to Florida as a gag writer.

> Guy swam out to the sand bar. But the bar was closed.

Jokes like that he'd do.

Hackett stumbled in one of his first big rooms, the Riviera in Fort Lee, New Jersey. The Riviera was a Hollywood set designer's idea of "class." Its periphery of window offered a view of the Hudson River far below and the George Washington Bridge and Manhattan twinkling in the distance. With its high-domed ceiling and acres of glass, it was a hard room. Its grandeur and size—four to five hundred dinner-show capacity—competed with the comic. In there Hackett had trouble.

Rickles did too. Unable to do the act he wanted to, he used the insults.

> This is it, fella. What do you expect, high mass?

a comedy not yet convention in those times. It got him bounced out of clubs more than once.

Not by design he ended a comic viper, doing a mad-on for an act. It was his answer when all else failed—the serious bits that were fine for the drama school he'd been to but not for the clubs. If the routines failed, the shpritz did not:

> Look at the guy. A German. Ever notice all Germans walk like they have timber in the crotch?

He was quick with it. It came like a gatling gun, too fast to fend against, pace that made it sleek sting-ing art. It was a sound he found made audiences snap to. It gave him the wild figure to work out of.

Rickles himself was a likable kid whose mums, Yetta, had to keep an eye on the bar tabs he ran up for strangers when she traveled along. Audiences, though, took him on his word. Some long nights.

So it was with the Hacketts and Greenes and Rickleses. Big paydays were ahead but for now it was some dues to pay. As they went, they were find-ing the rhythms with which the worst of gags could be bumped to a laugh. It was, Lenny Bruce was to say, like sending the audience off a cliff. Da da da whaa—the beat committed them to the laugh. Berle subscribed to the notion. To prove it, he once switched the punch line of a gag to nonsense words.

So coiled was his line he got the audience to laugh anyway.

It was part of comic presence, the ease in public that marked a pro and made him invincible in the sacred precincts of his ego. Tongue in cheek, Berle told a story:

"Jan Murray and I went to see Youngman on a late show in Miami Beach, place called Five O'Clock Club. And Youngman, if you know Youngman, he has forty-five minutes and he's gonna do it whether the audience laughs or not. Now it's dim in there and Jan and I go up, as we walk past we say to the maître d', 'What time does Henny Youngman . . .?' Well, he's about to go on right now. So we went and sat down in the back. The announcement comes over. Typical nightclub. 'Ladies and gentleman, the comedy star of our show, Henny Youngman!'

"Well, he fears no one. The music plays 'Fine and Dandy.' And he walks out. Now let me explain something. Youngman is a *non sequitur* comedian. He hasn't got what we call a block, a monologue. If you're gonna do a monologue on show biz, you talk complete show biz. You do a monologue on hotels, you talk about seven jokes. He always has one joke each subject. 'Take my wife . . . please.' 'I was going to the ballgame.' A putz. A real putz.

"He walks out. He don't know Jan Murray and myself are out there. The spotlight hits him right in the eye, he can't see the people. It's about forty people out there. He don't know if there's three hundred and he don't care.

> This morning, I was cracking my knuckles when—

"Jan Murray: 'Sir, sir, you said you were up this morning cracking your knuckles. Could you continue telling us about that?' And the guy's only got one joke on that. Henny goes, 'Oh yeah, yeah yeah sure.' That to him is an ad lib. Says,

> You go to a nudist wedding. You can always tell who the best man is.

"Jan stands up: 'You were at this nudist wedding. We'd like to hear the rest of that. There's more lines on that, isn't there, sir?' And Youngman says, 'Give that man a mickey.' And then,

> My wife went to the beach. She talked
> so much, her tongue got sunburned.

"Same thing. Jan interrupts. Asks him to expand. Now there's a joke that was made up—I don't know who made it up, I don't think I did—about forty years ago. To stop a heckler with a squelcher, if somebody happens to throw a penny on the stage, you pick it up and say, 'There's only one animal that throws a (s)cent and that's a skunk.'

"That's the stopper, right? But somebody has to throw a penny. So he's running out of what we call 'savers,' 'stoppers.' So he says, 'There's only one animal that throws a (s)cent and that's a skunk,' and nobody threw a penny.

"Show's over. They're playing bow music. He's about able to take a one bow. Applause. Lights go up. There's no way of him getting out of the club, he's got to come through the front. Lights go up. Jan and I run out in the streets. We say to the captain, 'Look, don't say anything. We're gonna walk in.' So he came out through the front of the fucking club and we came in. 'What time you going on, Henny?' He said, 'You missed it?' Said, 'Yeah. What time?' He says, 'What do you mean? I just got through. I killed them.'"

The incident showed the cocksure feeling a comic had to have. Without it, he was a goner. An audience sensed fear. So comics made themselves larger than life. Their talk brimmed with the overkill idiom— *murdered 'em/did real damage.* Even their failures were invested with verbal gigantism—*bombed/died/ down the tubes, man.* Twenty years later, new comics would have kept that (if little else) for legacy, saying, "I wrecked the motherfuckers, man. Laid them OOOUUUT." Or, in bad times: "Went down the commode and out into the Hudson, face up, jack." Comics' managers talked that way too. One of them, describing an audition, said: "Albert killed them, man. I mean, they were throwing up." Even the tape cassettes later comics kept were labeled "killer" or "double killer."

Comic conversation was revealing too. Sentences came in jabbing thrusts that sometimes ended with blah-blah-blah or dit-dit-dit or bup-bup-bup, filler phrases that allowed them to race to the next thought. It caught the staccato pulse so many of them had.

It was always at work. The race was never run. They were always toying. Noses were fixed. Names were switched. At one point, Keefe changed his to Roger Duck and back to Keefe. Even hairlines were altered. Pat Henning, returning to England with a toupee years after he appeared there bald, found it worked. Management told him he was better than his old man.

But such changes were only cosmetic. Comics that succeeded did it with their acts. They "tried things." They stood in a room and figured how to use it. The ability to seize a laugh out of a passing instant was the mark of a comic. It meant he was ready, not rote, willing to step out of act and chance a tumble.

A comic who worked in a Chinese-run club in Cleveland got nutty one night, ripped his shirt off and carried on. He was about to button up again when he saw a waiter. He signaled him to the stage, handed him the shirt and said,

Have it back by Thursday.

In the Greenwich Village Inn, Joey Bishop once followed a comic who did his jokes from cards he threw away after each one was delivered. When Bishop came on, he picked up the cards, flipped them over and said, "He shoulda looked on the other side." Bishop did his own material, pretending to read it off the flip side.

Shecky Greene, giving it another try, wound up in the Preview Lounge in New Orleans. One night as he worked, he spied a pair of cockroaches moving across the floor. Quickly conveying it to the audience, he dropped to his knees and did Clem McCarthy calling a race between the two.

Another time in the Preview, Greene saw a grasshopper. He picked it up and pocketed it, and went on with his act, from time to time giving a from-the-hip twitch, as if metamorphosing on stage. It was great comedic wit. Robert Ruark, in the audience that night, wrote his newspaper column the next day on Shecky's ingenuity.

A point of honor it was as well. Not to think quick when a moment arose was a blow to comedic *macho*. It was like being a gunfighter with heavy thumbs. Or, in Berle's phrase, a putz, a real putz.

Keefe, not a boy anymore, was learning it. Though the act still used the old standbys, he made them emerge in new ways. A sense of style he was getting.

One routine had an army platoon of movie stars, and included George Sanders, who was going to fight the enemy in his own way: *I shall write a nasty letter to The Times*. It ended with a Jerry Lewis imitation—

> Beans, beans
> beans, beans
> send a salami to your boy in the army.
> The navy gets the gravy but the army gets
> the beans, beans

and vamp out.

No great shakes. But Keefe's head was filling with some weird ways of putting things together. Once in a while, he'd try them in the joints. Down the can, man.

It was back to mimicry and

> This drunk in the movie theater was lying across the seat, going, "Uhhh, uhhh." And the usher says, "Cut the racket; will ya? Sit up in your seat."
>
> And the drunk just goes, "Uhhh, uhhhh." And the manager can't move him. So they get a policeman. Cop says, "All right, sit up in your seat there or leave the

39

theater. Stop making all this noise. What do you mean behaving like this? What kind of behavior do you call this? Where are you from anyway?"

Drunk says, "I'm from the balcony. Uhhhh. Uhhhhh. Uhhhh.

Even in doing just jokes, Keefe was educated to the game. In a club where he asked the audience to suggest impressions for him to do, a customer shouted out, "Lassie."

If you'll be the tree,

Keefe snapped back.

Another time, he got into a coughing jag that he came out of with an upraised finger and the suggestion,

Buy Christmas seals.

Moments like these he remembered and soon was building into his act. Memory was part of the game. And endurance was too. It had to be if a fellow worked the "toilets." In them it got to look like a dead end after a while. Jack Roy thought so. He got a shot at the Latin Casino in Philly, bombed and decided not to go back to places like Bayonne, Union City, Newark and Passaic, and work on top of the bar same as the strips did.

Roy got out and went into the siding business—last refuge for quick-talking rascals. Starr was out soon after, and down in Miami selling paint jobs with the storied Doctor. There he ran into Lenny Bruce, who'd left New York too.

In those days, Lenny was going with a stripper named Honey Harlowe, and his conversations were mostly of her. *Oh, she's too much. Her head. She's so funny. She grabs me, she tells me she wants to fuck me in the ass.* Always talking about Honey Honey Honey.

As a comic, Lenny was getting by. A gig here or there. Others beat on. Hackett, while at Billy Gray's

Band Box in Hollywood, was seen by the movie colony and soon was in films, appearing in a 1954 Universal release, *Walking My Baby Back Home.*

Some made it through the new medium—television. Will Jordan fooled with an Ed Sullivan impression he'd done before and changed it from a carbon to a caricature. From 1954 on, it was Will Jordan the comics imitated, not Sullivan. As Jordan put it: "I made up the expression *rrreally big,* which Sullivan had never said. I made up *big shooooo.* I cracked my knuckles, shook my shoulders, rolled my eyes. Burped. All gestures that you think Ed Sullivan does. He did none of those. If he did what I did, he'd be funny."

It spread Jordan's reputation from beyond Hanson's across the country by 1954. For a while he was on Sullivan's "Toast of the Town" so often that old man Hanson asked, "Veren't you on Sullivan?" And when Jordan said he was, Hans told him, "You kin hang around here." He thought Will had become a regular. When he found out he was not, he'd say, "Qvit hanging around here. Vat do you hang around here for?"

Jordan became so linked with Sullivan that his own identity got blurred. All the time he got "Hey, Sullivan" on the streets. Even people in the trade called him that, including Dean Martin, whom he'd known from way back. It got to where Jordan had a business card printed up, saying,

PLEASE!
Don't Call Me Ed Sullivan
(He's a Great Guy)
But My Name is
WILL JORDAN.

In the early and mid-'50s, a comic could get hot in a club and be booked for a long run. It had a tonic effect. He'd cultivate an audience he'd feel cozy enough to wig with, derring-do that made a comic grow.

Shecky Greene, in New Orleans' Preview Lounge and the Wits End, became a favorite of the "rounders" there—gamblers, drinkers and hookers. Those ladies he'd recognize by the hats they wore and, as they came into the room, he'd say, "Evening, Miss Lulu." And so on. Some nights he'd disappear with one of them until the next day.

In the early '50s in New Orleans, Shecky was liable to do anything for a laugh. One night he ran down Bourbon Street in an ape suit. On another occasion, he turned up at the funeral of a policeman's mother with a comic pal of his, Frankie Ray. It was Ray's idea—he thought of it as a goodwill gesture for the Wits End, a club he and Greene were running at the time. *Figured the cop sees us there, we can get away with more in the club.* Respectfully, Ray went to one knee and genuflected. As he did, he heard a strange sound back of him. He looked over his shoulder and saw Greene in a yarmulke, the skullcap he used in his act. Shecky was chanting in Hebrew. *And all these Irish guys— the cop and the rest of them—are looking at me. Well, I grabbed Shecky and got us the hell out of there.*

In those days, Greene went from one club to the next, always eager to do a few minutes onstage. The only problem he had was at the Preview with an older woman who sat in the balcony and did a running commentary on his act. *Uch, why's he doing that? Or, it's not de de dah dah dah, it's de dah dah.*

It was Greene's mother, a woman in the tradition of Jewish stage mums like Berle's and the Marx Brothers'. With her it was, as Joe Delaney, a chum of Greene's, remembered, "like two tapes, one slightly behind the other." Delaney, later a Las Vegas columnist, figured out what to do. "Shecky one day was saying, 'Joe, I'm not going over big as I should.' I said, 'Well, you've got to shut her up and send her home.' So that afternoon, when he got back from the racetrack with me, he saw his mother and said, 'Mom. I want you to go home.' She said, 'Why?' He says, 'I was talking to this fellow and he thinks you ought to go home.' So I walked in that night about twelve thirty. And I got hit by a purse. It was his mother.

"Fifteen years later, Shecky was working at the Riviera [in Vegas] and now I'm a critic. He introduced his mother from the stage. So I went over and said,

'Mrs. Greenfield, you don't remember me, my name is Joe Delaney and I was in New Orleans when Shecky . . .' She said, 'I remember you. You're the rotten bleep that told my son to send me home.' It was fifteen years later, and we never had any contact in between."

With his mother out of the way, Greene was free to do the dah-dah-dah he wanted and to visit the horse parlors she objected to also. From an extended stay in New Orleans, it was into bigger and better rooms. Joey Bishop went the same route—a long run in Chicago's Vine Gardens and into the city's posh Chez Parée. In clubs like Chez Paree, the Latin Casino in Philadelphia, La Martinique in New York, comics made reputations . . . or went bust. A few were known to find their speaking voices in the falsetto range with their first words.

The pressure was on, particularly at the Copa. What the Garden on 49th Street was to the prizefights, or the Metropolitan to opera, the New York Copacabana was to entertainment. Tension was in that room too, more so for the boss of it.

He was Jules Podell, a short stout man with a rough chiseled face and a voice that came from downtown, the deep cartoon sound of Popeye. He had the heavy tread and tight neck action of an enforcer and a readiness to be one. King Kong, the help called him behind his back. And it suited him. He was quick-tempered and violent. People under him he grabbed by the hair or neck and pushed against walls. With the women, it was, "Hey, broad, come here." The men got it worse.

It made time with him sticky. No telling when he was going to flare up, or over what. Keefe worked the checkroom of the Copa in the '40s on a day Podell tripped down a flight of stairs and struck his head against the wall as he fell. It was early in the afternoon. The club was empty. Podell got up, shook his head, mounted the stairs and at the top step, asked, "Who pushed me?" There was no one to answer him. He came back down, walked out front and fired the doorman. "Son of a bitch, son of a bitch," he muttered on his way back in.

He ran the Copa like a Caribbean despot, with an eye on all operations. When food came out of the kitchen, he was there to look it over and demand it be sent back if it was not up to his standards. He worked twelve to sixteen hours a day, and was possessive about the place. When singer Connie Francis walked into the kitchen one night, Podell snapped, "What are you doing in my kitchen? It's my kitchen. Get out of here."

In the main room, he sat in the back and, if he didn't like what he saw, rapped his onyx pinky ring on a table, a signal that alerted Copa captains. "One night," said Lee Tully, "I was working onstage. Now if you know the Copa, every time they get crowded, your stage gets smaller. And this night the stage became two by two. And one group, sitting to my right, maybe two rows back, was not only boisterous but vulgar too. And as I'm talking, I hear rap rap rap. And then all of a sudden I see two guys come down. Podell's boys. Very discreet. They merely take the table out.

"With the table gone, each one locks a customer's arms behind him in the back and whispers very quietly, 'We'd like you to leave or we'll beat the shit out of you.' And they take these guys out. You can see the guys are not walking on their own feet. It's like they're walking on air. And I'm watching this and telling jokes, but this is much funnier than I am."

With performers, the Copa policy was no-nonsense either. If a comic wanted a cup of tea, he paid the same price for it the customers did. And when Podell did not like one, he let him know: "You stink," he'd shout.

He was one boss not to be kidded from the stage. In 1955, Shecky Greene did a line in a voice that sounded suspiciously like Popeye's. Seconds later, the lights went off and the microphone was shut. "This was opening night for Nat 'King' Cole," Greene said. "And they turned the microphone off. So I walked off the stage and somebody says, 'Mr. Podell wants to see you.' I go into the kitchen where [in Podell's voice] 'Hey, I wanna ask you, why did you do that?

Who wrote that for you?' " Greene, who never heard Podell before, became hysterical.

"It was a real joke to me," he said, "and every night I got on the stage after that I did what I wanted to, and they closed the lights on me. The band started playing. Three weeks I had of that. Three weeks of closing the lights, the microphones going off."

It took all kinds to run the clubs. The German couple that had a rathskeller in Brooklyn spent the night sitting in chairs by the kitchen oven, visible to the comic working onstage.

> They're getting the oven ready back there, any of you people step out of place

was the line comics did, inspired by the sight. It forced the couple to advise the agent that booked the place—no more Jew comics, *danke schön*.

Jack Ruby was down in Dallas. He had a strip joint there. Sammy Shore used to have coffee with him, and would whistle glory-glory-hallelujah when Ruby went star-spangled on him. Ruby was a real patriot. Shore remembered he kept pictures of the presidents.

In San Francisco, there was Bimbo, who would take out his false teeth, put them in his hand and pretend to bite a listener with them. Another owner in that town was a former Nedick's counterman who'd started a place he called the hungry i ("i" for intellectual). He was Enrico Banducci, a man who owned more than two thousand berets and operated in an eight-thousand-square-foot cellar in what was formerly a Chinese gambling den. And just outside of Boston was a club run by a blind man who was suspect of comics that got laughs on sight gags. When Keefe did a silent movie routine there, word was sent to him. "De boss don't tink you're funny."

Few of them, in fact, had an eye for talent. Those that did were regarded as strange—their clubs were called, "chichi" rooms. In the mid-'50s it was in those places—Bon Soir, Le Ruban Bleu, Mr. Kelly's, Mocambo, the hungry i, the Purple Onion—that new comic sounds got aired.

Even before them, Max Gordon's Blue Angel was a haven for comics who had an eye for the small whimsical truths, soft-spoken oddities like Wally Cox. Cox was around in the late '40s, prefiguring a time when comics were regular in their pulse rates. He himself was a mild and amusing fellow, of a kind easily overlooked. Indeed, as a boy, he drew attention to himself by wearing a wristwatch upside down so when asked the time, he simply raised it to his chest and let people see for themselves.

At Cox's death, the actor William Redford wrote *The New York Times*:

> Twenty-five years ago, he [Cox] motorcycled a backstage friend to Rockland County and taught him to distinguish yarrow from Queen Anne's lace. He also trained him in bird-calling. . . . When he owned his Connecticut farm, they fluttered into his hands every morning. It wasn't just for food. It was also conversation. Some sort of matutinal ceremony with Wally as dominie. One human visitor wanted so badly to receive a chickadee in her palm she practiced the pitches for weeks. No go. They chirped but wouldn't approach. Then she got smart. She put Wally's fedora on her head and wrapped herself in his mackinaw. Seconds later, she was festooned with birds.

In the mid-'50s, the chichis were where comic irregulars went. It was there, for instance, Orson Bean could tell shaggy dog stories like the one about the two Martians talking. One says, "Took my kid to the zoo to see the googoo. And the kid was playing with the googoo. And the googoo was playing with the kid. And the kid was teasing the googoo. Next thing I know the googoo ate the kid. So I went to the zookeeper and said, 'Hey, the googoo just ate my kid.' And he said, 'So, you'll go home, make love to your wife, you'll have another kid.' And I said,

'Oh yeah, what for? Just to feed your goddamn googoo?' "

Cox, Bean, Roger Price were comics who at one time or another had been in the chichis. Theirs was another sound, one not revved to the gills. What a comic said began to count. It was why when the hungry i's Banducci heard Mort Sahl, he didn't mind that the delivery was inexpert. Sahl had a line,

> The McCarthy jacket is like the Eisenhower jacket except it's got an extra flap to go over the mouth

and Banducci liked what it said about the mind that managed it. That was a change.

There were chichi comics, and they ranged from Cox to Zero Mostel. And there were a few comics that just worked dirty. One known as Ting-a-Ling would come out with a cigarette in an enema holder, and do the jokes. He'd work with a floor-length apron around him. At the end of his act, he'd turn and bow to the band, and show a naked bum to the audience.

B. S. Pully talked tough. He'd do jokes like,

> On this guy's joint was written the word "Shorty." And part of the therapy in the hospital was to make it with the patients. But none of the nurses wanted to make it with him because written on his was the word "Shorty." Then one of the nurses decided to try. Came in the next day with a big smile on her face, she looked just great. They said, "What happened? You have a smile on your face. You made it with a guy that had 'Shorty' written on his extension."

> "Ah yes," she said, "but when he became excited, it said, 'Shorty's Pizzeria and restaurant, orders to take out, prompt delivery from Wednesday to Friday, TUlip

47

four-two-six-one-three. In New Jersey, BIgelow . . .' "

Pully worked "rough" dates.

Marie Alvarez, who went back to silent-movie days, did an act like that too. In the '40s, she was in a Greenwich Village club doing lines the gays dared her to say.

> I once goosed a ghost.
> What'd you get?
> A handful of sheet.

Oooh, she said it. She said it. Alvarez graduated to stags and smokers mostly, with material that was more hard-core.

Most other comics did commercial acts that insulted mother wit. Some of them had wild heads that served them more in their day-to-day scams. They smoked pot up in the Paramount dressing room of Martin and Lewis, or had sex in paperback circumstances. What ideas they had, they kept to themselves. On stage, they were just rim-shot dandies.

Of all the comedic jekyll/hydes, one of the more engaging ones was Lord Buckley. Ah, the Lord.

Bobby Baxter met him in the late '30s. Baxter was then a kid who'd go from joint to joint to do a few minutes of dance 'n' gags and then pass the hat. "Busking," it was called. Or sometimes, it was for floor money—coins thrown up on the stage—he worked. If so, he'd mark a few quarters and hand them out discreetly to get the money rolling.

In Chicago, in a club in The Loop, he asked the boss could he busk and was told to see the emcee. "So I go over to the emcee and I say, 'Listen, I do a little comedy, a little juggling, a little dancing and I wonder if I could just work for floor money.' And he looks at me and says, 'Ah, a traveling mountebank is it? A mountebank, 'ey? Of course, my boy, of course.' "

It was Lord Buckley he was speaking to, a man

who once met was not soon forgotten. "I remember," Baxter said, "he used to say

> There was an old hermit who lived in a cave. And he had an old dead whore that he fucked. Now it might seem strange to you, but think of all the money he saved.

"Well in those days to say 'fuck' on the floor, that was like fantastic, you know what I mean? And during the act, he used to smoke pot. Nobody knew what it was. They just thought it was kind of wild.

"Anyway, he introduces me. 'I have a traveling mountebank here, ladies and gentlemen.' In that affected English accent. Mustached. Tall. Elegant. He could be exhausted and not sleep for three days. Tired, physically ill and everything—and still his back was like a ramrod. So he introduces me and I go out and I work. And he takes an ace. Lays an ace on me. Throws a whole dollar bill at me. You know, took the hat out of my hand and passed it around.

"So now I thought, 'This is a great guy. Look what he did for me.' Then he says, 'Over here, son . . .' And there's three girls he never met before, and he's talking to them. And he says, 'You're a lovely lass indeed.' And he puts his hand—'Oh, say there. That is solid meat. You are built, dear. What a lass.' And he takes and puts his hand right up her dress. And the girl didn't know him. He says, 'Feel that, lad.' Takes my hand and he puts it right up her cunt. Oh god, what a guy. This is a hero of mine. You know, jiminy crickets. So I'm following him around the club.

"Now he goes into the dressing room. There's a girl singer there. He stops and puts his cigarette down, unzips his pants and pees in the sink. Had a big cock. Pees in the sink. And just talks with the girl. 'You did a nice number, honey. You did a hell of a show. Blah blah blah.' And puts it back in. This nonchalant thing. I said, 'Gee, this is the business for me. Show business. Pee in the sink.' To this day—I was sixteen then—to this day, to pee in the sink, that's real show business."

The life of Lord Buckley played like pure theater. A consummate con man, he was in and out of jams with grace and self-possession few men have. Early on, he invested himself with royalty, and built around him a whole courtly system, one he lived twenty-four hours a day. His Christian name was Richard. He insisted on Lord. More than a decade after his death, the last of his women still referred to him as "his Lordship" and preferred to be called "Lady" rather than Miss, Ms. or Mrs.

Buckley was a hedonist, indulging all pleasures with no qualms, costliest of which was his alcoholic intake. It led him to antics onstage early in his career that gave him a bad name among agents. The scarcity of jobs kept him living on the fringe, a position he occupied with wit.

Mere lack of money never set him back. Buckley lived like the Lord of his eye, well beyond his means. He managed it with a flair for schemes and the charm to execute them. He had the sweet persuasion. Often his capers ill-served others. But most forgave him because of the spirit in which he undertook them. Buckley's was high fellowship.

As a performer, he started in dance marathons and tent shows, and later moved into the clubs, mostly around Chicago. On stage or off, he had the stiff-spined carriage, and a voice that rolled up from the deeps. With a mustache he kept waxed and an imperious eye, he looked the Lord. He played it too. He took his act as a royal prerogative, and did what he pleased.

One time, it was said, he proposed a toast from stage, and threw the goblet into the club's fireplace, inviting the audience to join him. They did, much to the owner's consternation. Other times he ridiculed the patrons, which the racketeers that ran the joints loved.

During World War II, Buckley performed for the GIs on tour with Ed Sullivan. Then he went into the theaters with the act he had—eight to ten minutes in the lordly manner. To "Pomp and Circumstance," Buckley would walk out in tails, a cigarette in his fingers. He'd stand there, fix the audience with the royal eye, and then draw on the smoke that theater signs prohibited—*eat your heart out*—blowing elegant puffs out of the curled tongue. Then:

> Ladies and gentlemen, I should like to take you on a trip through the realm of spontaneous humor. I shall from the audience take members of either gender to assist me. IF—

in the rising evangelical style—

> IF you should be so fortunate as to be ahsked, you will get up immediately and none of your blasted dilly dallying . . . are you there?

the cigarette pumping all the while.

That said, he went into the audience to look around. When Buckley saw a "volunteer," he'd thunder, "Selection number one, that'll be you, mate. Get up there. Up, you bugger." And so on.

Charles "Tubby" Boots was a child performer when he first saw Buckley at the Hippodrome Theater in Baltimore. Years later, as a three-hundred-and-fifty-pound Miami Beach comic, he recalled how the Lord's word went with audiences. "He never had any trouble getting them up onstage," said Boots. "And I used to wonder about it. I'd see him again and again. Played hookey all the time. And finally one day I was sitting next to a man he picked and the guy—*but I don't want to*—and Buckley got down very close to him and said, 'Get your ass up there before I knock it off.' "

Once he had three men and a woman onstage, Buckley's act became tag-team Señor Wences. He stood back of them, doing Amos 'n' Andy dialogue out of them. He'd tap a man on the shoulder. The guy's mouth moved. And

> I swe-ah, I never saw such a lovely moon in all mah life,

in the Lord's lady voice.

Then he'd reverse it, and have the girl respond as a man:

> Momma, you comin' on with the come-on, you talking that sweet stuff to me.

Five minutes of that he'd do—moving it so quickly he often caught his help unawares, which delighted the audience. He had a Satchmo impression, a hat-switching game and then:

> The flowers. The gorgeous mystic multi-colored flowers are not the flowers of life but people, yes people, are the flowers of life. And it has been a most precious pleasure to have temporarily strolled in your garden.

And off with a bow.

A square act it was, and only the impeccable Buckley air made it work. It intrigued Boots, who was ten when he first saw Buckley. Two years later, when the Lord came back to Baltimore, Tubby paid his way in again. At the time, Boots was a regular on a local radio show and also a Saturday theater spectacle called "Uncle Jack's Kiddy Club." He'd been around performers and was used to oddball characters. Even so, Buckley was a revelation.

After the show that Boots saw, he watched Buckley step outside the Hippodrome and approach a policeman. "Officer," he said, "I want to report a dope addict. That gentleman"—he pointed to an innocent passerby—"be very careful, he's watching us." As he warned him, Buckley took a drag on his smoke and blew it into the lawman's face. It was marijuana.

A few months after Buckley was in Baltimore, Boots was working as a female impersonator in a place on a night it got busted. Caught between the law and parental discovery of what he'd been up to—he was living with an aunt, his folks thought—he went to New York, leaving the aunt to cover for him. He ended up at Buckley's doorstep, asking could he stay. At the time, the Lord lived in a step-down apartment in the

West 70s with his wife Elizabeth and the children, Richard and Lori. When Buckley heard the troubles Boots had, he said sure, he could camp in the royal court.

Boots was a blimp of a boy, well over two hundred pounds at the time, and he went to work in the Three Deuces on 52nd Street as an emcee. The money supplemented what Buckley made in infrequent presentation house appearances. And still, cash was short —a pity, for, as Boots said, "Buckley should have been born with money because I think he thought he had money."

It did not keep Buckley from living the life of a Lord—gawd no. He had jolly good times in his place, even managed to stage swell parties, using his wits to obtain what he needed for them. Remembered Boots: "He'd go out and tell the butcher, 'My god, I'm having a party, Fred. And I'm having it in your honor. Every Hollywood star is going to be there. Da-da-da-da. I know you're going to want to put the meat in the party.' And he would invite the baker and say, 'By god, Jules, I'm having a party in your honor because you've been in this neighborhood so long. Da-da-da-da.' And the guy would be so thrilled that he was going to a party with all these stars that he would donate all the bread. And before you knew it, Buckley had all the trimmings to give a party for a bunch of people. The fun came when the baker and the butcher showed up and thought they were the guest of honor. Buckley avoided 'em like the plague. But he did invite them.

"So anyway, he was in debt, always in debt. Bunch of bills. This bill. That bill. But people loved him because he only took advantage of his friends. That's one thing I always admired about Buckley. If he liked you, he'd con you. If he didn't like you, he avoided you."

Boots learned it firsthand. One night, the spigot-and-faucet unit to the bathtub came undone while he was having a bath in Buckley's apartment. Hot water shot out of the exposed pipes. It pinned the *Journal-American* Tubby was reading against his face and scalded the rest of his considerable manchild, burns that landed him in the hospital.

"Now every day," Boots recalled, "a telegram. Every day. 'We miss your sunshine at the castle. Please get well, Prince Charles. Love, Lord Buckley, Lady Elizabeth and the children.' And every day Buckley would come by and bring me a box of candy. And I'd say isn't that nice. How thoughtful. . . . And then I turned on the television one day and he was doing a quiz program called "Play Ball." And the sponsor was a candy company.

"Anyway, I didn't have any money or insurance, and I thought, 'Oh god, what am I going to do about the hospital bill. So I get dressed and Buckley was doing the television show, so he couldn't meet me at the hospital to take me home. So I go up to the desk and I said, 'Well, I'm awfully sorry, but I can't pay you.' 'You don't have to worry about that. Your bill was paid by Lord Buckley.' I said, 'It was?' They said, 'Oh yes, he paid us cash.'

"Tears came to my eyes. I said, 'I don't believe this.' So I go home and I said, 'Dick, you paid the hospital bill.' And he said, 'Uch, anything for you, Prince Charles, a member of the Royal Family. And here, I've got a plane ticket for you to go down to Miami Beach, Florida, because you must rest for a couple of weeks. And here's five hundred dollars for your pocket. And I want you to go down there and have a vacation.' Well, I broke down and I cried. All the months, he'd taken my salary at the Three Deuces and never let me have a penny. And now he's come through like a champion. And he takes me to the airport. And I go down to Florida. Now once in Florida, I receive a notice from an insurance company. Said, 'Due to the fact that we've already given the $25,000 claim to your uncle, we have to have your name on this thing.' I said, 'twenty-five thousand dollars!' "

Buckley and the insurance company had come to a quick out-of-court settlement. It was not the sum he managed that bothered young Boots but the Lord's going behind his back. Had he told him up front, Tubby claimed, he would have endorsed the scheme gladly. When he asked Buckley why he did it, the

Lord sweet-talked him into agreeing it was for the best. Besides, Buckley claimed, he was "in hock to the government up to my ass."

The Lord's ways were never routine. He did things with a flair. When he worked at the Suzy Q in Chicago, Buckley hired a hearse and rode in it while on his back in a coffin, dressed in tails. When cars pulled alongside the hearse, Buckley drew the curtains open and rose up from the dead, a sign proclaiming, "The body comes alive at the Suzy Q."

He was Aquarian long before it was the age of. When he went out, he'd carry packs of gum and Lifesavers and dispense them to people he met, even strangers. With old acquaintances, he was good cheer. A real gusto Buckley had. Visiting for dinner, he would greet company by the elaborate titles he issued —Prince Owlhead, Lady Renaissance—and then give his noisy appraisal as he ate. "Oh! Oh! I must say. Very fine," thumping his fingers on the table.

At a soiree he once threw, he invited people to watch him bathe in a tub he filled with ice, a feat he managed without a goose bump. Later, dried off, he had a lady of his remove her blouse and offered the guests "feels," exclaiming, "I say, those are tits!"

Meeting a group of jazzmen later, Buckley so enjoyed the time, he had his woman lie on the couch and do nude poses while he flicked the lights on and off for dramatic focus. With still another lady, he had her dress in Oriental styles and walk three steps behind him. For Buckley, masquerade made the days run. At one time or another, he affected the look of a cleric, sailor, huntsman and squire.

It was the high-anglo Lord he was stuck on, a role he managed with utter conviction. He once stopped a car on a street and announced, "I'm Lord Buckley. I'm late for a very important engagement." And he got the ride. Another time, he arrived at an army base to perform and introduced himself as an English officer. And he persuaded everybody, American officers included, to go through calisthenics.

There was a dark side to Buckley, and it'd flare up when given the stimulants' boost. "One night," Bobby Baxter remembered, "we were at the Latin Quarter in

Boston. It was guest night and he followed Sophie Tucker. He was stoned out of his head from drinking and from smoking pot and was in a mean belligerent mood.

"And he made some cracks about Sophie being an old fat woman and the audience turned on him. And he got nasty. There's my idol and he's telling them, 'Piss on you.' And so on. And they introduced me and I got up and I said, 'Ladies and gentlemen. Buckley's had a little too much to drink.' I was at the Copley Plaza then. Doing pretty good. When I'd met him, I was busking. Now I was trying to save his hide. And I said, 'Buckley is just sort of clowning. He's had a few drinks. He don't really mean anything. He's a very kind, generous man.' And he was. He would only get really insulting and nasty when he was in a bad mood or when he was high or something. Usually, he was like Lenny Bruce. He was very conscious of people's feelings. If he ever met you on the street, you'd always walk away feeling good from Buckley."

In Hollywood in the early '50s, Buckley wound up in an improbable place he called The Castle. It was a mansion that had once belonged to the silent film star Barbara La Marr, and was, at the time he saw it, empty. The old woman who owned it was living in a Methodist home and Buckley persuaded her to let him have it for a low rent. It was a far cry from the place he'd been living in in the hills of Pasadena, a sorry hole he called the Pigeon Coop.

Once in the Castle, Buckley installed the thronelike chair he had wherever he lived, and from which he conducted court. A certain protocol prevailed at the Castle. Lady Lisbeth, the mother of Buckley's two children, was greeted with a bow and hand-kiss. And then Buckley, on the throne, fingering his waxed mustache, would hold forth, talking in a voice of whiskey-soaked eminence, a deep sound with a hard cutting edge.

At one time Sinatra was there, and Tony Curtis. And there were jazzmen and junkies and no-goods and nothings of every shade of the ethnic rainbow. Cannabis would burn and booze was used, but in a mood of easy company. And the names the Lord gave them—Hair Head and Cougar Head and Princess Water Lily.

By day, Buckley walked nude about the spacious castle, not caring who was around, striding royally through the place, singing *The body is booo-ti-ful.* Sometimes, he ended up in a tub, where he'd take one of his several baths a day. He'd put a board across the tub and do paperwork on it. Or, still naked as a jaybird, he'd step to the balcony, giving the shock of her life to his Hollywood neighbor, Beulah Bondi. *Loooove Hollywood every moment,* he'd croon.

Dressed, he might walk over the small moat at the castle and out to the garden, where there was a miniature Japanese house and marijuana in the hothouse. At some point in the day, he'd ease into the Fairyland Express, an Austin he'd charmed a fellow out of for a ridiculously low price.

The car was bright red. Buckley got an acquaintance to do the interior in white and mount an American flag on the aerial. In the Fairyland Express, the Lord would tool around Hollywood, smoking joints. The afternoons he did business, he'd order, "Lisbeth, dress the props," Buckley's term for the children at such times. He'd take them along to influence prospective buyers.

Buckley worked scattered jobs—once in the valley with Lenny Bruce and Sally Marr, other times in Palm Springs and Reno. He had a small role in the 20th Century-Fox release, *We're Not Married,* a film that starred Ginger Rogers and Fred Allen and, in secondary billing, Marilyn Monroe.

But with the grand scale the Castle ran on, money was always short. In that respect, the reappearance of Tubby Boots was a boon. Boots was working at the Rhapsody Club in Peoria, Illinois, when he heard the old scoundrel Buckley was alive and well in Hollywood.

As Boots put it, "I made the mistake of calling him. It's a few years now since I've seen him. It's been a long time between. Why hold a grudge? What was done was done. I call him. The minute he hears it's me, 'Ah, Prince Charles, so beautiful to hear your voice. I felt so bad about what I did to you . . . with that thing with the insurance. I must make it up to you. I have a beautiful home in Hollywood Hills, I just made a motion picture bup bup bup. Let me make it up to you.'

"So I give up my job, which was paying me seven hundred and fifty dollars a week. Nightclub job and radio show I had. And I get on a plane and I hop out to California, expecting to see a band greeting me at the door. Like Buckley did everything with a flair. And I figured, 'Oh god, there's going to be a band to meet me and fans holding signs welcoming me to California and everything.'

"As I get off the plane and walk down the ramp, here's this black boy with paint all over him and Lady Buckley with her hair all disheveled, paint on her face and on her hands. 'Come on, Prince Charles. Lord Buckley's waiting.' And they scurry me off in a little sports car up to Hollywood Hills.

"And this is the exact scene that went on as I walked in the door. Buckley is on the phone saying, 'I have an act for you. My god, he's fabulous.' He turns to me. 'What do you do now, Tubby? . . . Oh, he sings and dances and does comedy. He could open tonight. A hundred twenty-five? Sold.' He was sitting on the phone, trying to sell me that night to open. At a lousy hundred and twenty-five dollars at a cafe on La Cienega.

"I had just given up seven hundred and fifty dollars a week to come to California to live in the lap of luxury and this bastard is on the phone selling me for a hundred and twenty-five. And meanwhile Buckley's got all these actors there. Larry Storch and his brother, and Russ Tamblyn, who later did *Blackboard Jungle*. And everybody in the house is starving.

"When the rent was due, the old lady—Lady Curl, he called her, or The Witch—would come and he'd con her out of the rent. I mean . . . well, he had a movement. His wife was a very good ballet dancer. So he would have this thing going, he called it "Swing for Life," where we would all get in ballet togs. If you could see us all in these stupid tights—all these comics who never knew the first thing about ballet. And she would come and he'd say . . . he would get us up the morning she was due. And he'd say, 'Well, troops, Lady Curl the witch is coming to collect the rent. And we must meet her at the fortress. So when she comes in, you'll all be gracious to Lady Curl. . . . Well, the minute she hit the door, she'd say, 'Lord Buckley, about'—He'd say, 'Lady Curl, you are looking more beautiful every day. Get into your ballet costume, we're going to have the "Swing for Life" movement *now*.' And he would get her into her ballet costume. And we would get there and we would do these ballet exercises. And then whatever was left over, I would cook and throw chives in and make a special dinner in her honor. And he'd take a glass of wine and he'd say, 'Well, I'll see you next month, Lady Curl, same time?' And put her out the door.

"It got so bad Buckley took to selling the furniture in the house. And when Lady Curl asked about it, he'd tell her it was out to be cleaned. But Buckley had a thing about him. He could come out of anything on top. He was never upset by anything. And he was always at his best when he was broke. When he had money—working on a movie or in a nightclub or something—that's the time when he looked like he was in the most trouble of all. He didn't know who to pay first or how to get rid of it. In other words, if he was broke, he knew how to get it. But when he had it, he didn't know how to use it."

The swashbuckle style often worked against the Lord in business. A musician friend of his, Dick Zalud, arranged for Buckley to read for the voice of a cartoon character. Buckley did, and was so good he was offered all the voices for a sea-captain cartoon being worked up. As Zalud was working out details, Buckley stepped outside.

The building was designed as a square with open ground at its center. On the open ground was a mound of dirt that Buckley repaired to. There, he rolled a joint and lit up, visible to the cartoon people thinking of hiring him. That was the end of the deal.

Still, life rolled on at the Castle. The income Boots was making served Buckley and the rest. In the evenings, they'd entertain each other with songs and comedy, the Lord invariably stage center on the throne, the others on scattered pillows around him.

Occasionally, he would dress up in a tuxedo for the ceremonial nod he gave new members of the court. The time he knighted jazz musician Benny King, he had artists draw up a scroll that he gave King after dubbing him with a sword and the words, "I give you the title of Prince Benny of King."

But what the Lord gave, he took away too. When Clyde Jones, of the jazz Jones Brothers, incurred his displeasure, he sent him a telegram, "You are no longer to be referred to as Baron Clyde of Jones. I have taken away your title."

Piece by piece the furniture went but Buckley kept his motley band going. Lord of all he surveyed, day after day on the balcony, he bayed to the world,

LOOOOOOOVE HOLLYWOOOOD
EVERY MOMENT.

And he did. He fit the place.

Wild as he was off the stage, on it he was bup-bup-Buckley, nothing special.

His act had too little of the Lord's fanciful head in it. That changed.

In the early '50s, he began to experiment with a new sound, one that used a syntax of its own, a hot manic jazz line.

"Hipsomatic," he called it. It was a jive language in extravagant tales of Christ (the Naz) and Gandhi (the hip Gan) and Hitler (the hip Einie), a mutha-tongue that suited spaced-out souls more than dead-level ones, word-tripping he did best in jazz rooms.

More a high-flying elocutionary lick than a comic one, it came down like this:

> Yeah, here I is again, that's me. And dere's you. And I dig all you cats out there, whippin' and wailin' and jumpin' up and down and servin' up that fine juice and pattin' each other on the back and tellin' each other who the greatest cat in the world is. Mr. Malenkov and Mr. Da-

> linkov and Mr. Eisenhower woozen wee-
> zen wizen woozen and Mr. Westhill and
> Mr. Beechhill and Mr. Churchill and all
> them hills, they gonna get it . . .
> STRAIGHT. If they can't straighten it,
> they know a cat that knows a cat that's
> gonna get it straight. But I'm gonna put a
> cat on you was the sweetest gaaaaawwwn-
> est wailingest cat that ever stomped on
> this sweet-swingin' sphere. And they call
> this hyar cat

—his voice pitched low—

THE NAZ.

It was Buckley's way of introducing the Christ tale.

Whatever he talked of, it had the long-
gaaaaawwwwwn sound, the dervish gyrations and syn-
tactical shimmying of hipsomatic. Buckley's rewrite on
the Gettysburg Address:

> Four big hits and seven licks ago, our
> before-daddies swung forth upon this
> sweet groovy land a swingin', stompin'
> jumpin' blowin' wailin' new nation, hip
> to the cool groove of liberty and solid-
> scent with the ace lick that all the studs,
> chicks, cats and kitties, red white or blue,
> is created level in front.

What Buckley did was to work out of his own impulse. It was the way comics began to go in the mid-
'50s. Mort Sahl was the first to do it with any impact.
With a rolled-up newspaper, in a cashmere sweater and
shirt open at the collar, he'd come out and

> Stalin carried it a bit too far, killing doc-
> tors. No wonder they don't make house
> calls.

Sociopolitical material he did, always with the cyn-
ic's eye. Korea, Khrushchev, Eisenhower—all were

grist for Sahl's highbrow mill. He even offered a standard disclaimer to Senator Joe McCarthy.

> I didn't mean to be a subversive, but I was new in this community and I wanted to meet the girls.

It was a new sound, calmer than what Lindy's comics did, a zigzagging professorial line whose untracked moments were part of its continuity. *So . . . well . . . where were we . . . Oh, yes.*

The business did not quite know what to make of it. In Sahl's early days, an agent at William Morris advised him to stick to writing. He was a new kind of comic, one with jokes to jar small truths as well as laughs. It was a literacy he brought to the cafes, one at odds with the yadda yadda that came down from vaud-e-ville days.

When Sahl said something like,

> Reminds me of the fellow in the statistical analysis course who'd never use sigma. He preferred his own initials instead

and it got a single laugh, he'd tell the man that if he understood that joke, he didn't belong there:

> You had better call the government. You're desperately needed.

Or, when he spoke of a cultural spa in Arizona and was interrupted by a man who said, "I spent two years there with those queers," his reply

> I wasn't talking about deviation . . . which is a Marxist concept anyway,

suggested a new comedic shorthand.

Sahl made it so comics could speak their minds. He brought the cafe IQ up a few points and altered expectations. It did not change audiences altogether. Many a comic would hear the smart line clunk in the night and know he'd better do the old jokes if he wanted to last the engagement.

Yet Mort gave comics a clue. He offered the proof that wit could make wages. He staked out new ground, and did it with a perverse glee. "Is there any group I haven't offended?" he liked to ask.

Some of the comics that came after him did the kind of material that once suffered the chichi stigma. Now it was *smart*. Either way, the material was more than a cartoon. It had an uneasy echo.

> I can never believe that Bartok died on Central Park West

was what Nichols and May would say, as lovers trying oh-so-**hard** to "relate."

Comedy now marked the times' confusion. And it came out of the rubbed nerves any art did. Mike Nichols and Elaine May, in the Compass Players, a Chicago improvisational troupe, did impromptu sketches that forced them to dig within for their small shiny moments.

It was the same group Shelley Berman emerged from. He was a man who looked as if he'd been dragged out of a bad night's sleep. His fretful expression was not the usual comic accessory. Berman was an actor, often unemployed. With the Compass Players, he did a solo improvisation with a telephone as a prop. The routine got laughs and Berman used the phone regularly as a device, even when he moved into nightclubs as a stand-up comic.

Shelley was a new one on audiences, not a bow-tied boy out to smile his way into their hearts. With the nervous pauses he took and the serrated edge his voice had, he was, as the media called him, "an Everymanic-depressive," decrying the routine chaos, the petty snafus that plague day-to-day lives.

A speck of dirt in a glass of milk, a bureaucratic tangle, the idiocy of airline hostesses: elaborating on them, Berman created scenes that asked—more than gag-premise comedy did—to listen-up. Mood mattered. And if a crowd cared for Schenley's more than Shelley, he was up a creek. It was what happened at the beginning. Berman was fired after one performance from his first nightclub job.

"It was in Milwaukee," he recalled. "Some nightclub in Milwaukee. And the guy said, 'Your stuff just goes over everybody's heads.' And I remember, I had borrowed money to go out there 'cause I had no money. I bought a suit. Because it was my first nightclub job. And I thought, 'Wow, big stuff.' And I borrowed money to take some pictures of myself because I had no pictures.

"And they fired me. I never even got paid for that first show. I remember the room had a kind of South Sea atmosphere. I mean there were palm trees all around me. And it was sort of like everything but Tiki gods, you know. And the most I ever got was chuckles.

"After, I took the next bus home. I packed and I went home. I packed my suit. Black mohair suit. And the people back home asked, 'How did it work out?' 'Well, I got fired.' 'When?' 'After the first show.' I remember it cost me so much money and I was hoping that I would get paid for my first show and I never got paid."

The act a Berle or Youngman did was no guide to the man. Most of what they said was bought and borrowed, and held together by technique and/or charm. Straight-out nonsense, expertly done. The Sahls and Bermans were not content to leave message or magic out. What they were onstage was a clue to what they were off it.

Or wished they were. The father that speaks to young Berman in a gruff ("They are sissy boys, Sheldon. All the actors are sissy boys") but loving ("Listen, Sheldon, Sheldon, don't change your name") way when he asks for a hundred dollars to go to acting school in New York in a favorite routine of his was not . . .

Q [*Berger*]:   —not really your father?

BERMAN: That's correct.

Q: Then how did you—

BERMAN: Did you ever hear of wishful thinking?

Q: This was the father you wanted?

BERMAN: I suppose so. I suppose. I don't think I could be so totally ungrateful to my father and my mother. 'Cause I think they tried hard. And I think they were all right. And they did help me. But the relationship that I'm demonstrating in *that* father and son routine, the relationship between these two men was far more important to me than the substance of the material, or the idea that I presented. The idea that I presented was that I wanted a hundred dollars to go to acting school. My "father" resisted. Eventually, he gave it to me because he loves me. What was far more important for me to show is the affection that stood there. That was paramount. And that bridged this great, great cultural gap. That particular essence was almost nonexistent at home. It was not that way. My father was not a sweet, fine deep-down-underneath swell Jewish guy. He was very ordinary with lots of weaknesses and some strengths. He certainly had no Jewish accent and he had very little of the depth of understanding that the father I portrayed had.

Q: What was he professionally?

BERMAN: He was a pimp.

Q: Literally?

BERMAN: He was a cab driver. And cab drivers in that time in the city of Chicago could make a good living doing that. And he lived a very, very hard and disgusting and disappointing life. And there was just nothing else for him to do. Nothing else he knew how to do. He bought a tavern but he drank too much.

Q: Got out of his taxi—

BERMAN: Yah. He drank too much and he lost that business. He was not an insensitive man, and he wasn't a fool. But he was an un-educated man who cursed his luck so loudly and so often, and I think maybe in some ways he was right. But he cursed luck too frequently. And I don't believe in luck. My mother suffered a great deal with him. She died very young. She was very young. She had me when she was nineteen. We were able to talk pretty well when I grew up. 'Cause she was only nineteen years older than I. . . .

I remember once when I was a teen-ager I'd met a girl in Grant Park in Chicago and I'd gotten myself all excited with her, and then she turned me off. And I came home and I was in considerable pain. And I couldn't tell my mother about that. I came in, I was practically doubled over. I had rocks. I mean, I really had pain. And I was just doubled over when I came in. And my mother said, "What's the matter?" And I said, "Nothing." "Well, something. You don't walk like that and nothing's wrong." "Well, I got a stomach ache," I said. "Maybe it's appendicitis."

She said, "Where in your stomach?" I said, "It's in the low part of my stomach. I'll just lie down for a while and it'll be better." Oh god, I was in agony. Well, there was a long pause. I sat down in a chair. And she made me a cup of tea or something. Yeah, she made me a cup of tea. And she was sitting . . . There was a long, long pause. And she said, "Were

66

you with a girl?" I said, "Yah." And she said, "Get yourself a little excited?" I said, "Yeah." She said, "Just a minute."

Then she walked into the bathroom and I could hear the tub running. She said, "Come on." She said, "Get in the tub." I said, "Oh, none of that cold water bit, Mom. Don't do that." She said, "No, it's a warm tub. It's a warm tub of water. Sit down in the warm tub of water." And I said, "All right. Just go away and leave me alone. And I'll sit in the tub of water." And she said, "I don't want to go away."

I said, "Mom, I don't want to undress naked in front of you. I don't want to do that." She said, "Well, I don't want to go away." And she closed down the toilet lid and sat down. And she said, "If you want to hurt, you can hurt. If you want to feel better, you'll sit in the tub and we'll talk." Many years later, when I read *Franny and Zooey,* I learned that I wasn't alone. And my mother and I had a long chat about girls who do that kind of thing. She had a great depth of understanding. She was marvelous.

Q: And your father?

BERMAN: It was hard for me to communicate with my father. It was hard. I was scared of him a lot. . . .

So it went. The act that used its own strange sources to make comic Rorschachs now did it in public. It was out of the Brooklyn flats and Broadway street corners and into the clubs—and with material that had the mark of the man on it.

No mistaking, for instance, what Jonathan Winters did. He was one of a kind, a clockwork zany, whether in the proper suburban village of Mamaroneck, New York, where he lived, or at the improper bar of Toots Shor's, where he resided.

In either setting—not to mention nightclubs and TV studios—Winters was a quick-change artist, able, in a blink, to create the sound and sauce of a character, and fit him with funny things to say. It was a skill that was, when he started, a reflex. Jon was "on" all the time.

Shortly after Winters moved into Mamaroneck, he wandered into town, stopping at the local drugstore, where, in quick succession, he informed the startled pharmacist:

1) He was Jesse James' brother Frank, in need of a fancy comb like the one Jesse toted. When the man looked startled, Winters became

2) A Mexican outlaw from just up the line in Mount Kisco. Called himself, he said, the Kisco Kid. When the druggist looked alarmed, Jon changed his story again. This time

3) He was Mrs. Woodrow Wilson's lame-headed nephew, out on a day's pass from the sanitarium.

In Shor's, Winters was whiskey's comic voice. On the drinks Toots' regulars slid up to him, he obliged the entertainment, jumping in and out of characters, bits so original that Catskill comics hanging around whipped out pads and made notes on lines Jonathan himself was unable to recall the next morning. Those lines came on whacko tears he did with the odd repertory in his mind—yokels and Yalies and octogenarian ladies.

He started as a beer-pub whiz in Dayton, Ohio, doing speedway motor sounds for chums. The laughs he got convinced him to try it for a living. By the time he arrived at Shor's he was nationally known, a status that inhibited him not at all.

It made for laughs in Shor's or the other rooms he moved through. Here he was a man losing his grip on an electric carving knife, apologizing to guests,

> Sorry. Sorry . . . Oh, you're the lucky one. You got the ring.

There he was a pilot interrogated on a plane of his that never landed:

Q: What did you do with the plane?

PILOT: Well, I did what anybody else would do. I give it to my little boy.

Winters was a keen observer. His skill with idiosyncratic detail enlivened characters. In Shor days, the comic Pat Harrington, Jr., had a character of his own, an Italian golf pro named Guido Ponzini. One night he was at Toots' bar, giving tips on the game in pidgin Italian to unsuspecting bar habitués. Then Winters came in. "Ponzini" was introduced to him. Winters gave the Italian golf pro the once-over, said, "Irish," and walked away.

Back then Winters' genie was in the bottle. He was a steady drinker, who used liquid spirits to make the good times roll. Occasionally, they didn't. One weekend in 1958, he went on a bender that saw him insult a number of people, the dim memory of which led him to moan, "I'm sorry, I'm sorry, I'm sorry, I'm sorry," the Monday after to anybody within earshot.

One of them was Tom O'Malley, the talent coordinator of the Jack Paar show, who a short time later heard that Winters had vowed to give up drink for good. Jon did—but not before climbing the rigging of an old sailing ship on Fisherman's Wharf in San Francisco, the result, O'Malley theorized, of too abrupt a withdrawal from alcohol.

He was not the only comic with a midnight source. Far from it. As Marty Kummer, a manager of comics, put it: "The more you find out about comedians, the more you're going to find out about hang-ups. They have them more so than other people."

Among Kummer's clients had been Shelley Berman, a fair proof, he claimed, of the proposition. Berman's stage figure was of a man aggrieved by a slipshod world, an accurate projection of Shelley himself. Or so Kummer attested.

"First, let me say this," he said. "Shelley Berman is really a decent human being, a nice man. If he could find happiness, that part of him would come out. I'll give you a perfect . . . There was a writer by the name of Marvin Marx, a very good comedy writer, had a stroke. And was in the hospital for eight months in Florida. Without any publicity, Shelley wrote Marvin Marx. I'm talking about when his wife used to say, 'We think he understands what we're saying,' but he —he could not talk because of the stroke. 'You have no idea what your letters have done for him.' Shelley Berman quietly was writing Marvin Marx. Not that they were—they were never bosom buddies. But it was the right thing to do.

"Shelley Berman is also a professional Jew. Same as Ed Sullivan's a professional Catholic, so called. Shelley Berman is a professional Jew. A nice Jewish boy would do that. If Marvin Marx was in town, Shelley Berman would be the first one over there, like the Jewish mother with the matzoh ball soup, you see . . . Shelley Berman has done more in his own little way, getting involved with the United Jewish Appeal and the B'nai . . . as we say, the B'nai everything. Shelley Berman always got involved . . . as a citizen. . . . He'd give up his time for those things, because he believed in it. He believed in it. Quietly. Many little things. Many little things that you wouldn't believe any performer would have time to do, Shelley Berman would do.

"And on the other hand, to show you the other part of him, he goes berserk because one of the big problems in this country is the lack of service and pride in service that employees have. All over, except in California, you very seldom find a good waitress. They get annoyed very easily. They don't care. There's no pride in a good shoemaker. Well, that kills Shelley Berman. I hate to tell you the times Shelley Berman has gone on record with airlines, and the letters he's written complaining about service and misinformation. Phone companies, utility companies, things that bug us. He tries to do something. And you say to him, 'The time you spent on that, why don't you write a new piece of material?' "

Even Sahl, who ran down the news with surgical precision, came to think he was part of it, a figure (he said) the CIA was out to kill, never an impossible notion with the politically involved but one that time and Sahl's continuing existence eventually seemed to disprove.

For demons, though, Lenny Bruce was the dark prince.

Even when he did *oogen ge shplugen*, Lenny was past it in his head.

He was, as Joe Ancis put it, "the loose maniac."

It was a quality he kept under wraps in the late '40s. Most comics from Hanson's remembered him as a nice fella, on the quiet side.

There was more shakin' with him though. The Miami Beach police arrest report on Leonard Schneider (Bruce's given name) was dated April 23, 1951:

> *Received a call to investigate a man dressed as a priest soliciting funds for a lepor colony.*
>
> *Found subject at the corner of 48th street & Alton road, dressed as a priest, subject stated to the undersigned that he was soliciting funds for some non-sectarian organization that had sponsered a lepor colony.*
>
> *Subject had no identification of any nature on his person, and stated that he was not working, but that maby he would go to work this week end. Subject stated that he was a comedian on the stage and appeared localy under the name of LENNY BRUCE. . . .*

On the Coast, Lenny became a changed man. When he arrived in LA in the early '50s, Bruce was married to the stripper Honey Harlowe, and madly in love with her. Offered a screenwriter's job at one of the movie studios, he took it on the condition that he could work irregular hours. Bruce wanted to be by his Honey when she woke past noon, after late night's work in clubs.

The feeling he had for her in prenuptial times, *Oh Honey, she's too much, man,* never left him, even when the marriage went bad. Lenny torched. Hurt hipped him to the whole mad bag he could do. The wigged edge was wedded to a growing awareness, a conscious push to empower his comic. Shecky Greene remembered giving him a vocabulary-building book that Bruce went through like a Times Square zealot does his Bible.*

Words, ideas, tricks old and new Bruce filled up with, next to useless in places like Strip City on Western and Pico. There the comic did jokes in between the girls' acts and covered the fifteen-minute break the band took. The entertainment was continuous and so was the noise when the comic came on.

In there, it was cooz that counted. Not for Lenny. One night when a party from one of the local newspapers heckled him, he ran out between acts and got a pie tin he filled with whipped cream. Next time up, he enticed one of the gents onto the stage and gave it to him, as the phrase goes, right in the kisser.

He got wild with the words too. In the dives he found that the musicians had an ear for his more demonic sounds. He began playing to them. Their laughs were what made his comic pump.

In a strip joint called Duffy's Gaieties, the ex-druggist name of Rocky who ran it took a shine to Bruce. He thought Lenny was the last word on comedy, and let him work regularly, bumping other comics if he had to. He'd tell them—blow, you crumb, Lenny's coming back.

In Duffy's, Bruce put the words in strange places. Surreal premises were pursued—what started as a quick flash turned into elaborate routines. In a nasal voice that often went whiney, Lenny wound up in orbits that the musicians were crazy for. He did a bit

---

* Even later as a big-name comic, Bruce remained a student. While in Chicago to headline Mr. Kelly's, he enrolled in a late-afternoon typing course. Each day, he'd enter the classroom, bow graciously to the elderly teacher, and leave an apple on her desk.

on a junkie hornman up for a job with Lawrence Welk's band that some of the musicians in that aggregate came in to see. In it, Welk—or Mr. Wig, as the hornman called him—told him what a fine bunch it was, a spiel the stoned musician never reacted to.

WELK: How come you don't talk to me?

MUSICIAN: (*drowsily*): Like, you know man . . . can't make it, sweetie, you know. Lot of cats put you down, Mr. Wig. No matter what they say, man, you're the best banjo player . . . whatever your ax is . . . I know you swing, you know. That's the main thing. To swing with your ax, you know. I knew Bird very well, man. I got Bird's ax. I saw Bird, man. He was really tore up. I knew all them people. I knew Miles. I knew Basie before he could count. Okay, you know . . . So, like really, if you want to do the thing, baby, like you dig?

WELK: What the hell are you talking about?

MUSICIAN: Hey, really, you're pretty wild. Hey, I don't want to bug you, but can I get a little bread in front?

WELK: You're hungry? You want a sandwich?

MUSICIAN: No man, I need some money. I need . . . Wait 'til you get to know me, man. I'm really a good-natured slob, man. I . . . give everything away to people and, you know. I even gave my bed away. That's why I'm sleepy. And I need some money just to . . . to take-my-aunt-to-the-hospital.

WELK: All right. I'm going to sign you. 'Cause I'm good judge of character.

MUSICIAN: Hey, I hate to cop out, Jim. I got a monkey on my back.

WELK: Oh, that's all right. We like animals in the band.

Every other week, Lenny was into Duffy's with new slants, not for the stiffs in off the street to ogle sweet Betty's buns but for the musicians and other LA comics and maybe celebs like Hedy Lamarr, Ernie Kovacs, Steve Allen. *Too much, too much,* they'd tell Rocky, and the ex-druggist would nod, knowing it was Rx—just what the doctor ordered.

Lenny worked with acerbic tongue, twitting blown-up politicos and notions and nelly sweethearts like Sophie Tucker. And then he'd go back to the flat and jot down a key word or two to keep each bit in mind. A pro. *Oogen ge shplugen* no more. No mimicking of other voices. Bruce found his own, sort of. Traces lingered.

The frenetic sound Joe Ancis put down in Hanson's or in Brooklyn pads was part of it. Diverse word elements, straitlaced Funk and Wagnalls rubbed cheek to cheek with gutter phrases or the Yiddish and jazz idioms Ancis used into the '70s. Joe spoke of "digging Pushkin's ass" when it was the body of his work he meant.

Old city cronies who went out to the Coast heard Lenny say, "Yeah yeah, I'm doing Joey now." Later, when he came to New York as a name comic and spent some time with Ancis, neo-Joe was in the act again. Ancis' psychiatrist remarked on it after he saw Lenny work. Bruce's description of Monet's painting was precisely Joe's from an earlier session. Ancis had seen the Monet exhibition at the Museum of Modern Art and told Bruce about it.

The use of hip talk and the Broadway eye-view on any subject smacked of Will Jordan's style. Some of Bruce's ideas were suspiciously close to his. Lenny had the rabbi with the precious pulpit sound that vent de odda vay once he was through.

Later he was to do a bit on Adolf Hitler that came from a Jordan original—the idea of Hitler's life as a 20th Century-Fox musical. Will created it one night backstage at the Roxy. When he journeyed to LA he got up at the Cobblestone and did it for Lenny and others to see. The Führer began appearing in Bruce's act shortly after. When Jordan asked him how come, Lenny told Will he was known as a commercial mimic. "Why would you be doing this?" Bruce asked. "So I might as well do it."

He did it—the idea was of Hitler as a "find," the Hollywood myth of stardom. In Bruce's routine, agents seeking a dictator-type (Bremerhaven/1927) call Central Casting. No good.

1ST
ACTOR: (*aggressively German*): Das ist ungespinnert alles gefrimmer, ya!—

AGENT: Ah, that method crap! Get out of here with that Brando jazz, you kidding mit that? Ok. Paul Schneider. Paul? Do ze bit, alright?

2ND
ACTOR: Das is ungespinn—

AGENT: You fruit! Get out of here! Don't bug us no more . . .

It begins to look hopeless. Then one of the agents notices something.

AGENT: Don't look now, but dig the guy on your right dat's painting the vall.

2ND
AGENT: Vere?

AGENT: Don't look right away. He'll think you're putting him on. The *zhlub* with the white uniform. And the cap on. . . . (*Sings a few notes.*) Sonny, put down that painting. You'll do that later. C'mere, c'mere. Dat's right. Look at his face. Is this an album cover? Woo! Ziz iz a weirdo.

If Lenny was not above pirating a phrase or more, it was not a habit with him. Even Jordan acknowl-

75

edged it. When word first filtered back to New York that Lenny had taken "the Hitler," Will's reaction was —Why would Rockefeller steal from a shoeshine boy? Lenny had the reputation for relying on his own wit. He was prolific, heeding what old pal **Georgie Starr** later prescribed as the only **way for** a comic:

> You've **got to fuck and** suck it and eat it **night** and day. Work on the **material.** Work on it. Work on it.

It was what Lenny did. He'd put what he tried onstage on to paper to keep it in mind. Always with the scrap papers Lenny was, getting ideas down. He'd use matchbook covers, napkins, memo pads. Even at his apartment he'd try notions out. One afternoon, when another comic came by, Bruce pointed to a story in the local press about miners trapped beneath the earth. Soon he was in his kitchen, the blender going to simulate the rescue drill and the miners conferring on how best to exploit the caper once it was over. *Look, diggit, you say while I was down there, I was smoking Chesterfields and*—The tape of it he tried on an **LA record** firm. The head man there took one listen and pointed to the door.

A fine anger fed Bruce in those days. He was outraged by sham. One night he saw Ed Sullivan on the TV he rarely watched and the hooey theatrics sent Lenny to Western Union to fire off a multipage telegram to Sullivan. *Where do you get off with* . . . dit-dit-dit. The memory of hyped Brucean messages no doubt made Sullivan gun-shy when Lenny later was proposed for the shooooo.

For all that, Bruce suddenly could turn mellow. He'd rip a person from the stage and then meet him and like him and scrap the material. And when he kidded with friends, he didn't misuse them to get laughs.

FRANKIE
RAY: In real life, if he did anything funny, it was to make you laugh. It was never—

Q: Cruel?

RAY: No. He was very kind. The side I know of him. Later, when he started getting high, he respected me, he would always say to me, "I know you don't dig that, that's where I'm gonna go."

Q: You said, "kind"?

RAY: Well, like I'd been separated from my wife for oh, three years. And one day we're sitting in his apartment and there was no money. And he started asking me questions about my wife.

Said, "Why don't you call her up and say hello to her? I'll pay for the call." And the conversation that we had on the phone —my wife and I—was kind of a sad conversation. And when I hung up, he was sitting there, and he was crying. Because he could almost tell what she was saying. And I guess he saw it was a hopeless type thing.

A mixed bag he was. When Ray got hold of a jeweled ring in tainted circumstances, Lenny, asked to spirit it away for safekeeping, pretended to do so. Later, the "ring" was dug up and found to be worthless. Some time after, when Ray said he was wise to what happened; Bruce confessed to selling the ring for six hundred dollars. Only then did he give Ray his three-hundred-dollar share.

He was not always true to the comic word either. Onstage, he talked seriously about the sexes. Off it, he was not so thoughtful once it started to go badly with Honey. Women were a passing fancy. All he wanted, he'd say, was "to squirt the poison and run." And he did, leaving the ladies cold.

It was the same Lenny who'd perform "abortions" on musicians in his act, *All right, sweetie, spread 'em*, using a vacuum cleaner as his major surgical device.

As the operator of a Tijuana abortion mill, he'd assure them, *Eez not going to hurt you.*

Other nights, when it was time for him to introduce a strip, he'd hop across Duffy's stage like a jackrabbit, altogether naked. Once, he came out in the buff and angered patrons there with their wives. They wanted to knock him around.

Some of the so-called "sick" Bruce routines came with a reverse lining, though he was capable, to be sure, of the gratuitously sleazy line. The one the news-weeklies later seized on was the extenuating circumstance he worked up for Leopold and Loeb:

> Bobby Franks was a snotty kid anyway.

In Duffy's, a line like that got paroxysms of laughter from Bruce aficionados, less concerned for moral fine points than the soar of comedic invention.

Bruce was acquiring a reputation in LA as a hip comic. It was why when in 1957 he was booked to open Slate Brothers, a club with a legitimate "Hollywood" crowd, he felt good about it. He figured it'd be abracadabra for him in popular acceptance.

It didn't turn out. First night, he walked on and *bzzz bzzz*—it wasn't Bruce but each other the people wanted to hear. Lenny was past playing twinkly-time comic. Over the din, he shouted for them to give him a break, all he wanted was to tell them one joke.

It was a gag he'd heard from Buddy Hackett at the bar before the show. An oldie:

> Did you hear about the kid that says to his father—"What's a degenerate?" And the father says, "Shut up and keep sucking."

Lenny didn't stop there either. He kept at them:

> Half the girls in this audience are hookers and the joke offends them. And

bah bah bah.

Bruce had a thing he did in the '50s. He'd turn his

back to the audience, raise his jacket and shake his ass. That night he did it and ran. Later, he sent a telegram to the brothers Slate, canceling out.

It came at a time the marriage was going under. In those days, Bruce often tried to be rid of her. He never quite could. He'd hole up for a day or two with Maynard Sloate, one of the owners of the Crescendo, an LA club Bruce worked. While there, he'd swear to Sloate that he was through with the Mrs., but always he broke and went back.

Even after the divorce, he saw her, and it was rarely for the good. Bruce's pals, years after, referred to Honey Harlowe as "the woman" or "her"—never by name. There was a tacit feeling she brought him hurt and a drug connection, the combination of which led him to infernal last years.

Lenny remained bewitched, a sucker for red-haired women. Once, he decided to settle a financial debt to comic friend Jackie Gayle by getting him a high-class hooker. He went to see the girl to arrange it, and discovered she was a Titian-haired beaut. He stayed the night(s).

In LA, he worked the Crescendo, Duffy's and up and down the Strip, still playing to the band. Sloate of the Crescendo remembered some nights he'd turn his back to the audience and do his first five minutes to the musicians. To keep them amused, Lenny changed his act, turning out routines by the dozens; material that caught on at Ann's 440 in San Francisco. It was there Bruce's career got rolling. On and up: From San Francisco to the Cloister in Chicago, and on into New York. From ninety dollars a week, he went to ten times that.

The relevance Mort Sahl initiated, Lenny jazzed up. He talked about sex, drugs, religions, show business, race and politics—but with a head-rattling anglo, a mix of whirling words and ideas that sometimes crashed through to a small revelation. He didn't tiptoe either. "Are there any niggers out there tonight?" was how he got into a shaman's riff on the absurdity of racial slurs. Religions he depicted as a cash conceit.

His assemblage of leaders of the Judeo/Christian faiths is greeted in this fashion:

Good evening, gentlemen. Nice to see so many boys heah tonight. Most of yew religious leaders ah haven't seen in many yeuhs. Ah just was talking to Billi this aftanoon. Ah said, "Billi, yew came a long way, sweetie, long way." Who woulda thought back in '31—we were hustling baby pictures then and siding. We're swinging, you know—we didn't know what the hell we doin'. The CC camps were startin' to move, yeah. Ah didn't know mahself, y'know? An' just lahk that! We came on it, y'know? The Gideon. An' bop! An' theah we were. Hah!

Bruce was far from the *oogen ge shplugen* comic he'd been a decade before, a species he viewed as hopelessly out of it. Dinosaurs. Hacks. A type he got down in his classic routine on the comic that wanted to play the Palladium in London.

Here was a *zhlub* looking to have the Palladium's prestige rub off on him, which even his manager perceived was impossible. Warned by him not to play there, the comic scoffs at the caution:

I got my act tight now. I got twenty-four minutes of dynamite. I know every laugh. I can work all kinds of people too. Work the Jewish people. I learned how to say "toe-kiss," alright? Now, when I work to musicians, I do a bit called hep-smoke-a-reefer. Alright? Got them right in my pocket. Work to the eggheads, I do the Stevenson stuff. I got it down. Twenty-four minutes—wherever I go, I kill them.

A pure philistine with not a thimble's worth of a notion. A mind that reduced thoughts to trivia and, when brought to the Palladium stage,

Well, folks, I just got back from Lost Wages, Nevada. Funny thing about . . .

is met with silence save for the courtesy applause of two usherettes who ball every act coming through.

The house booker tactfully tries to persuade the comic he is not right for the Palladium, resorting even to the line that he is too hip for its crowd. But the comic is no fool when it comes to his survival. He recognizes what is on the booker's mind, and storms and fumes and finally begs for another chance:

> I didn't even do my fag at the ball game yet.

Against his better judgment, the house booker agrees.

Same thing again. Silence. Faces staring. Fifteen hundred people. An oil painting. By now, he's tried everything. Nice tasty Martha Raye bits. Picking his nose. And it's granite out there. Jefferson. Washington. Lincoln. So he throws a phrase out to the Britishers. SCREW THE IRISH. It's the first line the audience picks up on—and more than even the comic figured on. Chaos that ends with the booker exclaiming,

> Ooo-eee, goddamn, son. Oh. Oh. I don't believe what's going on out there. Go ahead, you sadist. Get a nail and do it up right. Oh. Oh. I don't believe what went on out there. Just don't believe it. You're a bloody mau mau. I swear to god, son. Robert Ruark really missed something with you. Now look, son. I don't mind these boys who come out and they start with the same word every night. They finish with the same word. Perhaps, they're not too creative or funny maybe, but goddamn, son, you've got a knack of making people vicious. There's a difference in not getting laughs and changing the architecture of the theater. You're not funny, that's all. I mean, face it. How old a man are you? I should say thirty-four or thirty-five. It's not too late, you know. Take the cloth, something. Forget it. You might be good with those evangelist things, saving

> people. What the hell are you staring at
> me for, you idiot? You don't use narcotics,
> do you? Here, son. Sign it [a release]
> where it says "witnesses" while you've
> still got the fingers to do it with.

It was the length to which a comic would go who
hadn't the mind over matter. He was, as Vonnegut
would say, "stuck in time," and the time was the
twenty-four minutes his act was. With such a comic,
even the tiniest apocalyptic moment was unlikely. It
was where Lenny differed. He operated so he could—
and did—shift gears.

Shecky Greene saw him in a club in Chicago, working to an audience of prom kids from a local Catholic
high school. "And he was," said Greene, "a little bit
nuts that day. And he said to these kids,

> Yeah. What do I talk about to prom kids?
> Yeah, yeah, yeah. Let's see. Let's talk
> about clap.

"Did ten minutes on clap. And a kid stood up and
I swear this is a true story. I was there. And the kid
says, 'Mr. Bruce, we came here to be entertained. We
don't want to hear about that.' And Lenny went,

> Koo koo koo koo. That's great. Hey, man,
> that's really really . . . that's really wild.
> How old are you?

"The kid says, seventeen. Lenny says,

> That's really wild. That's magnificent that
> you would stand up and you'd say that to
> me. That's great.

And he asked the kid did he play football. And the
kid said he did. Lenny says,

> Yeah, if I was really to talk about that
> after you told me no, you'd really whack
> me, wouldn't you?

"And he got into these kids that way . . . little by little. And he didn't talk about clap. He talked about something else. And what it was to go to a prom. And it was the goddamn cleanest show I ever saw him do in a long time. He had these kids spellbound."

He schneidered them in some places, in others he didn't. But usually he worked on the rim of danger. He let the weird notions run. When one clicked, it'd lock in in Bruce's mind, and he'd get the rush all comics do who move off the moment.

Bruce did it more than other comics did. He took the chances. He was not afraid to fall flat on his arse with new material. There were those that saw him go gurgling down the drain one night and make thunder the next.

He did the unexpected and not just in performance. What he did off the stage added to his antic reputation. One night in a hamburger joint on Sunset Boulevard, a motorcycle tough came in and said, "I'm going to kill me every Jew in this place." Customers tensed and hoped the thing would blow over. Then a song was raised in that room—

> When Israel was in Egypt land,
> Let my people go-ooooo

in the unmistakable voice of Lenny Bruce.

Hearing it, the hood reached for the nearest man handy and bashed him in the face. Into the battle charged Lenny, in time to be thrown through a plate-glass window.

It battered body but not spirit. In the police cruiser that took him away, he was on the two-way radio, spieling, "The perpetrator is a white male, in his twenties, no distinguishing scars"—to the amusement of the law officers.

In Las Vegas, Bruce once arrived to see Shecky Greene work at the Tropicana. From the stage, Greene kidded him,

> What are you here, to steal my job?

to which Lenny replied,

> You kiddin'? I wouldn't work this shit house,

a remark overheard by a hotel official, who took it seriously. Bruce was asked to leave.

Later, he stopped by the Flamingo to see Pearl Bailey. "And," said Frankie Ray, "a guy from the band told her, 'There's Lenny Bruce. He's a comedian. Whyn't you get him up?' Pearl Bailey says, 'Well, I hearda Lenny Bruce. Lenny Bruce is a very funny man. You come on up here, Lenny Bruce.'

"And Lenny said, 'No, cool it, cool it. I just came to see you. Thank you very much.' And she says, 'Ahm serious, Lenny, come on up here.' And he says, 'I don't do this kind of shtick.' She says, 'I don't shtick shtack. Come on up here, we're gonna have some fun, Lenny Bruce.'

"So he went up there. And he's standing there. And she just forgot about him. Just let him stand there. So he remembered when he was in the navy, he used to have fun with those fire extinguishers. He said, Fuck it, and ran backstage and grabbed the fire extinguisher. And instead of coming out foamy, it dripped. It was watery. And hit her in the face. And she gave her big speech, 'I guess our people will always be bah bah bah.' In the meantime, the guards are trying to catch Lenny and are falling on their asses, slipping all over the stage. The musician got panicky, and he ran. And she forgot about it.

"But then he had to go write one of his letters again. She read his letter—'You got a lotta nerve telling me what you've done for your people, and bah bah, you going around with that Stepin Fetchit bullshit, you throw them back fifty years.'

"And she goes, 'Git him ooooouuuut.'

"And they went upstairs. And he was sitting on the toilet. And they kicked him off the toilet. And he said, 'I'm a good friend of [Flamingo owner Morris] Lansburgh.' So they called Lansburgh. And Lansburgh heard about it already and said get him out.

"And then Shecky and me went looking for him to give him a couple hundred dollars to get him out of town. Couldn't find him. We're in front of the Sahara. And I'm saying, 'Shecky, I can't find him.'

"All of us, when we needed the fucking money, we had to go to Shecky. Even though he'd scream and holler, we'd still get it. So he had the two hundred dollars and I'm getting nervous, 'cause Shecky'll run and throw it on the dice table. And all of a sudden a guy goes, "Pssst, psst.' Now, you know those post-cards when you see an Indian sitting on his haunches with a blanket. Well, Lenny was there, sitting with the blanket. 'They're all looking for me.' I says, 'You fucking nut.' So then we went in to cash the check at the Sahara. And on the way out, Lenny says, 'How do you do this shit, Shecky?' And Shecky says, 'That's roulette. Throw something.' So he threw five dollars on the roulette and won. And he says, 'I like this.' And he took the money and scrammed."

Not everyone went for the new comic sound.
For some it was sick. For others it was just nothing.
When Bruce appeared at the Duane Hotel in New York, a popular refrain among detractors was,

> Where's Lenny Bruce?
> Down the Duane.

Crimped times. The sleepy Eisenhower era had the gray view of change. In comedy, it meant new notions drew guarded response. Not just the ideas expressed either. The very *sound* of a comic could do it.

It was the case of a Talmudic scholar from the Lower East Side, a quizzical kid who gave up the rabbinate to be a comic, a change that occurred to him while he orated to his congregation. As he put it: "I would talk from the pulpit about the sacrifice of oithly pleasures and while I was talking, I'd notice there was a fan-tastic girl in the third row."

Jackie Mason, son of an orthodox rabbi, had been persuaded against his better judgment to be (as his brothers were) a man of God, an affiliation that suffered for his lack of belief in a deity. What he put his faith in were gags and girls, interests mutually inclusive in the life of a comic. No accident he went straight to the Catskills.

There he did jokes in a Yiddish rhythm that a Yeshiva upbringing had given him, syncopated beat he had the temerity to think he could do in mixed ethnic company. Summers in the Catskills, winters on the bar mitzvah circuit, all the time Mason wanted to branch out, move into the cafe circuit, a notion preposterous to people in the business.

"I was in the mountains, let's say two summers," Mason recalled. "After the second summer in the mountains, I decided that I could be a fantastic comedian for Gentiles . . . but I wasn't sure. . . . And every time I tried to get a job in a nightclub, they said I was too Jewish. And the ones who said it most severely were the Jews. And the ones who were most fearful of my trying to entertain the Gentiles were the Jews. They thought . . . they thought if I told a joke in front of a Gentile audience, all Jews in America would be wiped out. Because they thought that it's the most offensive thing you could do . . . to sound so Jewish in front of American people.

"So they started to beg me to take speech lessons. And one after the other, every important agent or manager or anybody I met in show business said to me, 'You can't go like this in front of the American people. These people will kill you.' Some of them reached the point of getting furious. 'What do you mean you're going to entertain people when you talk like that? People don't want to hear that. How's it going to reflect on the Jewish people? I've got a brother, I got a son. American Jews are finally making progress in this country and they're starting to achieve an identity, and you're going to talk like this?' "

Mason pushed on anyway, booked into rough *goyische* joints. "The first," he said, "was a strip in Massachusetts and it was a bunch of wise guys in a small-town kind of a neighborhood bar. And I went on the stage and before I introduced the stripper, I did some of my cultivated classy-type jokes, which was a million miles from what they were interested in hearing. They thought a guy would say, 'Lemme tell you a fucking joke.' Instead, I came in, I'm doing my psychiatrist routine. They didn't know a psychiatrist from a purple heart. They didn't know what the hell it was. And I'm stinking the joint out. As I'm stinking the joint out, I introduce the stripper. By the time I finish introducing, I was already fired. The boss came over while the strip was on and said, 'Get your stuff and get the fuck out of here.' When they fire you in those places, they don't say, 'I'm sorry, sir. It didn't seem to be the propitious moment.' They come over and say, 'Get your fucking clothes and get out of here, you prick. You call yourself a fucking comedian?'

"Next was in Rome, New York. Same thing identical. A woman owned that club. She walked over to me, she said, 'What the fuck makes you think you're a comedian?' A woman said this. A fat old lady. 'What the fuck makes you think you're a comedian?' I was stunned.

"By now, my best friends were convinced that I was an idiot, that I was kidding myself. That I was suffering from sick egomania. That I was refusing to face reality. Buddies. Family. Friends. Guys on corners. Philosophers. Psychologists. Dancers. Whoever I met. Whoever knew me well or long or cared. They would say, 'What are you kidding yourself? It's two years already. You were a hit in the mountains, you saw that anybody that knows anything about show business is telling you that this mockey accent is not going to sell and that this can't go big time. What makes you think you know better than William Morris? Who the fuck are you, a shmuck that's not working, that's going to tell the William Morris office what's going to sell? They're selling stars a million years and you can't get a fucking job except a bar mitzvah and you become an expert. Why don't you get wise to yourself?' And while they were talking, I'm saying to myself, 'This guy is a shmuck.' "

Eventually, Mason got himself booked into Slate Brothers in LA on a night-to-night basis so that if the Lower East Side sound wasn't funny, he could be shipped out fast. He stuck around. To the Coast crowd, he was a weird little yid, cocksure—

and sharp.

His lines were those of a reformed loser. He told how he used to be so self-conscious that at a football game, he thought that in the huddles the players were talking about him. And:

> I went to a psychiatrist. I said, "How much do you charge?" He said, "Twenty-five dollars a visit." I told him, "For twenty-five dollars, I don't visit. I move in."

He was a hit with the jokes. Even when one missed, he'd look the crowd over and say,

> It's the foist time I ever saw dead people smoke,

or ask ingenuously,

> You understand what I'm saying? Does anybody out there know what I'm talking about?

with the Delancey Street delivery that was a wholly unique comic experience.

It was a smash with Angelenos. He was at Slate Brothers for a long stay, leaving theorists back East to reassess their ideas about ethnics.

TV moved his price up. From $300 a week at the Slate Brothers, Mason went to $8,500 a week within two years. TV was rapid transit from the late '50s on. It was a starmaker, particularly its late-night talk shows. TV changed the business around.

In the early days, it was considered a second-rate operation. When Will Jordan went on Arthur Godfrey's "Talent Scouts," the program was simulcast on radio and TV. In fact, back in 1949, when Groucho Marx did "You Bet Your Life," the radio budget was $12,000 per program, and TV's was $2,500 per. By 1961, the average TV budget was $40,000 and there was no radio. Keefe remembered a show that Johnny Olson did in the basement of a New York department store in TV's early days. Payment for appearing on it was a Speidel watchband.

"There was," Keefe said, "one guy I worked for. His wife wanted to be a comedienne. So he figured an idea, and got it on TV. It wasn't hard then. The idea was that people wrote in and gave the panel of comics [and the producer's comedienne-wife] a category to make a joke on. Each comic did, and then the audience decided which one was best—an applause meter and all. Of course, nobody wrote in to a show like that in those days. The producer made up all these fictitious letters. The show reappeared every so often as 'Tag the Gag' or 'What's the Joke?' "

TV often was not geared to the comic. Bobby Baxter was invited to take over a show on which other comics had fared badly. It was held in a studio where the audience sat in the balcony—so far away from where the comic worked he could hardly hear the laughs. Later, the show was moved to another theater, and Morey Amsterdam and Jackie Gleason were the costars. Eventually, Amsterdam left and Gleason took over, bound for stardom.

In the late '40s, Berle was the big man on TV. On Tuesday nights, stores closed down early so people could get home to see the slapstick shtick Uncle Miltie did.

Makeup!

he'd roar, and a stooge would rush out and slap him with a sack of flour. Pies flew, and so did the old Berle nonsense:

Thank you, ladies and germs. I wuz—

The mock horrific expression would turn to the goof-toothed grin.

In contrast was Max Liebman's "Your Show of Shows" with Sid Caesar. "Double-Caesar," Liebman called him, for Sid had a voracious appetite then— he could down two chickens in a sitting. Caesar, Carl

Reiner, Imogene Coca and Howard Morris were not, strictly speaking, stand-up comics. "Sketch players" was the term, but their laughs came from wit that was years ahead of TV time.

In a spoof on the Western classic *Shane*, Caesar appeared at a ranch to refresh himself and his horse and drew the attention of Coca, in the part Brandon de Wilde had played.

COCA: You seem mighty thirsty. Have a long ride?

CAESAR: No—I had a herring for breakfast.

The laughs on the show were the result of writers Liebman hired—Neil Simon, Mel Tolkin, Lucille Kallen and Tony Webster. Also around was an ex-Catskill comic, Mel Brooks, who, Liebman remembered, stalked the corridors. "Sid liked him," Liebman said, "because he was entertaining. At first he wasn't officially connected with the show. Sid paid him twenty-five, thirty dollars just to hang around. He'd go with him to the Gotham Health Club. Into the steam room. Always joking around.

"First time I met him was backstage at the old Broadhurst Theater. Sid said, 'Oh, this is Mel Brooks.' He said, 'Mel, why don't you do what you did for me? Why don't you do it for Max?' And to me, 'Mel's an entertainer in the mountains, he has a little act.' And Mel said all right and went out onstage and there was that work light there and he went into this little thing he did. He sang,

> Hello, hello, hello
> I've come to start the show
> I'll sing a little, dance a little
> I'll do this and I'll do that
> And though I'm not much on looks
> Please love Mel Brooks.

"And then he got down on one knee and made a mammy-type gesture."

Eventually, Brooks joined the show on a salaried

basis. In the sessions Liebman had with the writers, Mel was no shrinking violet. Liebman often threw lighted cigars at him to shut him up.

But Brooks was irrepressible. At parties he and Carl Reiner did skits based on a character of Mel's, the two-thousand-year-old man. He had an answer for every occasion—and more often than not it was funny. One time, when the writers worried over what occupation to give a character, Brooks quipped, "He shouts prayers to crashing pilots."

Comics came tumbling down too. TV discarded them as fast as it popularized them. Material ran thin when shown on a regular basis. So did the public's interest. It meant a comic had to manage his appearances so they'd have impact. Handled right, TV could speed a career along. Comics did what they could to get on it.

One afternoon, in the theater the Paar show came out of, there was a knock at the door of talent coordinator Tom O'Malley. Into the office came a young lad who bowed and announced, "I have the pleasure of presenting to you the great Lord Buckley." It was his son.

Buckley was back. And if the material was changed, little else was. He remained the same grand figure, again installed in quarters clearly beyond his means. The Lord worked in small jazz spots and partied long into the night, his resolve to give the bottle up apparently forsaken.

Keefe was in on it—Sir Adam in the floating court Buckley had. "He'd drop," Keefe said, "like five, six mescaline tablets into a bottle of vodka, shake it up and drink. I drank a thimble's worth of it. And I was up for three days and three nights with my eyes wide open. The world was technicolor.

"Between that and lovemaking, he had a time. He'd be balling every few minutes. Not necessarily with the door closed either. You could see if you cared to look. You'd certainly hear them because Buckley made love like a rhinoceros. MMMM AHHHH. MMMMMMM. AHHHH, MY DEAR. MAGNIFICENT. A REAL COUNTESS."

To the end, he took his royal prerogatives. Musician

Dick Zalud remembered, "One day my wife and I were working in New York. We were going up to the Catskills. And just before we left, Buckley called. He said, 'Owlhead, I need sixty dollars immediately.'

"I said, 'Buckley, I don't have any bread.'

"He said, 'Immediately, Owlhead. I want you to jump in your car and come down here and give me sixty dollars. I need it immediately.' And I said, 'Buckley, I'm just leaving for the mountains and we're packed and leaving. And I'm going up to the mountains and we'll pick up money there. I'll send it to you.'

"And then he started to get on me. 'You Jew bastard, you son of a bitch. You dirty . . .' And I hollered up to my old lady that he was calling me a Jew bastard. And she said hang up on him. And I hung up. And we got into the car. We were driving up to the hills and I said, 'I feel terrible that I hung up on him. I really feel bad.' So the next morning I got up and I called him. I called him back in New York. And the first thing he says, he picks up the phone and says, 'Aha. Conscience!' "

TV didn't ring the Lord back. Hipsomatic never got the run he would have liked it to on the airwaves. It was mostly confined to the small jazz clubs where he was His Wigged Highness until his death at age fifty-four in 1960.

If TV made stars with a speed not previously possible, it ruined the cafe scene. Clubs went under, a few in fires of suspicious origin ("kerosene cans," in the trade). The job market tightened, a squeeze that took some of the fun out of the comic colony.

The camaraderie that had existed in Hanson's changed. With TV, careers turned so rapidly it embittered comics. Even ones that made it. Success spoiled Buddy Hackett. Jovial as St. Nick before he made it, he was not after. In the late '50s, he'd be by Hanson's and the B&G next door, saying "You guys are aw-ull losers. Scwoo you's. You's aw-ull stink. You're never gonna make it."

It worked the other way too. TV phenomena caught heat. Jackie Mason was an example. On the Lower East Side, Mason, a bumbler with wall-to-wall eye-

.brows, was discounted by the Catskill comics who ran the basement social club he belonged to.

When he became a star, it was hard for them to live with it. He was not the same man. He'd had electrolysis for the brows, and psychiatric help for his insecurity. Along the way he'd learned to write and tell jokes. And courtesy of TV—he was a star. Likethat.

They began to badmouth him. Stories that he was bogus goods/the accent was unreal/he was never a rabbi/he was rotten to his parents/he got a *schvatzah* pregnant. So on, so forth. Sometimes, they'd come to see him work in clubs. If he went over after to say hello, they'd get up to leave and curse him on the way out.

He got it from the big-timers too, who resented his quick success. In the Stage Deli, Fat Jack would be on him. *Errh, errh, calls himself a friggin comedian.* Off to do a nightclub, he'd discover Alan King had told an owner he wouldn't play unless he got more money than, in Mason's phrase, "this hot mockey comic."

All sorts of slanders were circulated. There were those who said he was not in his thirties, that he was far older. One day at 1650 Broadway, Mason met comic Sonny Sands, who dragged him into the elevator, pointed to a mirror there and said, "You're not thirty-two. Lookit the wrinkles. I hear you're fortyseven."

Up against TV, the nightclub was no longer an attraction. Its small extortions and sleazy commercialism were antiquated when a man could sit in his jockey shorts and get the action for nothing.

A minor consequence of the decline of the cafes was that their operators had to bargain with comics they'd shafted in better times, which Shecky Greene, for one, enjoyed. When Podell of the Copa called to ask if he'd come work there, Greene told him no—in the Popeye voice. "I don' need the job," he said.

And he didn't. Las Vegas was paying salaries clubs couldn't match. The new comics did not rely entirely on the fancy rooms either. For them there was money to be made in record albums. Sahl, Berman, Bruce,

Bob Newhart and Winters all made cuts. Berman's were major hits. Concert tours were lucrative too. *Variety* reported Sahl's take for a twenty-seven-city itinerary in 1960 was $120,000 on an overall gross of $246,370.

The clubs they played were the ones known as chichi in the past. Now rooms like Mr. Kelly's, the Blue Angel, the hungry i were places where a comic could make a living. In 1960, Bruce earned $108,000 —a good portion of it in those boîtes.

Not that the places were heckle-proof. Often the old-style mugs infiltrated, which some handled better than others. It was a question of style. Sahl's was cerebral, but gag-oriented. No strain for Mort to detour:

> I'm glad you all think more of relevance than having a good time,

he'd say when he didn't get laughs. Or, when he did,

> I'm not geared to total acceptance.

Sahl was no patsy. Years later, when a drunk female heckled him at the Bijou Cafe in Philadelphia, he quipped,

> It's obviously not the first time you've failed in the dark,

which sent her into a glass-throwing tantrum.

With Berman it was another case altogether. His comedy was a more fragile construct. O'Malley of the Paar show remembered the first time he saw him: "This was in 'fifty-seven when Shelley was starting. He was nothing yet. And he came in to audition. Had a white shirt on that was tattered at every end. And he looked awful. He had acne. He looked completely unlike a performer. And he said [in nasal tone], 'Eh, could I have a stoo-uhl?' And I said, 'Let's pretend that we . . . you know, have a stool. You can just sit in the seat there.' And he said, 'Uh . . . I have to . . . have a stooo-uhl.'

"And I was new at the job and like a jerk I went across the street and got a stool for him from a bar. I said, 'Could I borrow this stool? I'm with the Jack Paar show.' Said, 'Ok, bring it back.'

"And I gave him the stool. And he sat on the stool. And then he went like this—he put his hands to his eyes. And he's like that for a while. And I said, 'Any time you're ready, Shelley. Go ahead.' And he didn't even answer. Didn't answer. Just sat there with hands to eyes, getting in the mood. Then suddenly he took his left hand and he put it up to form a telephone and he started dialing."

In the business, Berman had a reputation for tantrums. Other comics, in talking of blow-ups onstage, would say, "He did a Berman." When Shelley worked LA's Avant Garde, he would insult people to the point where they wanted to fight him. "We had maître d's that had to stop them," owner Maynard Sloate (formerly of the Crescendo) recalled. "He had no finesse in telling off a customer. He could be a mean and miserable man. He had traumas of his own. And like ok, one night I'm standing in the doorway and he's on the stage, saying, 'What's that noise, Maynard?' And I'm trying to hide now because everyone's looking at me. So this goes on for about fifteen minutes. And I'm shaking my head. Every five minutes, he finished a routine and says, 'What's that noise, Maynard?' So finally, fifteen minutes into the act, he stops and says, 'I know what it is. It's the refrigerator motor.'

"Terrible, terrible. Anybody say anything, he'd just tell them off without humor. One time he come in, there was a comic name of Phil Leeds playing. And Phil Leeds was a lovable little fellow who all comics loved. Never a major comic. And that's why they all love him. Because comics love people who aren't successful. That's how they judge a good comic. So Phil was appearing at the Avant Garde. And Shelley came in as a customer. He came in to see Phil. So he asked if he could eat in the showroom, which normally we didn't do because we had a small dining area in front. So Shelley is sitting and watching Phil Leeds, and Shelley is giggling hysterically at everything Phil Leeds says. And nobody else is. But Shelley in his compassion or whatever for Phil is just giggling and giggling. And I know nothing of this. I'm just sitting at the bar in the other room, which is separated from this room by swinging doors. So Shelley is giggling. And Phil is working. And apparently at the table next to him, there are two couples. And they start doing lines on him like, 'Who is this fag?' And Shelley finally comes back and complains, 'I'm heckled even as a customer.' "

Comics were always bucking against it, linking in strange and often unknown ways.

In 1957, when Lenny Bruce was out at Slate Brothers, Rickles was rushed in to replace him. And in that celebrity-studded room, the insult style caught on.

When Rickles said to Sinatra,

> Make yourself at home, Frank. Slug somebody,

everyone cracked up. Don's star was in ascendancy. By 1959, he was out of the crapper for good.

A strange daisy chain it was. In the '50s, when Shecky Greene worked Billy Gray's as an unknown, the favorite there, Buddy Hackett, would come in and sabotage his routines with misplaced laughs. Years later, when Hackett browbeat Catskill comic Morty Gunty, Greene warned Buddy off. And what of Gunty? Dealing with Morty (among others) drove a kid gag writer named Richard Lewis to try it as a comic himself.

With Keefe, the connections always turned out wrong. In the late '40s, he was a part-time usher at the Capitol Theater when Jackie Gleason came in for a week's engagement. Gleason found he was a man shy for one of his sketches. Keefe was enlisted with the promise that Gleason "would take care" of him.

In the sketch, he played the Arab manservant to Gleason's Foreign Legionnaire. He carried Jackie's incidentals onstage and waited to be tipped. At his exit, Gleason quipped, "See ya at the Luxor," a Broadway steam bath.

"After a day or so," said Keefe, "he stopped doing

the line. Maybe he forgot, or whatever. I'm almost all the way offstage and I don't hear the line. So I stopped and said, 'See ya at the Luxor Baths.' And he does the double take. And the band falls down. So from then on, I got away with that. And I did it the next show. So then I came out and I started doing Walter Brennan. Then he made me up in blackface. So naturally when I got out there I did Jolson. So it was a happy week. He was living on beer and Benzedrine. Trying to lose weight. Between shows, he'd ask me to get him beers, and I would—out of my own pocket. Meantime, the guys working for him are building him up to me. 'Oh, Jesus, Jackie is the greatest guy in the world. He's a sweetheart.'

"I figured he was gonna slip me a hundred dollars, fifty at the least, who knows what he's gonna do? All week long I'm building this up in my mind. Like what kind of bread is he gonna lay on me? So comes the big moment. 'Send the kid in.' I'm waiting outside the dressing room. And I come in. And he writes this check with a flourish, signs it, rips it off and hands it to me with a big smile on his face. It's a check for ten dollars. I said, 'Mr. Gleason, I'll tell you, I was making twenty dollars a week as an usher.' 'Well, haven't you,' he said, 'been ushering?' 'No, I've been going out and getting you beer. The manager told me you were going to take care of me.' 'Oh yeah. Well, if you're not satisfied, you can quit. I don't need you. Forget it.' And he fired me.

"So then I go around Hanson's. And a guy there goes, 'You shmuck, you putz.' I said, 'What? What did I do?' He says, 'Aren't you the guy working at the Capitol, and Gleason had you stooging for him?' I said, 'Yeah.' He said, 'What a putz. You really are a shmuck. 'Cause he told everybody that he really loved you, he thought you were great. And he was going to put you on the TV show and everything. And you tried to hold him up for money.' "

The next time Keefe had a shot at big-time TV was when an agent got him an audition for "The Arthur Murray Show." Keefe devised a routine that involved Kathryn Murray's learning how to mimic Cagney. Both Arthur and she liked it, and told him he'd be on the show. Then his agent appeared. "He was one of these guys with a cigar in his mouth. He says, 'How much you gonna pay him?' They said twelve hundred dollars. The agent says they can get me for eight hundred. They say no no, twelve hundred. He doesn't know what he's doing. So he offers Arthur a cigar. No no, he doesn't want it. Then he goes and offers Kathryn a cigar. No no, she says. And he lowered my price again—to five hundred. By now Arthur is looking over the agent's shoulder and shaking his head. I was finished. The agent had never been near the big time, and he panicked. He was literally trying to push the cigar on her."

By 1959, Keefe was a mimic/comedian with a skull full of notions, still working the places he had a decade before. Most of 1959, he was in the strips on West 52nd Street or in the Village, doing,

> Next week on our stage, right here on our stage, we're gonna have a really big shooo. Primo Carnera's shoo,

nonsense to get him through another night. More elaborate riffs he had were useless.

> Weather report: Tomorrow will be muggy. Followed by Tuggy, Weddy, Thurdy

was what a fellow did until it came time to bring on the ladies. Then,

> Here she is, performing the remarkable ritual fire dance by Sterno

and off.

The strips didn't do for him what they had for Lenny. With Keefe, it was bup bup and away. It was like being imprisoned in a B movie as still another stripper confided, "I wasn't always like this."

One of them even fell for him. The feeling, sad to say, was not mutual. It put the stripper in a state. One night, she got drunk and, in the wee hours, chased him through the half-empty club, declaring, "I wuv you, I wuv you."

He worked one place that tried to be a French review more than a honky-tonk, a struggle it waged with small distinction. One time as a female singer leaned against a "Parisian" lamppost, her song was filled with hitherto unheard vibrato, eerie sound caused by an electrical short.

Nights like those drove a man to drink. It was for the bottle's comfort that Keefe headed one night to Greenwich Village.

Greenwich Village by 1960 was a hub of pop amusements, its streets lined with cafes that featured folk song and spoken verse.

On Bleecker, Macdougal, Sullivan and so on, kerouac-y souls wandered in search of sex, sin or revelations of the mysteries of life.

There were tourists too, who'd give it the amused eye and go back to their towns to blah blah the beatniks.

The cafes and coffeehouses were the pulse of the Village, fancifully named places like Cock-n-Bull, Fat Black Pussycat, some for sitting 'n' sipping, others for entertainment. Small rooms most of them were, with back spaces filled with great vats of syrup to concoct cheap beverages out of.

It took penny precepts to survive. In the Cock-n-Bull, owner Manny Roth poured coffee, mopped floors, cleaned toilets and barely covered the two-hundred-dollar-a-month rent. So tight was it that Roth once collared a customer on the street whose check had bounced, and demanded restitution right there. The fellow tried to stall him but Roth insisted he would have satisfaction—one way or another. He got his money.

The performers relied on busking mostly. In the Village, it was prefaced with a pitch, which often inspired more originality in the singers than their music did.

This is the only idea I've ever stolen from a church, but for God's sake, give more was the kind of line heard. And around went the basket.

What came back was a pittance and—added insult—occasionally included a heated nickel. A folk singer named Dick Davy had to be restrained one night from going after the joker that gave him one.

At first it was mostly folk singers and poets in the Village. Then came comics, the better of them to make petty wages per set. At the Cafe Wha?, the entre-preneurial Roth's second place, the going rate was up to five dollars a set. It was the Wha? that Keefe wandered into on a night meant to be a bender.

"And I said to the guy," he remembered, " 'I'd like to get up and do something.' And he said, 'Well, what do you do?' And I thought, Well, I don't want to tell him that I'm a comedian because he's liable to say, 'We don't use comedians.' It was mostly folk singers and poetry in the coffeehouses then. He said what did I do, and I told him I just talk about things. He said maybe he'd try me out, but that night he didn't want to. So I went around the corner. Was another place called the Cafe Rafio.

"Had a stage in the window which was some kind of old grocery store that had been turned into a coffee-house. It was a very small place. If they got twenty-five people in there, it was packed to capacity. And the place was empty. There were two people sitting there who were so stoned they wouldn't know if there was a show or there wasn't. Anyway, I put the same story on this guy in there, Rafio. I often wondered what happened to him. . . . He was a guy who was an advertising agency man who just decided he was going to become a "beatnik" and opened up this coffee shop. Anyway I got up and started to do my act.

"To these two stoned-out people. And the act is very physical and it's right up there in the window. And all of a sudden the whole joint filled up. And so when I came off, he said, 'What's your name?' And I was thinking. I didn't want to give him my name, which was *Bob* Keefe at that time, because I was thinking about the union. So I said, 'Adam Keefe.' And he said, 'Will you come and work for me?' And

I said okay. And went to work at the Rafio. Twenty dollars a night."

In the Rafio, and later at the Wha? and other Village spots, Keefe began to try the bits and pieces he'd done infrequently out on the road. Now he put them together—

> A few thousand impressions that have been keeping me out of the big money for some time now,

running them to a beat that built as he went on, the rolling-stone effect that the good comic got. It was the same highriser the right matador managed in his fixed form, or the fighter in his. An energy that was made contagious.

Keefe worked the sprung second they did at the Roxy, trying to jump-start an audience. It was parry and thrust, this-don't-work-maybe-that-will:

> Here's one—one of the finest comedians on the stage today. Mr. Alan Ladd in a scene from *This Gun for Hire.*
>
> LADD: You pull a rod on me, and I'll shove it down your throat,

affecting a quizzical look when it—

> Oh, I see. It's a much more sophisticated group. So I'd like to do my tribute to America's greatest living actor, Louis Hayward in a scene from *The Man in the Iron Mask.*
>
> HAYWARD *(muffled)*:   Lemme out, lemme out,

and he'd add, wryly,

> He's in a mask, can't get out, and neither can I.

And then,

Here is Alan Ladd, in a scene from *Two Years Before the Mask*.

LADD: You pull that mask on me, and I'll shove it down your throat.

Bap bap. The words danced in and out. The laughs he got fed the glow he had when onstage. In the Village it was abetted by a drag or two of marijuana he liked before he came out. No less nimble was he for it. He had the easy gait he did as a kiddo in F-f-friar's saloons. He looked much the same—a sharp-etched face with aquiline nose, slit mouth and cool gaze.

And on he went:

George Sanders in a scene from his own personal life. I call this real George.

SANDERS: Zsa Zsa, come he-uh. I under-stahn it's yo-ah burthday. It is? Happy burthday. Now make breakfast, you pig,

to a clubhouse roar.

Thank you, fellow brutes.

Keefe had many of these swifties, some of them on the flip side.

Spencer Tracy in a scene from *The Last Hurrah:* "Hurrah."

John L. Lewis: "Strike."

Walter Pidgeon: "Coo coo."
Be surprised how often that lays an egg.

And now here's a man who's known as . . . me,

with a quick shuffle step, palms extended. On nights

he put them in the right mix, he'd get a hand for just being K-e-e-f-e.

> Thank you. Wow. That's what I call a spontaneous demonstration. They scare me a little bit, I'll tell you the truth. I keep remembering what happened to Stevenson,

he'd say, adding,

> Actually I don't do any political humor. I did want to say I'm going to vote for Nixon—

and when that got laughs—

> It's very gratifying to have an audience that really knows political humor when they hear it.

In the Village, he'd start with quick hits of mimicry before more elaborate concepts. At the Wha?, the lights would dim and, to prerecorded piano, Keefe would perform an entire silent movie in two minutes. Over the spotlight, Manny Roth would flutter a piece of cardboard to create a flickering effect as up onstage, Keefe flashed title cards—*Enter the villain/the hero/ the heroine/the mortgage . . . Enter the villain/the Indians/the cavalry*—that he acted out, never failing to remember what the henchman of the blind club owner told him, "De boss don't tink you're funny. . . ."

And then a few assorted licks. Eddie Fisher meeting Eddie Cantor:

FISHER: Hello, Eddie.

CANTOR: Hello, Eddie.

FISHER: Gee, you made a lot of stars.

CANTOR: So did you. But I didn't marry 'em, kid.

He'd mimic Gene Kelly singing in the rain, a song
that ended with gurgled voice; Maurice Chevalier as
Jolson ("Ma-mee, ho ho, look at me"); a gramophone
Bing Crosby with the technical difficulties; and Brod-
erick Crawford's sister—

> So how come you never get me any fellas?

in Crawford's voice, naturally.

He moved fast, and sometimes he'd miss. Or get
a solitary laugh. But, like Berle, he could do something
with it:

> Could you run around the room and make
> that sound as a group?

A Keefe specialty was Bela Lugosi as a nightclub
comedian. Lugosi with the tongue-flicking delivery and
big-eyed look. He'd turn his back to the audience and
when he wheeled about, he gave them a horrific face,
one that looked as if the flesh were petrified:

> How do you do-bl-dooo. Allow me to in-
> trroduce myself.

The Transylvanian accent made jokes cumbersome.

> My tongue is so long, I am de only man
> who can seal a letter after it's in de mail-
> box . . .

A panicked look and a repeat on the punch line—

> After it's in de mailbox. . . . These are de
> djokes.

His Lugosi was not easily discouraged.

> Did you hear de one about de two be . . .
> boppers were standing in front of de Eiffel
> Tower? And the one be . . . bopper said
> to de other, "Man, dig that crazy hypo-
> dimic niddle. . . ."

You don't . . . care for the djokes?

Bela did it all—Cag-a-ney impressions, Transylvanian songs ("Everybody . . . sing along") until he'd bring on Boris Karloff, the physical creation of whom invariably got a response. Karloff, no spoilsport, acknowledged it with—

> I hear ap-plause in the
> la-BOR-a-tory.

It went over in the Wha?, Rafio and other places, though sometimes the tourists couldn't keep the pace Keefe set. One night, an older couple who didn't know Lugosi from linguini got up in the middle of the Transylvanian's riff and walked out, the gentleman pausing to say to Keefe, "Oogldy boooogldy." Keefe just laughed. "What could I say? The point of what I was doing went completely past him. To him, it was just some jerk up there trying to scare people."

Some nights a tall goateed fellow named Noel Stookey would drop into the Wha? late. He and Keefe did stories—Stookey creating the narrative line, Keefe acting it out, each prodding the other.

Keefe got to thinking there was an act in it, but Stookey talked of a folk trio he was involved with. Keefe told him he was crazy, the woods were full of folk singers. Stookey changed his name to Paul. The group became "Peter, Paul and Mary."

Keefe's own career soon was moving. Eighteen months after he'd gone downtown, he was booked into Art D'Lugoff's Village Gate. From the Gate, he went to the Blue Angel. And then came a shot on the Sullivan show in 1961—well over a decade after he first did the amateur nights.

A long hard time it'd been, full of odd twists, too many for the worse. Once he thought an agent of his was going to turn the career around. What fooled him was the material she kept giving him. *I thought she was a genius. Of course, I had never seen Orson Bean.* It was Orson's act she doled out. She'd managed Bean very briefly.

It didn't surprise him. Nothing did. The nickel/

dime comic circuit was a cram course in sleazo psychology. One afternoon, he was in an agent's office just after getting booked for a job when another comic walked in and asked for it. The agent pointed to Keefe. "This gentleman's working it," he said. The comic looked Keefe over, said, "Fuck him. Put me in there. I'm better than he is."

As Keefe began to play name rooms, he remained wary. Still in mind were the times in crummy places for short pull, and the economy measures they brought —the cardboard stuffed in shoes and the chalk to whiten shirt collars. After years like that, it was hard to be sure the new action was for real. The night he was seen coast to coast on Sullivan, Adam Keefe had torn underwear on and holes in his shoes.

In time, it changed. He was booked onto the Gleason show—Jackie avoided mention of their past run-in. When he did the "Tonight Show" in New York, Johnny Carson noted Keefe's custom-made shirt from Lew Magram, who billed himself as "Shirtmaker to the stars." Comics that hit it stopped in there to get the tuxedo shirts in colors, styled beauties. In Hollywood, he picked up the $350 tux to go with them.

He was moving: Mr. Kelly's, the Purple Onion, Playboy, earning up to seven hundred dollars a week. TV too was regular. He was ready for club or studio. The years had made him savvy with crowds. On the cafe circuit, he'd feel his way. If the audience was straight, he'd do a few jokes up top:

> Was listening to the news. Said a woman shot her husband with a bow and arrow. And when they asked her why, she said, "I didn't want to wake up the kids."

Or,

> Did you hear about this fellow who had laryngitis. And he walked into the doctor's office, and said to the nurse: "Is the doctor in?"

> And she said (in a sultry whisper, beckoning): "no, come on."

Jokes, mimicry, Lugosi—he did the fast minutes he'd polished in the Village. He even took requests, zapping a "Lassie" with

> If you'll be the tree

and a wink.

But the routine associated with Keefe was the "spliced movie." He took a film with cracked and faded footage and reproduced its sound track, down to the scratches and multiple splices. Its manic cuts and the dexterity with which Keefe did them gave it a lunatic quality. "If Ionesco wrote a 15-minute soap opera, it might sound something like this," said *The New York Times* reviewer.

RICHARD
 CONTE: For seven years, for seven years, I've been in this lousy stinking cell waiting praying hoping for *TP*

   / now *TP*

   you
   say you'll help me but what do you do *TP*
   that is what you

   do about me *TP*

   no matter what I
   say *TP*

JIMMY
STEWART: *TP TP* Wal, I 'spect that's how you feel, but thar's one thing *TP*
   will you be ready—

and so on.

It gave Keefe memorability in clubs. He worked them with ease, jumping from one thing to the next, always calculating how he stood. Nothing threw him—not after the time he'd put in in the boondocks. On a night in San Francisco, when the feature attraction, singer Nancy Wilson, came in and put a toy pussycat onstage while he worked, he did as she asked—placed the thing on the piano. Then he turned and said,

Thank you, Nancy. I knew if I hung around here, you'd hand me your pussy.

He turned the toy upside down and said,

Hmmmm, a spade one no less.

Shecky Greene was there that night. He came backstage after. "And he runs over to me," said Keefe, "and he was doing like . . . the Mad Russian. He's doing like, 'My God, I never saw anything like you in my life. Come here.' And he pulls me and drags me up the stairs. Halfway up to the men's room, pushes me against the wall, like Jules Podell or somebody, and says, 'Where'd you come from? I can't understand it. You're great, you're fantastic. You ought to be the biggest star in the world. . . .'"

On coffeehouse budgets, comics could afford to be bad in the Village when they started.

And some of them were—Woody Allen *in extremis*.

Allen was a slight man with a startled look about him, as if just caught in an unspeakable act. He wore glasses and, on appearances, was automatic last in the batting order.

As a comedy writer, he'd sold gags to working pros while in his teens. But as a comic, it was another story.

Starting in the Duplex, just off Sheridan Square, Allen was, as even his manager Jack Rollins conceded, a flop.

ROLLINS: He was totally embarrassed because he was a solid pro writer at that time. He was making several thousands a week as a writer and recognized by his peers as an excellent comedy writer.

Q: Any signs of what he felt?

ROLLINS: Well, he would walk like a small caged lion, up and back, up and back. He'd wear out a path. He worked the energy off by walking up and back.

Q: In the dressing room?

ROLLINS: Yeah. And one day, he said to us [Rollins and partner Charles Joffe], "Listen fellas, do you really think I should continue this? You know, I make a very good living as a writer. And I'm making nothing here." He dropped his writing to work on this. He says, "Does it make sense?" We said to him the only answer we could give him. To us it made sense. But that's to us. He has to concur in some way.

Q: And what about audience response?

ROLLINS: Zero.

Q: Was he getting hecklers?

ROLLINS: He was heckled once in a while and he didn't answer them. He would stoically go through with his lines and do his twenty-five minutes like they weren't there, kind of look at them out of the corner of his eye. He would get up there and wrap that cord around his neck. You thought he was going to choke himself . . . I mean, he just . . . you had to see him. It's hard to describe.

Q: Were there other nervous—

ROLLINS: Oh, filled with nervous tics. Nervous, nervous. It was a sight.

But Rollins and Joffe sensed something when Allen read the sketches he wrote for TV producers. They were not alone. In the late '50s, when Woody was a sketch writer at Tamiment in the Poconos, he struck others as funny too. The Village folk singer Dick Davy was there then, and recalled: "Like we'd be sitting around a lunchroom and it would be time to leave. And he'd say, 'Well, I got to go back to the cabins to do the husband bit.' You know, his wife was there. It was just funny. Everything that came out of his mouth. And he'd say about how he got married for the first time when he was like seventeen to a girl named Harlene—she was always called Mrs. Woody —and they didn't know anything about sex. So they went to a marriage counselor or a rabbi before they got married to tell them what to do about it. He says, 'All you do is mount her like a young bull.' That's Woody telling it, and to hear him say it . . . it's just like really funny. I remember that phrase. He says, 'And you mount her like a young bull.'

"Another time, I asked to talk to him. And he said, 'Well, where will we talk?' And I said, 'Well, I'm out there playing the guitar by the lake, like in the afternoon.' And it was the first time all summer that he had been out there. And that's the main thing that they do at resorts. Lay around on these chaise longues with their music and their gin and the watermelon and making out. And Woody looks at it like it's a scene from a strange movie. And he got all excited. 'Is this what goes on here all day, all these naked women? Wow, you must have a ball. Wow.' And he's looking at all these girls. And he really uses all that in his movies. I see all that in his movies. All his fantasies. And he was like very uncomfortable . . . a fish out of water, looking around. 'Cause he was always writing. He had stacks of spearmint gum. You know, for the nervousness and writing.' "

To manager Rollins, Woody was a "one-r," crossword puzzle jargon for a unique type. And indeed there were few like him around then. Even those comics whose "hook" was the loser type came out like the other storm troopers, doing the hard-luck lines in the same rim-shot rips:

> I spent a thousand dollars to have my nose fixed, now my brain won't work.

> Last week, I met a girl from Buffalo. Why can't I meet a girl from normal parents?

Bup, bup bup.

The futzing around Allen did onstage was the gestalt of a comedic antihero. The elliptical pauses, the scratching, the hesitant voice: true neurotica.

The times were ready for it. Years before, jokes like,

> Two psychiatrists pass each other on the street. The one says to the other, "Hello, how are you?" The other says, "I wonder what he meant by that?"

were considered daring. No more. Freud was a household word and no magical mystery tour. And Allen was the logical and laughable extension of Herr Kafka himself. And, in Franz' fashion, he couldn't see what all the fuss was about.

ROLLINS: We said to him, "Woody, we see something that we can't explain. We just think that you . . . But we're not up on that floor suffering every night. You are. And if it's too difficult, you certainly should not continue it."

Q: And?

ROLLINS: And he was the most . . . uncomplaining . . . he's one of the seven wonders of the world, this kid. I mean, I adore him as a human. This guy will never, never place his troubles, his burdens, his neuroses—and god knows he is neurotic—he'll never place any of it on any other human being's shoulders. I mean, that's—

Q: So he stoically kept going?

ROLLINS: He stoically went through it, and he asked us did we think . . . ? And we said, "Well, we think so if you can bear it."

In the Village, Allen learned to use the shrugs and quivers. He made them part of the stage Woody/wouldn't-he. It worked for him, adding to lines like

I don't believe in an afterlife, although I
am bringing a change of underwear,

or

When we played softball, I'd steal second,
then feel guilty and go back.

In the clubs—Mr. Kelly's, the Blue Angel, hungry i
—there was an audience for the words and psycho-
music he made. In fact, as he grew in reputation, fans
of his held him in an almost proprietary regard.

It ran the age spectrum. Small fry sent him jokes,
which manager Rollins, tongue in cheek, said were put
to good use: "If you see his movies, you see he uses
them all." College types who identified with Allen
wanted to work free for him. Girls sent him phone
numbers and statistics—occasionally photos came with
the letters. The girls that mailed their pictures, it turned
out, were never up to Woody's taste. One girl asked
if he'd send her one of his socks. More normal were
Allen buffs who wrote him regularly after a movie or
New Yorker piece appeared—to say how much they
liked it.

What made Allen a prodigy was more than his Sig-
mund sound. It was the reams he turned out. Woody
was prolific. With TV, he had to be. To do "the tube,"
it took material, a regular flow of it—the right kind,
of course. The networks were not queuing up to ask
Lenny Bruce on. Steve Allen used him; others avoided
him.

Another Rollins comic, Dick Cavett, did clever material, too clever for his own good, a network man told
the manager. "He'd be very funny at Yale but not for
our audience," he said, an opinion subject to change,
and not in Cavett either. TV held no opinion that time
and toil could not alter.

Cavett worked, one of many in the Village in the
early '60s. It was easier than the old club scene fast
fading. J. J. Barry, who shuttled between the Village
and more commercial precincts, saw the difference. It
was up top with the men who ran the places. The
Village owners tended to be chummy with comics.

"They thought," said Barry, "they were one of us. They could rap with us on, quote, our level. But when you stepped out of the Village, and worked for the Frazzini Brothers, it was a different level altogether. Half of them wouldn't talk to you, and half of them thought, 'Hey, as long as you're funny, kid.' I had one owner once told me in a place in Massachusetts to *mix*. And I said, 'What?' He said, 'I want you to mix.' I said, 'What do you mean, *mix*?' He said, 'Come on, have some customers buy you a drink.' I said, 'Wait a minute, man. I'm not a broad.' And the guy said, 'C'mon, c'mon. I'll give the agency a bad report on you.' I mixed. I didn't even drink. I mixed. I'd tell a guy who wanted to buy a drink I had an ulcer. And I got a bad report anyway."

Not that cash didn't count in the Village. Downtown came with its own ground rules. "It was," Dick Davy recalled, "*the* place to come to when you were in New York. And so there were all these tourist traps. And the main thing for a folk singer was to sing loud to get the people off the street—to bring 'em in and charge 'em a buck and a half for some kind of sugar water.

"And I didn't sing loud. I was much more soulful and quiet . . . intimate . . . and it wasn't making it. But I'd be talking in between, and people would laugh at things I said. So I'd start out like very traditional— 'Barbara Allen,' about forty-seven verses of that. And people weren't listening after a while. And because nobody's paying attention, I'd just start talking and they'd laugh. And then the room would . . . laughter is a funny thing. Like three or four people laugh really loud, other people turn around to see what they're laughing at. So I'd keep talking and they sort of liked the country way I was talking.

"And whatever I'd say, they laughed at. And I really felt bad that I didn't have more things to say because I really had 'em with the first few things I said, and they were ready. . . . And then I'd go back to singing another song, and they'd go back to bedlam. So I started writing down . . . whatever they were laughing at, I'd write it down when I got home. So then I started writing little chunks of material. But I always played the guitar. I always sang songs. I never really had enough material to be a comedian.

"At the beginning, I thought I was going to be the world's greatest folk singer. But then I saw guys that were really good at this. I mean guys like Noel Stookey and Len Chandler. And what's-his-name was just starting out then and he was lousy, man. He'd go to all these hootenannies, and nobody paid any attention to him. Bob Dylan. He'd be singing 'Blowin' in the Wind,' and everyplace it was bedlam. He stunk with . . . with the guitar . . . a baggy cap on and a harmonica in his mouth. And he'd go into every hootenanny. Monday night was hootenanny and amateur night and they'd announce him. And he'd get up and sing and nobody ever paid any attention to him. It was bedlam. He never won nothing. Nobody paid any mind to him.

"The woods were crawling with guitar players. Hundreds of guys. And even to pass the hat it was competitive—they don't want to have just anybody because they're charging the people a lot of money coming off the streets. So I had a little bit of a reputation. So I could work these places as a folk singer. But it got slimmer and slimmer. In fact, the lousier you sang, I found, the more money you got for passing the hat because they felt sorry for you. Anyway, in those little joints where they squeezed in every tourist possible, there would be other guys with guitars and girls and trios and they're all hungry to get your job even though you're not getting paid for it, just passing the damn plate or hat around. And I started losing even those jobs. And started doing comedy."

Davy, who looked like a grown-up version of Carl (Alfalfa) Switzer of the old "Our Gang" comedies, was a strapping six-two son of an orthodox rabbi. It made him, in his phrase, "a sad miserable little Jewish Portnoy kid," the worst aspect of which was with women.

With the guitar it changed some. He made wages and women both—and did it with a between-songs character, a cracker-barrel type who spoke with a Southern drawl. The first time he was asked where he was from and said New York, he saw it was not what people wanted to hear. After that, he told them Texas.

Born and raised on New York's Upper West Side, Davy began to cultivate the dialect. He knew a North Carolinian with a rich drawl, a fellow he personally found grating. In spite of it, he ran around with him to get the accent down. "I told him I was from Arkansas because I didn't want him to think I was making fun of him or something, talking the way he was talking."

In the Village, he did a hillbilly that could have played the Grand Ole Opry. The laughs came from the naiveté he had with big-city ways. Ticketed by a police officer for parking in front of a fire hydrant, he said,

> It's for water? It don't look like it hold much water. Besides, how they know the fire goin' be right there?

As his sotto voce failed in the coffeehouses, he relied on comedy. He'd settled his geographical roots by then. The Arkansas Fellow Traveler was who he decided he'd be.

If he'd hoped the accent would be, as he put it, "my open sesame," it wasn't. Nothing so startling that he gave up his day job as a teacher of emotionally disturbed children. In fact, he began to phase out of the Village, and do mostly civil rights benefits.

In the early '60s, blacks began to move to right inequities they saw in the sociopolitical system. And Davy, in an era before whitey was odd man out in civil rights, was there with them. He was at benefits to raise money for movement groups. To Harlem, to Brooklyn, all over the city he went, his material beginning to deal wtih racial issues—and in mixed company.

He kidded the bigots—

> This House Un-American Activities Committee investigatin' the Klan. Ain't that something? But the Klan ain't gonna last long anyway. They going out of style. They the only ones in the country still buying white 'stead of colored sheets.

but didn't forget so-called moderates:

> Liberals—they same as bigots. Feel the
> same way like the bigots but they ashamed
> of it. So they get a whole pile of Ray
> Charles records in the house in case some-
> body come over.

He took the very notion of equal rights to its absurdist
ends:

> I seen a colored girl in the Playboy mag-
> azine, right in the middle where you pay
> the money for. She don't wear a whole
> lot. White Citizens Council been trying to
> get equal time. Get a white lady be Aunt
> Jemima for a month. . . . Tryin' to get
> Mrs. Faubus right on the box.

It wasn't always the whites he knocked either:

> The times is changin'. A whole lot of
> fellas going out with colored girls now.
> You know who's even going out with
> colored girls? Ohh . . . Duke Ellington,
> Count Basie, Billy Daniels.

With Davy, things weren't just black and white.
There were shades between. And in the comedy scene
it was a shade of difference.

With black comics, the joke was always on them.

In the '20s, when Pigmeat "Here come de Judge"
Markham was starting, he played in all-black tent
spectacles that were part of otherwise white carnivals.
They were called "jig shows."

Chances were few for black funnymen in radio days.
The character of Beulah, a Negro maid, was at first
played by a white man. So were Amos 'n' Andy played
by whites.

Hollywood's concessions to equal opportunity were
the eyeball-rolling Stepin Fetchit and Mantan ("Feets,
do your stuff") Moreland. Indeed, W. C. Fields referred to blacks on screen as "iggerolas," "sweet little
pickaninnies" and "Ubangis." And Marx Brothers
films mistreated them too.

To work, black comics had their own circuit. Markham, talking about the eastern seaboard theaters he played, referred to them as "around-the-world." By black geography, it was.

On their own, the colored comics (the phrase old-timers used) stuck to stage conventions. They worked with baggy pants and used burnt cork to blacken their faces and exaggerate their lips. When Frank Schiffman of the Apollo Theater in Harlem tried to do away with burnt cork in the late '40s, he met opposition from the comics themselves. Distorted blackness made them more secure.

It was rare for a Negro comic to play in white clubs and, when he did, it was not apt to be on his terms. When Timmie Rogers showed up at a white club in Hollywood, it was in a dinner jacket and not the zoot-suit costume the owner previously had seen him in. Rogers' insistence on wearing it got his engagements cut short.

It wasn't until after the war that things changed on the Chitlin Circuit. That was when monologuists came on the scene in numbers. The majority of black comics were sketch players before. Now Nipsey Russell, Slappy White, Redd Foxx walked out and did jokes. They worked fast and were gag-oriented, and the lines were often blue. They were lightened up later when Vegas money could be had:

> Told my barber Angelo I wanted the Afro look. Went to sleep in the barber chair. Woke up. I had a bone in my nose.

It was a while, of course, before it got to that. In the '40s, Nipsey Russell worked the Baby Grand in Harlem. And Foxx and White did a double until 1951. Redd wore a hat over a Mohican haircut and, when he took it off, the crowds went crazy. As Foxx said, "Those spooks laughed for five, six minutes."

With the '60s, black comics began to work to white audiences. Foxx appeared at Basin Street East. Godfrey Cambridge was trying it at the Cafe Wha?. And Dick Gregory was figuring out what he had to do. He'd run it over and over in his mind.

I've got to go up there as an individual first, a Negro second. I've got to be a colored funny man, not a funny colored man. I've got to act like a star who isn't sorry for himself—that way, they can't feel sorry for me. I've got to make jokes about myself, before I can make jokes about them and their society—that way, they can't hate me. Comedy is friendly relations.

> Just my luck, bought a suit with two pair of pants today . . . burnt a hole in the jacket.

That's making fun of yourself.

> They asked me to buy a lifetime membership in the NAACP, but I told them I'd pay a week at a time. Hell of a thing to buy a lifetime membership, wake up one morning and find the country's been integrated.

That makes fun of the whole situation.
Now, they're listening to you, and you can blow a cloud of smoke at the audience and say:

> Wouldn't it be a hell of a thing if all this was burnt cork and you people were being tolerant for nothing?

Now you've got them. No bitterness, no Uncle Tomming. We're all aware of what's going on here, aren't we, baby? Now you can settle down and talk about anything you want.
One other thing he was ready for. The old bugaboo. *Nigger.* He knew it'd come and he'd have to handle it. In his home, he had his wife, Lillian, call him nigger when he least expected it, and he'd react to it with a remark. It was verbal quick draw.

When it happened in a blue-collar club, he was ready:

> You hear what that guy just called me? Roy Rogers' horse. He called me Trigger.

He eyed the crowd, blew out cigarette smoke and added,

> You know, my contract reads that every time I hear that word, I get fifty dollars more a night, I'm only making ten dollars a night and I'd like to put the owner out of business. Will everybody in the room please stand up and yell nigger?

Gregory wanted the whispered issue of race out in the open. To laugh at it was a way. The question was whether he would get to do it in the traditional comic markets.

He got a chance in January of 1961 when double-talk comic Irwin Corey canceled out of the Chicago Playboy. Gregory pinch hit for him, working to a mostly Southern-white audience.

> Good evening, ladies and gentlemen. I understand there are a good many Southerners in the room tonight. I know the South very well. I spent twenty years there one night. . . .

> Last time I was down South, I walked into this restaurant, and this white waitress came up to me and said: "We don't serve colored people here."

> I said: "That's all right. I don't eat colored people. Bring me a whole fried chicken."

He got bravos when he finished, and ended doing double the time he was booked for that night.

Soon, he was in the smart rooms at top buck, using the kind of lines a black man hadn't before:

> I sat at a lunch counter for nine months. They finally integrated and didn't have what I wanted.

It took poise to handle the sticky moments the racially insecure times brought. For Gregory that meant off the floor too. He was at the bar in the Blue Angel one night after a performance when a well-meaning Southerner took the highball out of his hands and said, "I want you to know how liberal I am. I'll even drink from this glass." He drank from it, then handed it back to Gregory, who put the glass down and said, "I'm sorry. I'm not that liberal."

Working the Apollo Theater, Gregory had the same steely grip. When he was heckled repeatedly one night there, he squared away and told the man, "You be quiet. If it was Bob Hope, you wouldn't open your mouth. Don't open it to me."

For him, comedy was on-the-job training.

GREGORY: See, it's a growth thing with me. When you're doing social commentary and you're poor and ain't got no money and ain't never been on a jet plane, you never been on a train, you never been out of the country, you automatically limited to what you can do.

Q: By experience?

GREGORY: Right. You grow. And America grows too. You go back and look at a lot of that stuff I did then. I wouldn't be caught doing it now. But that's how the whole country have grown.

Years ago, Gregory had a joke about a prisoner being strapped into the electric chair, and asked by the priest could he do anything.

Yeah, when they pull the switch, hold my hand,

the condemned man said.

That joke was refined to

If Jesus Christ came back and was elec-

> trocuted, you'd all be walking with elec-
> tric chairs around your neck,

a more incisive view of ritualized religion.

To get to that point, Gregory risked his career by involvement in the civil rights movement—against the advice of associates. He took his chances.

> Q: In the early Sixties, you'd travel across the country to demonstrate, and then travel right back to perform, right?

> GREGORY: Right.

> Q: At what cost to you?

> GREGORY: Didn't cost me nothing. I had a credit card.

> Q: Eventually you gotta pay, no?

> GREGORY: Or they take the credit card like they did.

> Q: Is that what happened?

> GREGORY: Yeah. I commuted from Chicago to San Francisco every day for thirty days and . . . but see, that's something that I never . . . I never worried about it 'cause anything I ever wanted to do, I'd always find the money to do it.

From 1962 on, Gregory was where the black action was. Mississippi, Alabama, all over the country. In September of 1963, the day after the bombing of a church in Birmingham resulted in the deaths of black children, Gregory was to meet with a writer to discuss collaboration on an autobiography. The writer, Robert Lipsyte, came into Gregory's New York hotel room and found him in his shorts, crying.

"He was on the bed," Lipsyte said, "and it was obvious he forgot he was to meet with me. I asked him why he was crying. He said, 'Haven't you read the paper?' Then he went into a nonstop monologue for hours, talking to the ceiling. He wondered if there was any point in going on in show business."

Gregory continued to put his body on the line. He was jailed, beaten and, later in the Watts riots, struck by a bullet. Still, he kept a sense of humor about it, envisioned the day he could open a restaurant whose name—"Nigger"—would be in bright lights. The place, in Gregory's scheme, would have the best of everything. Anybody, he said, who came into a place called Nigger deserved it.

In the Mississippi summer of 1964, Dick Davy was there.

He went South, as he put it, "to be in the mass meetings and rallies and the churches and the living and sharing of the terror. They were trying to open up voting in '64. You know, there was the three guys killed [Andrew] Goodman and [James] Chaney and [Michael] Schwerner in the beginning of June. I went there July."

When he came back to New York, it was with the feeling that he was finished with the Bleecker/Macdougal scene—he'd confine his Arkansas Fellow Traveler to civil rights benefits—and that would be that.

"At one of the benefits in 'sixty-five though," he said, "a little humpbacked guy comes up to me afterwards and says, 'Who represents you?" I said nobody. He was crippled with arthritis of the spine. He says, 'Where you working?' You know, people come up to me after they've all been laughing and they think I'm a big shot. And I told him I'm not working anywhere. He says where would I like to work? And here I'd been working all the joints on Bleecker Street and Macdougal, and there's a couple of good places in the Village that I never dreamed of playing. He says where would I like to play? I say the Village Gate. He says—okay, he'll get me in there next week. I say, yeah, sure."

The gnomish figure was Art Steuer, a man who'd made a reputation as a writer just out of college. Then he'd come down with the crippling arthritis and his interest shifted to comics. He hung around with Lenny Bruce (serving as one of the collaborators on the Bruce autobiography, *How To Talk Dirty and Influence People*) and was a confidant of Dick Gregory's (arranging meetings for him with people like Mark Lane, the radical thinker).

Steuer began to manage Davy. He got him into the Village Gate and was urged by Davy to try the Apollo Theater. Steuer thought it was a waste of time: there was no money in the black scene. But Davy had a feeling it'd make his career. He'd been there for an amateur night early in 1965. He'd sat in the basement with the other acts, had his named called and gone upstairs to play to black faces.

That night, he did a couple of minutes—

> Down South, they trying to get voters registered. I know one fella finally got inside the courthouse last year. They threw him a ballpoint pen and a piece of wax paper. "Write your name, boy." They handed him a Chinese newspaper. "What's it say, boy?" "It say I ain't gonna vote this year,"

before Honi Coles of the Apollo came on stage to get him off: *Okay, man, I see you're good. We'll book you back in some night regular.* Davy protested that he was getting laughs and could do with more time. The audience, though, apparently saw enough. It voted him third prize.

Backstage, Coles told him he'd bring him in when the headliner was right—say, Miriam Makeba, an act that drew a thoughtful clientele. From the few minutes he was on, Davy knew he'd be a smash if he could play the Apollo. That night he felt an audience with more affinity for his material than even crowds in the Village had.

He took to phoning Coles. The first time Honi told him soon, man, soon—and sounded as if he meant it. But each time Davy phoned him after that, he could tell Coles was no longer of a mind to make good on the promise. If he persisted, it was because he knew the Arkansas Fellow Traveler was a can't-miss proposition for black audiences.

No white comic had looked at the world the way the Negro community did. Indeed, most of them risked being shouted off the stage if they tried their acts up at the Apollo. Not Davy. He'd thought about race issues and confronted his own feelings. The liberal with the Ray Charles records that he joked about was once him—for all he knew, it still was . . . however much he'd changed.

What Davy had to say was a giant step ahead of what black audiences heard ofay comic cats tell them on TV. And Davy knew it. It was why he was not afraid to do the Apollo. White comics had been there in the past—Berle and Red Skelton had done benefits—but long before the racial situation had heated up. Now in Harlem—never mind the Apollo—the white man entered at his own risk.

Davy gave up calling Honi Coles, but when Steuer became his manager, he decided to try one last time. It was September 1965. He'd just finished at the Village Gate, and once again urged Steuer to secure the Apollo. Steuer phoned Coles, used Dick Gregory's name, and Davy was booked a short time after the power blackout struck the eastern part of the country.

The Apollo was a landmark. To the public, it was the big stage for Negro entertainers. Located on 125th Street, it was in the heart of Harlem. The night Dick Davy played it for real, most of the sixteen hundred seats there were filled, not for him but for Brook Benton, a black singer, who was the headliner. Still, when the crowd heard,

> The Apollo Thea-tuh takes great pleasure in presenting a wonderful guy. He came all the way from Arkansas and has no intention of going back. He's a very shy guy, so don't you frighten him. Here he is—the Arkansas Fellow Traveler DICK DAVY

and saw ambling out of the wings a six-two sandy-haired honkey in flannel shirt, chino trousers and high-top brown boots, it laughed amiably and wondered who in hell the cat was.

A stool in one hand, he moved to the center of the stage with a disoriented look, as if he'd been told it was the holiday crowd at Radio City Music Hall he'd be working to. Scratching absently, the way hill-country boys in every Ozark flicker out of Hollywood do, he sat on the stool. Then he took a wad of chewing gum out of his mouth, and stuck it to the side of the microphone. And in a drawl that had the bumpkin's long octave, he said,

> Howdee. I used to say hi y'all. It's just a way a greetin' in Arkansas but up here I found out I say Hi y'all, it's a way to a beating. Even little kids poundin' on me 'cause of the way I talk.

As he spoke, his voice broke in spots, doing the high diddly of the hayseed, a sound more likely to find a friendly ear in the Apollo than, say, Basil Rathbone's:

> I was backstage there. Over there, I think it was. Ain't that where I came out from? Was a fella there, he say, "Go on out there, whitey. They either gonna love you or lynch you." But everybody been real polite to me around here. Keep calling me MISTER Charlie.

They laughed. Davy was doing it by Dick Gregory's primer. Kidding himself first. It'd allow him to do more powerhouse lines later. For now, he talked with the molasses speech, telling of his reaction seeing Big Maybelle in rehearsal the other day:

> I was watching her for the first time, the way she singin' and movin' and doin' what she do. I asked her how come she enjoy herself so much? She said, "Honey,

if you could be colored for five minutes, you'd never want to be white no more. . . ."

Over the roar he added:

Well, I got home last night in time to say my prayers. I asked the good Lord to push these freckles closer together. I don't think he heard me so good . . . I'm gonna try again tonight.

A whitey with reverse-english. It was, as he figured —can't-miss. The laughter was in every corner of that room as Davy turned the old racial tales topsy-turvy. He told, for instance, how the Arkansas Fellow Traveler came to end up in New York—and without a job:

I tried to get a job pickin' up people's bags. I seen 'em fellas in the bus station. I went up . . . 217 West 125th Street. Brotherhood of Sleeping Car Porters, it say on the door. Fella behind the desk inside. And I said, "Sir, I need a job." He said, "Man, you come to the wrong part of town. You musta took some wrong fork in the road somewhere. "I said, "But I could pick up a suitcase, sir. I could pick up a satchel. Even carry a shopping bag from the bottom so the watermelon don't leak through." He said, "What are you trying to say, man? You some kind of triple-threat?" He said, "You the first ofay cat ever come through the door. Ain't no such thing as a white redcap."
Well, I tried to ask him about the Brotherhood like it say on the door, but he didn't say nothing for about a minute and I didn't say nothing for a minute . . . it was the same minute. Then he said, "I'll tell you what I'm gonna do, whitey"—real friendly-like. "I think I might just make you a case of token in-

tegration." He gimme this cap, almost fit on my head. And he sent me to this place called Port Authority. I mean I went there next morning. And the first one I see, an old lady with all these heavy bags. I took 'em away. I took 'em clear out to the sidewalk, put 'em in a taxicab and she got in. The cab started to go. I said "Wait a minute, ma'am. Ain't . . . you . . . forgettin' something?" She gimme a little card out of her purse. Card say, WAGES OF SIN ARE DEATH. I said, "Well, ma'am, everybody got a right to their own religion. Don't yours allow for NO tipping?" I worked a whole long day in that station. A fella come . . . my brother from the Brotherhood come over after. I asked him how come I didn't make no tips a whole day, just this little card and a subway token. He said something about I didn't pay my dues and he took the token. He said, "Too bad, man. Don't look like New York ready for no token integration."

He was ok-ofay now. The crowd was won over. The laughs were big bellowing ones, like the roar of a mighty black motor. He could do what he wanted— and did. Not hurrying any, he told of reading how the Grand Dragon of the Ku Klux Klan "killed hisself," and when it got a crashing laugh, he fingered his brow as if taken aback and asked, "You read about that too?" He elaborated, said another of the Klan in New Orleans almost killed hisself too:

He seen that the new Negro bishop had a fancier robe than him.

It was not, he allowed, all he read:

I like to read the newspapers in New York a whole lot. And when I want to read about you-all, I look at the *Amster-*

> *dam News*. The one I never miss is this
> one right here. They call that *Muhammad
> Speaks*. I get the issue every time. Always
> got this fella in the pretty hat, and seem
> like every issue he looks whiter and
> whiter. Must of run out of ink. If he keep
> on like that, he liable to make the cover
> of *Ebony* magazine.

Now he was working on his own terms, the com-
pleat racial monologuist. He eyed around the Apollo,
told the crowd it was a fine place—he thought it'd
make a nice barn. Or church. "That's just what Harlem needs . . . another church."

No question, he said, the times was changing. Sid-
ney Poitier was a good example:

> They give him the Academy Award for
> his convincing portrayal of a Negro.

And he noted equality in another way:

> Uh-huh. A little while ago, a colored cab
> driver passed *me* by. Not only that. He
> gave me his finger like this here. Lit up
> his off-duty sign.

And so it went, the words coming slow 'n' easy,
Davy's mind working considerably faster, tricked-up
with Dexamyl. He'd gone to the chemical cupboard
in the Village when he found he languished in the
laughs. It was, as he put it, "like a damned warm
bath."

That night he was on top of it, he had the dark
laughter rolling out of the balconies. He was snug-
gling up to it, his speeded skull was juggling all the
possibilities and racing on.

And when a muscatel-soaked insult came down
from the balcony, Davy crooked a finger and said,

> You shouldn't be doing that. Because up
> there where you are, you should be pray-
> ing to the good Lord to forgive you all

your sins. 'Cause that's the closest you'll ever git to heaven.

It wasn't easy. Good as he was that night, the ghetto instinct was git whitey. And more than once people tried to. Davy rolled with it and turned it to his advantage. And at the end, they sent him off the stage with a roar. As he went, he said to himself, I won.

And figured the hell with his day job as a teacher. He'd have his laughs while he could.

The Village was a crossroads in the '60s.

Every kind of comic came through there. It was a place to start. Woody Allen, Davy, Cavett got going in the coffeehouses and clubs. And in a way so did the veteran Keefe.

Others were around, swinging from place to place, five/six sets a night. One of them was a black man who, as a bartender in Philadelphia, made the patrons laugh while serving up the drinks and got to thinking there was a future in it. In the Village, Bill Cosby worked both the Gaslight and the Wha?, and was so good the Wha?'s Roth upped him from $5 to $7.50 a set right away. Cosby was a natural. No beginner's kinks in his style. He was the flimflam man from the start.

The Gaslight, where he was a fixture, was not a comic's room. It ran to folk song and poetry. Kerouac jacked around there. It took a rare comedic cat to make it in that place. Cosby did, working with a sure hand.

"Supercool" was the way he was remembered from Village days. "It was," said Keefe, "like he'd already made it. Like he had an air about him that was of success. Of not only success, but social position." To Roth, he was unlike other comics that came around the Wha?. None of the dit-dit-dit with him. He rarely talked comedy. "Other guys," said Roth, "you'd get, I shoulda done this. Or, did I do that wrong? Or, whaddaya think of this line? I/me, I/me."

Cosby was self-contained. He'd be at the Figaro playing chess. Or on the street corners talking to girls. Or at the basketball court on Sixth Avenue, across from the Waverly Theater. And he was always ready to work. One afternoon, he dropped into the Wha? in a sweat suit and did a fast twenty minutes, just after having shot baskets. It was informal there during the day.

Roth, who'd saved twenty-five hundred dollars in two and a half years at the Cock-n-Bull, was making double that a week at the Wha?, so busy he kept the place open eighteen hours a day, starting at noon. In the afternoons Len Chandler, who ran the Wha? by day, often rode his scooter to Washington Square Park to flush out talent.

Evenings, it was tougher. Not everybody got the guaranteed buck. Bernie Travis, small/zippy/dark-haired, would do three, four rooms a night for nothing. Into a coffeehouse, sign up and hope to get a weekend show out of it—a chance at busking money.

Some hard times in the Village. Winter nights, Travis worked in a coffeehouse window—no heat in the place and sub-zero Farenheit on the street. The pipes froze shut. The vapor came out of Richie Havens' mouth as he sang. Six twenty-minute sets Travis did in there.

Even when he made money, he worked like hell for it. On a weekend night at the Village's Purple Onion, he learned the comic at the place across the street had canceled out. The boss told him he'd double up. "And," said Travis, "he put a clock onstage. Set it at half an hour. He said, 'When the clock moves, you move. If you're not onstage, we'll dock you five dollars for every minute.' And I was making twenty-five dollars [for three 30-minute sets] at the Onion, and an extra fifteen for the other—forty dollars to do six shows. So I get to the sixth show and suddenly BOOM. The next thing I know, I wake up and they have compresses on me. I passed out completely. They ran me over to St. Vincent's Hospital to check me out."

Travis took the lumps. They all did. It was part of the game. Took it, and waited for a break. In one place, Travis had an agent come to see him work. And from the floor below the place, a fire started, the smoke spiraling upward in the middle of his act. For the agent, discretion was the better part of valor: he left. Travis heard himself say, "Wait, I'm not finished yet."

Each day brought new comics to the Village, guys who were funny in the neighborhood and figured to be a howl onstage too. And some were. The street corners and schoolrooms were what the minor circuits on the vaudeville wheel were to the baggy-pants comics, a place to learn their sound.

An actor named Robert Klein subwayed downtown to the Village one night with a comic routine in mind. He was a big-boned kid of twenty-two, a six-footer with a blunt sculpted face—clefted chin, a nose that gave sidekicks to call him "Porky" and dark hair done in what was known then as "the Princeton cut."

Klein was from the Bronx, part of a bunch that was always "on"—sidewalk philosophers that spoofed the neighborhood and its odd fellows. Like the Jewish tough who renamed himself Lefty Farrell and hung with a crowd of horse-trot partisans along the wall on Mosholu Parkway. At any five-second interval, a passerby was sure to hear Adios-this or that.

There was Shelley the Nit who was once in the David Marcus Theater on an afternoon the Klein crowd was too. The film was on and he was in his seat watching it. On the screen came a shot of a room with a clock in it. The clock said 6:45. Shelley was up with a start. "Oh, man!" he exclaimed. "It's late. My mother's going to kill me." And he left—with Klein and the rest of them doubled up with laughter.

At the twins' house, they'd sit and run it down—all the crazies out there on the streets of the Bronx. Duranko at the pool hall who opened a rack with a series of obscenities before—WHACK!—he stroked the cue ball. The science teacher at DeWitt Clinton High who'd pour sulfuric acid on sugar and announce as it turned black and levitated: "You're looking at a nigger's hard-on, fellas." Ace, a local rowdy who once pulled a zip gun on Klein from the rear (not knowing who it was) and asked for money. Klein turned and feigned a swoon as Ace, trying to revive him, went out of character. "Don't tell anybody, Klein. All right? All right?" Even as he was nodding, Klein was thinking how he could relate it for laughs to the boys.

They were a tight bunch—with their own fanciful expressions. To die was "to execute a duster join-up." To be high was to be "loopdeloop-luderts." Their poker chips were fancifully named. So were the nickel bags of grass they scored. "Sleepy-time gal" led to a condition referred to as "buttocks glue."

At the twins', they had the run of the place. The twins' mom, who looked like the unfinished portrait of President Washington, was called George, and was physically forced from rooms they wanted to be in.

Always it was for laughs they went. It carried over in the short stay Klein had at Yale Drama School. Once, he did an improvisation there from the point of view of a circumcised infant:

> Look at 'em. I'm bleeding to death and they're all having sponge cake. What kind of barbarians are these?

Even now as an actor, landing an occasional job, he found himself framing routines. In autumn 1964, Klein was living on West 153rd Street, just opposite a churchyard cemetery. After he dropped out of Yale Drama ("Did Eddie Cantor go to college?" his father Ben had asked), he worked summer stock and in an off-Broadway play for five dollars a week. When he complained it was coolie's wages, the producer told him, "Shmuck, it's a break." And in that business it was. So he took in extra money as a substitute schoolteacher.

In the meantime, a routine was moving around in his mind, one based on boyhood trips to the circus. Figuring he'd try it out, he showed up at the Wha? one night and did a few minutes, impressing Roth, who told him to check out the hoot at the Bitter End. He scored there too. The management firm out of the Bitter End even talked of handling him.

> The freak show. Remember the obese guy ... ? Six hundred and fifty. And the tall guy, nine-three. That's cute? And there's a guy who was born with just a neck. Nothing else. He types with his ears some-

132

how. My mother tried to make an object lesson. "See what that young man did with a disability. Don't complain when you have a cold."

The management people sent him to see a "real pro" work. To Klein, he was a rim-shot dandy. Robert was sure he was better. But for one reason or another it never amounted to much. And the laughs Klein got the first few times came hard after. And soon he wasn't stopping by the Village.

Another New York kid who was to come around the Village was George Carlin. He was from Morningside Heights, up by Columbia University, which romanticists among his crowd renamed White Harlem.

In the early '60s, Carlin was in Hollywood with a radio newsman, Jack Burns, the two of them going around to the local stations looking for a job. They'd walk in and launch into a B-movie musical shtick in the foyers of stations: "Here we are . . . in Hollywood."

The manager of radio station KDAY saw them and offered them three hundred dollars a week to be the Wright Brothers, an early-morning slot. Evenings they did comedy at a coffeehouse called Cosmo Alley for another ninety dollars a week.

The hours there occasionally made them late to the station. What they'd do when they arrived at KDAY was to throw a switch to put the station at moment's silence and then begin in midsentence—". . .'onderful morning today"—a hint of transmitter troubles in case the manager was listening.

Burns and Carlin gave up KDAY to work as a comedy double. Their act took, as one reviewer noted, "a sicker-than-thou approach [that] leaves no socio-economic turn unstoned." They got laughs on the Peace Corps, Jackie Kennedy, the John Birch Society. Carlin mimicked comic heroes like Sahl, Bruce and Berman, and his John F. Kennedy was said to be "worthy of a broad Harvard A."

As Captain Jack and Jolly George, hosts of a progressive kids' show, they were most outrageous. They took the smile-and-sell approach of those shows to new comic heights/depths, depending on the personal politics of listeners. Captain Jack and Jolly George offered the little 'uns a Junior Junkie Kit, asking the camera to dolly in for a shot of their eyes—they wanted the kids to know they were getting the real goods. The bent spoon to mix the fix came in Modern, Traditional, Provincial and Rosemead. ("Make sure you specify which patterns you want when you send in, kids.")

Carlin and Burns appeared at rooms with the hip standing of the hungry i, but there were too few of them for an act that hadn't the star clout of a Lenny Bruce or Mort Sahl, and too often they ended up in clubs mismatched to their material. "Some really great toilets," said Burns. "We played some little club, I think it was outside of Akron, I forget the name of it, but it was built on cinder blocks. And we got up and our audience was the bar softball team. They came in with their dates. They had just finished the game. And they had their cleats on, and their uniforms. And George and I are up there doing political satire. And they got up in about the middle of the first five minutes —we had no laughs at all—and a guy goes over to the jukebox and puts some money in and they start dancing and we're standing up there with these people dancing around us, man.

"It was wild. And the owner said, 'I'm taking a bath with you guys. I'm paying you big money, you better come up with something. Don't you guys work dirty?' I said, 'You want us to work dirty, huh?' And he said, 'Yeah. What is this stuff with . . . Christ's sake—with Kennedy jokes and Health, Education and Welfare? And Better Business Bureau. I mean, no one understands that shit.' I said, 'Yeah, nobody understands it here, man. That's right.' So George and I had a break. And we had another show to do that night. So we went down to a local Woolworth's and he picked up a fright wig, and I picked up a Yo-Yo. We just thought that would look good. And we came back and walked on. And I said, 'How're you feeling, Georgina?' And George was wearing a fright wig, and he said, 'I'm feeling pretty shitty.' And they broke up. And we just started doing crap jokes for about fifteen minutes and that got us through the week.

"Lotta jobs like that. We were always pissed off about it. We'd get stoned, man. And we'd get hostile. I mean, some nights where we would almost get into fights with the audience. In those days, I was drinking a bit. And George was smoking quite a bit. And between the two of us, we'd be really out of it by the third show.

"All these yelling matches, you know. And either one of us would say, if we got heckled too much, we'd say, 'We have no smart retort to that, so if you keep it up, we're going to punch the shit out of you.' Lines like that."

In 1962, the pair split. Carlin went out on his own.* By 1964, he was in the Village from time to time, working up an act with the magic of Lenny Bruce in the back of his mind.

Bruce himself stopped there once in a while—at the Gate or Cafe Au Go Go, a changed man from Lenny of long ago. Out in California, he'd marked it by emptying his closets of all the suits he owned.

When he came to New York, he liked to stay at seedy hotels. His own room he was fussier about. In one place, he hired painters for it. When he returned later to New York, he was unable to get it back. A permanent resident had settled in.

To his old city friends, he seemed a driven man now. "The cat never slept," said Joe Ancis. "Up all night. Writing. A compulsive driven cat. Just fucked. No eating habits. If it'd be raining, he just wouldn't bother to eat. He was very driven, Lenny. He'd rattle on and on. 'Man, I gotta do this, do that.' His movements were relentless."

In Chicago, he got it in mind to find Rocky from Duffy's. The ex-druggist who'd let Lenny have the run of the room back in LA now lived in Chicago. On an impulse, Lenny jumped in a cab and began to tour the Windy City's pharmacies. *Hey, you know Rocky? . . .* Out of one taxi, into another. He blew seventy-odd dollars that night.

---

* Burns later joined with Avery Schreiber as a comedy team.

He found Rocky in a bust-out joint later, cooking in the back. Bruce asked him how come he hadn't come to see him work. "Hey, Lenny," said Rocky. "What does it mean? I know you like me. I like you. What do we have to see each other?" Bah bah bah.

The laughs were few at the end. There were police busts for narcotics possession and obscenity onstage. He couldn't get work. Club owners feared the police heat. Old friends drifted away, spooked by the drug habit he had and the change it made in him. He was not as easy to be around.

He kept to his house in the Hollywood Hills, working on his court cases, or tilling the earth—planting flowers and vegetables, rooting out weeds. He was more moody now. Part of it was cop funk. In cities he worked, he'd switch cabs several times on the way to a place, suspicious the driver was an undercover officer.

Once, a friend of his noted that the furniture in his place was uncomfortable. It was, Lenny said, by design. That way, people were not inclined to hang around. He avoided some folks. And some of them shied away from him. Bruce came back to his house one afternoon miffed because he'd been standing at Sunset Plaza hitchhiking, and Mort Sahl had passed him by.

Georgie Starr saw him the last time he was in New York. "I called him up. He was at a hotel in the Village. 'Oh, man, come over. I'm lonely. Gotta see ya. We haven't seen each other.' And he was hugging me and kissing me. We hadn't seen each other in so long. . . . He was very involved in this legal thing. He had some guy he was dictating to. And there were legal briefs all over the walls. And letters from attorneys offering help. And little girls—I think he became a stud late in life. Little girls going in and out every minute. And finally [we] went in the john, the toilet. So we could talk.

"He was very handsome. He had long hair but was terribly bloated. His body was just misshapen. And he showed me his back was scarred, the whole length of his back. He told me he'd had a lung collapse. I didn't know that. And in the room—he had a whole case of sardines. He always liked beat hotels. Even when he was making money. So the sardines. And a lot of bloody towels too. . . . See, I'd met him a year or two before on Broadway. I ran into him. He said, 'I'm a junkie.' So I laughed, thought he was putting me on. Bloody towels . . . I didn't discuss that. I saw bloody towels though."

The impulse that sent Bruce into dark corners was routine in the business.

Even in Lenny's troubled last years, there were comics coming up who'd get bonkers at times.

A loose-gaited black, Richard Pryor, had that reputation, blowing hot or cool on a moment's whim. In the Wha?, where he was a regular, Pryor was given to whipped-cream hijinks, or bilious rages in which he'd fistfight patrons underwhelmed by him. The whole emoted spectrum he'd do—with an intriguing virtuosity.

Manny Roth, who managed him awhile, said, "With Richard, it's like you never stop loving your kids, no matter how bad they are. And he was bad. When he started getting gigs in the mountains, if I didn't give him an extra five dollars whenever he asked for it, he wouldn't show up. Pissed me off, man. And he'd come back, and he'd be very contrite. I remember one night, he was sitting in a bar and [crying] 'I didn't mean to. I don't know what I was saying. I'm sorry.' The whole thing. And I'm not sure if it was for real or a performance.

"He'd come into the Wha? and say, 'I have to pay my taxi, man.' I remember one time I gave him five dollars and the meter was like a dollar and a half. He gave the guy the five dollars, says, 'Keep the change.' I used to bail him out of more fucking things. Anybody hold out a piece of paper and give him ten dollars, he would sign that paper. He'd sign away his life. He never read anything."

Pryor seemed bent on abusing his chances. Quite the opposite was impersonator David Frye, who was also in the Village at that time. Frye, an intense little man, was driven. He lived best when he was onstage. And to that end, he worked at it all the time. In the 12th Street apartment he shared with Bernie Travis,

Frye was in the bathroom late into the night evoking the characters he did.

He worked from movie magazine snapshots of stars —and not voices. The physical contours of the photos, he recreated in person. Once he had the look of the character, the sound came readily.

With Frye, a mirror was crucial. When he performed in the Village, he needed to work to it before going on. In most places, the mirrors were in the men's room. That's where Frye would be with the photos, practicing. If biology sent him to a stool, he'd still do the voices, which once led a customer to ask a club owner, "What kind of place you running here?" when he heard several famous voices coming out of one bathroom stall.

In clubs with no mirrors, or ones too high up for Frye to angle a good look (he stands five feet, six inches), he'd bring his own along. Without it, he was lost. Georgie Starr discovered it when he fixed up Pip's, the coffeehouse he ran in Brooklyn. "I did some renovation," he said. "And in the bathroom, I installed a linen roller towel because the toilet would get stuffed up from the paper towels. And we had to remove the old-fashioned mirror, see. So there's only a little mirror that's higher up, and the roller, see? So David comes in. 'George, how are ya?' He's a great handshaker, he's always shaking hands. Goes into the bathroom. Comes out of the bathroom. 'George, this used to be my room. Now, I can't make it here anymore.' 'What's the matter? Nothing's changed, Dave.' 'No, it's no good, forget about it. This isn't my room anymore, George.' "

Frye was always in character(s). Travis would be with him at a coffee shop on 8th Street and hear, "Pahs the cream." James Mason. He'd ask him to stop it and talk to him regular. "Don't like my impressions?" he would answer as George C. Scott.

In those days, he had a Buick with a six-way seat. The seat would rise so that Frye was taller than his passengers. And even on his elevated perch, he'd carry on. Always the voices. Travis used to wonder which ones he did in bed.

Frye was a strange one. "I was emcee at a hotel in

Fallsburg," Travis said. "At that point, Dave was starting to move, and I booked him as the comic—he was paid sixty dollars, I think, for the late show. Now when he got to the hotel, he expected that he'd be given a beautiful room. But the staff, which I'm part of, stayed in a house. It was an old house. On logs. A depression house. It was like disgusting. And he had to stay in my room. And the building was tilted so if you dropped a ball, it would roll across the floor.

"So he's coming to the Gilbert Hotel, which is beautiful, and they put him in this old building like a haunted house. And I come in and he's lying in bed ready to go on. And he says to me, 'You invite me. I do a show. I come up here. And I'm in a room that's on the side of a hill. How can you live like this? How can you live a summer like this?'

"I said, 'Dave, do me a favor . . . You're booked for the show . . . I'm not asking for a commission. I got you the show. Don't bullshit me about the room. I live here all summer. I gotta cope with this every day.' He said, 'I don't deserve a room like this.' I said, 'Dave, do your fucking show and leave me alone.' And I walked out of the room.

"A friend of mine was the singer at the hotel. He sees me later. He says, 'I walked in the room. I thought you were in there. And I walked in and Dave Frye is like this, see: 'Why did he bring me up here? Did he do this to destroy me . . . who can live in, who can stay in a room like this? I'm Dave Frye.' "

Keefe, out on the Coast in 1966, was with Lenny Bruce one day in August.

KEEFE: Went up there with a friend, dropped in on Lenny. He was wearing this jacket that he'd gone into court to plead poverty with. [In 1964, his earnings were a reported six thousand dollars. In October 1965, he was declared legally bankrupt.] Somebody was suing him. And he had this old jacket. It looked like an old Italian immigrant's jacket or something. And he had worn that and a pair of coveralls to court. And he'd taken his jacket and he'd frayed the cuffs and edges of it with a razor blade and made a few slits in it and everything. It looked like the model for Harpo Marx. It was an old pin-stripe jacket. Was once a good one. No more, though. And the judge . . . after the . . . they had their business in court, the judge took him aside and gave him ten dollars.

Q: Was it the jacket that—

KEEFE: Yeah. Right. The way he looked. You know, poverty-stricken.

Q: Did the judge know him as a good comedian?

KEEFE: That I don't know. I don't know if the judge knew anything about his history or anything.

Q: How do you know that the judge gave him ten dollars?

KEEFE: Lenny told us the story.

Q: You think that part is true?

KEEFE: Yeah. Lenny wasn't full of shit about those things. He was laughing about it, telling us how he got the jacket ready and everything.

Q: Anything else?

KEEFE: Yeah. That day, there was this chick up there. When we drove up, she was hanging over the balcony, laughing, 'Ha, ha. I almost OD'd last night.'

The next day Lenny Bruce himself was dead of a drug overdose.

Part Two

The Avery Hotel is in Boston.

The actor Robert Klein was there in late 1966 for the pre-Broadway run of *The Apple Tree,* a Mike Nichols-directed musical he was in.

Afternoons at the Avery were TV-tuned. W-this W-that *click click* take a leak and back for more. And there in the pre-Cronkite gray 4:30–5:30 came a comic name of Murray Roman doing the dit-dit Lenny did, jingling hip that hoped to boogey up routine licks.

No way. It was a pass at gone magic. *Dig it. Dig this. Uh, the maa-un goes in and says* nada/nothing to Klein, sitting in BVD's next to the bedside table with the Gideon in it, watching and wondering what the hell.

It annoyed him enough to try his own hand. That night he sat in his hotel room into the early morning and wrote material, standing to do the gestures that elaborated the words. Occasionally, he laughed out loud. A regular vaud-e-ville it was in the Avery.

And when he was done, Klein vowed to run over to the Improv once he was back in New York, and try it out.

The Improvisation Cafe is located at 358 West 44th Street, due west of 8th Avenue's hooker traffic.

Once it was a luncheonette. Marilyn Monroe, coming out of the Actor's Studio down the block, was said to have stopped there for coffee. Later it was a Vietnamese restaurant with red-lacquered wood and mirrors and an electric bill that broke its owners.

When Gerson "Budd" Friedman, a sturdy chin-whiskered man, leased the place in 1963, he put in Tiffany lamps and theater posters to make it a late-hours hangout for show people. For a while it was. Broadway players came by, and many of them wound up on the brick-backed stage to do an after-hours turn.

In those days, Friedman even drew his kitchen help from the Broadway ranks. It so impressed actor Albert Finney, he'd tell friends, "It's a mah-velous place. They have a dishwasher who's with the Lincoln Repertory Company."

Eventually, comics found their way to the room and some of them got up to try out material, forcing Budd to ask the theater people to hold the noise down. They obliged by moving on to other watering holes. It changed the tone of the place. Soon proprietor Friedman was doing a fast line or two before bringing an act on.

The rise of the Improvisation came with the decline of the Village. Old haunts there disappeared or changed to a rock format, leaving comics without live crowds to work to. Their misfortune was Friedman's blessing. With the best comics money needn't buy, the room prospered.

Indeed the place had a charmed life. Early on, a pay phone there began to cough back coins inserted in it, enabling customers to make calls anywhere in the world for nothing. It increased trade. People in to freeload ended as Improv regulars.

If Ma Bell's charity brought people to the room, the comics made them return. They were the attraction, and in those years, Budd had some good ones. Through his door came Woody Allen, Dick Cavett, Milt Kamen, David Astor, Ron Carey, David Frye, Richard Pryor, J. J. Barry, Vaughn Meader, Sandy Baron and Stiller and Meara.

And one night for laughs, Robert Klein wandered in.

That Klein was there was a curious return on a Bronx prophecy.

The sight of Robert when he was a boy used to provoke a neighborhood lady to croon—*the comeeee-dian, the comeeee-dian.*

Moving through the streets of the Bronx—Gun Hill/Decatur/Bainbridge—he was a dervish presence. Whether at Divack's candy store (from whose roof its proprietor plunged to his death one night) or in the movie house or along the wall at Mosholu Parkway, Klein was a boyo Berle, imitating the class genius who'd competed against a local bank's computer and barely lost, or the colored kids whose sounds titillated the comic ear. *You gonna invite me to yoah bomb bitzvah?*

At the twins' house, which his crowd usurped for its hangout, the boys traded wisecracks the day long. It was their Roxy. One afternoon they sought to find which one of them could sing the most audacious "Rumania." *Rumania . . . Rumania Ru-maaaaaaaa-nia.* They'd trill the word like Caruso. Other times, they'd fashion cardboard placards and walk about the house as pickets.

They were a merry band, with a snot-nosed surety that the world was off its bean save for their nook in it. All of them had the stage instinct—from the twin who'd walk streets in dead of winter in T-shirt and trousers—no overcoat (he and his sibling had had prekindergarten psychiatric help) to No-Neck and Al Uger, who went for the punch line with a brawler's authority.

Klein too. Not the easy stance of Mister Hope he'd use as a comic but rather the club fighter's blunt hulk —and the straight-ahead sound that went with it. It came from a Bronx past, where to get a word in edgewise took the commando air.

Klein still had it at Alfred University in upstate New York. Driving back to the city for vacations, he'd do nonstop Amos 'n' Andy routines, creating the dialogue as he went. At school, he'd entertain Kappa Nu fraters

143

with routines that they'd recall years later meeting him on city streets.

If he'd gone to Alfred to be a doctor, he had a change of heart that led him to a postgraduate stint at Yale Drama School to train as an actor, a move that ran against the risk-free route. The Professions recommended and Bronx tenement moms and pops endorsed.

Show biz was a magic world, a glittery scheme, a "deludert" in the embellished vocabulary of Klein's past. And it was, when all was said and done, the attraction that afternoons and evenings at the twins had sped him toward. (Indeed Al Uger a few years later, musing on his newly earned degree in dentistry, would say to himself, "Teeth. It's all about teeth," and a short time after end up as a TV comedy writer.)

Comeeeeee-dian, the comeeee-dian. It was a while before he took the neighborhood oracle at her word. The brief fling in the Village showed him he hadn't the comic gismo yet. When a few months after the Wha? and Bitter End, he landed in Second City, an improvisational group out of Chicago, he still thought of himself as an actor.

Second City, though, was geared to laughs. Its blackouts sought the punch line and often got there with a few yocks going. For a raw talent like Klein it was an instructive time. In the Village, he'd gone at it blind —no notion of technique, the slick to focus a crowd.

At Second City, he began to find how comic things worked, educated to them, none too charitably in his view, by the unit's glamour boy, David Steinberg. Steinberg was a performer with a sparkly smile and literate mind. As the reigning wit of the outfit, he was used to center stage and resourceful enough to hold it, too often, Klein felt, by making a chump out of him.

If Klein was seated in a scene, suddenly Steinberg would be pacing around him, bewitching the eye with his moving figure. "Grabbing stage" was the expression. He worked that way with words too, using impromptu dialogue to browbeat collaborators, a tack that took getting used to.*

---

* Klein never forgot it though. Years later, on a gig in Bryn Mawr, Pa., a stranger asked him what he thought of George Carlin. Klein said he was a good man but that Dave Steinberg

In time Klein caught on. He learned to cope. And when he left Second City, he had tricks of his own. He knew how to move words beyond their alphabetical binds. He could doctor the mother tongue. Most comics did. Voices dropped like express elevators, or climbed like a coaster, giving a word a queer spin. There were comics that worked more to the whisper, in rhythms that hadn't the hype. But even a Woody Allen or Irwin C. Watson or Jackie Vernon used a sound so understated as to be a dynamic of its own.

Klein had his. And he cultivated it in Friedman's room, going there each night after the final curtain came down on *The Apple Tree*. On a puff of the magic drag, he'd fly from the Shubert Theater straight to the Improvisation, there to ply the comic trade.

With him went a Wollensak tape recorder, a reel-to-reel model he used to play back his performances. Afternoons in his Upper West Side flat he'd listen to the tapes and find the pieces and pauses that incited laughs, and go back and do them again, curious to see if he had a corner of a routine slicked, greased and couldn't-miss.

It was one thing to be funny among chums, with whom wit was often a case of cryptic flashes. Quite another story it was with strangers. It meant acquiring the rhythm and inflections that'd give him the whaaaa he wanted, the involuntary laugh that he'd double in the next breath. That was part of it, the comic wiring, so to speak. The rest was material. He had to find, frame and edit it.

In the '40s, comics started their acts in lending libraries, copying gags out of the books, or in the Broadway movie houses, committing Berle and the boys to memory. With Bruce and Sahl, comedy came from the bones. So did Klein's.

He took his experiences, and distilled them to the comic quick. In this, he was aided by a remarkable memory, one able to retrieve an inordinate amount of data. One night in 1973, Uger called out years from the '50s and asked Robert to elaborate on the desig-.

"sucked," a flip afterthought he regretted uttering almost the instant it was out. "Geez, I shouldn't have said that, huh?" he remarked moments later.

nated Catskills summer. Klein did, remembering names, places and resident loonies—and the anecdotes that went with them.

It was that knack for details of a '50s past that lent his comic fragments of it their liveliness. It was a period that shaped Klein, a time when the romanticist in him was wised up. In the cafes and coffeehouses in the years ahead, he'd remember it.

Like the afternoon when, eight years old, he'd gone to Macy's wearing his New York Yankee jacket and cap that, in his words, "had to be removed by surgery," to see a baseball hero of his.

> I waited on line there. I was first or second. There was a three-hour wait. What a tremendous thrill it was when the player . . . arrived drunk. And I said [*boyishly*], "Gee, man, how many games you going to win the series by?" And he went "UURRRP." Seagram's belch. That subway smell. He said, "You a Yankee junior?" Said, "Yeah, I'm a Yankee junior, you drunken bastard ya. [*Mock righteous*] I'm a young man. I might go the wrong road now. I seen you intoxicated."

It was nothing next to what civil defense did to Klein. Its megaton-minded indoctrination traumatized him. He had nightmares that the Kremlin would abuse the noon lunch horn by dropping the goods at precisely that moment, catching the Bronx at lunch in the midst of holocaust. In that case, Klein had escape routes figured: he pictured himself pedaling his bicycle like crazy up the Hutchinson River Parkway.

It did not reassure him though. For P.S. 94, doomsday was curriculum practically:

> We had all kinds of drills. We had one with three short blasts, two long blasts, one where we had plenty of time, one where they got over Alaska. And then the no blast, where they're over 135th Street. You hear the propellers, you run and . . .

put your ass to the window. Those were the official instructions. "Put your ass immediately to the window." Signed, Averell Harriman, Governor."

Klein had nightmares at the crimped quarters he was raised in, just down the block from a cemetery, nuclear fantasies he later insisted were permanently imprinted on his mind by the approach educators took. At P.S. 94, the highlight of the civil defense program was his teacher's instruction for the use of identifying dog tags. Passing them out, she'd say:

> "Nooo talking. Take these tags home. They're to be used in the event you're burnt beyond recognition in a nuclear holocaust . . . and nooo talking *during* a nuclear holocaust . . . I shall be taking names."

The shrewish schoolmarm was a figure he began to use in Friedman's joint. If the room was not quiet when he went on, he'd strike up the old girl's posture-perfect stance and tight-lipped hauteur. "No talking. No talking," he'd warn in pedagogical pitch. "Button your—" and here he'd put fingers to lips and "lock" them with a key.

Sometimes, if it was still noisy, he'd build a scene with her.

TEACHER: No talking. No talking. What did I just say? (*Pointing.*)

STUDENT: (*rubbing sleepy eyes*): I dunno . . . Peter Stuyvesant?

It usually did what he wanted it to. It made the crowds listen up.

Which was half the battle.

The Improvisation was a small room—capacity of 120—but when laughs rattled between its four walls, the bricks shook. A fine sound. Klein heard it regularly.

He heard good things from other comics too. One of them was a hefty man who'd once hung out with Lenny Bruce. It was Jack Roy, now working under the monicker of Rodney Dangerfield, back in business after more than a decade out of it.

For years, he'd made a good living in siding. He had the blather and con needed to sell. He sold. The money rolled in.

All the while, though, he was writing the jokes, an addiction not time or treasury notes changed. Into a duffel bag he'd cram the gags, occasionally dipping in to sell some to working pros like Billy Sands. Or Jackie Mason. Or Joey Bishop, who told him to use the side door when he came around.

Scribbling jokes was not enough. He torched for the mike. He'd talk about it while out on the road, hustling the siding. *Oh, man, gotta get back. Gotta get back.* For years, the closest he got were the Broadway hangouts. He'd stop by, a sweaty figure with a dyspeptic look.

Now in his forties, the woebegone face was a tale of mismanaged days. A classic comic look. To the look, he was to add an angle, a *hook* in the comic's term. He got it from old pal Georgie Starr, who now ran Pip's coffeehouse in Brooklyn, under his real name —Schultz. At Pip's, George convulsed guys with a character of his, a racketeer who, when queried on the violence he did to people, invariably stated, "He didn' show me respect. He shoulda showed me respect." *I don't get no respect.* It was a line to entwine around the hard-luck jokes Rodney told on himself. Dangerfield asked Schultz did he mind his taking it, and George said no.

When Klein first saw Dangerfield, he figured him for a hack, an old boy just fiddling evenings away on 44th Street. The more he heard him, the more he realized he was wrong. For Dangerfield had the comic mind: he'd keep checking in with new material, gags so good they began to show up in the patter of big-name comics, none of whom felt obliged to credit him. "So what?" Alan King told him. "Sue me."

A Roy by any other name, he was the same man-Jack. *No respect:* it suited him fine. No change from the '40s when every day was an insult to him. Rodney, like Roy, had the dim view, and he'd often spell it out onstage at the Improv, occasionally encouraged by the bottle of French red Budd laid on him. Those nights established him as Friedman's prime-time act and convinced Klein that the ex-Mr. Roy could whale. For Rodney often departed from his material and winged it.

The offstage Roy/Dangerfield intrigued him too. He was stoked by the same bilious source that his downtrodden comic was. Eh this/eh that. Dangerfield was a grand opinionated fellow. He and Klein got chummy.

The both of them would check out comic ideas with each other. *Hey, man, whaddaya think of this?* Klein, fooling with an impression of horse-race announcer Fred Capossela, wondered whether to have him use the staccato patter he did at the race track in his private life too:

> "Good afternoon, racing fans. This is Fred C-apossela. The track is fast, the day is clear and I talk funny.
>
> "And they're off. Tamburlaine first, Rickshaw second, Wilhemina's Baby third, Claptrap fourth and Lion Tamer on the outside fifth."
>
> He's always so objective. He doesn't care who wins, too smart to be betting during his thirty-eight years. It'd be embarrassing if he got involved. "Rickshaw coming up quick on the outside. Run you son of a bitch, run."
>
> Goes home, he's the same kind of man. "Good eeev-nin', Mary C-apossela. Here comes mother with the dinner. I want the fruit cocktail first, split-pea soup second, roast beef third, mashed potatoes fourth and the coffee on the outside."

The bit came together when Klein put Capossela at the dinner table, and Dangerfield blurted the phrase, "... and the coffee on the outside." The idea to serialize the menu struck him then. What Klein did with that bit and others impressed Dangerfield, who got on the phone to Jack Rollins, a high-powered manager of comics, to tell him about Klein.

Early in 1967, Dangerfield began to get big beyond 44th Street. TV shots spread his name. The jobs were for a better dollar. Often Klein tagged along with him when he worked. Up to the Concord, where audiences banged wood sticks at tables to spare them the effort of laughing. Or, down to Miami, familiar turf for Rodney.

He'd gone before to hang around with comic pals that worked one-nighters down there. Club-date comics. Old New York boys making anonymous paydays in the sun. In coffee shops and luncheonettes, they'd huddle and recollect the old days. Rodney was pipeline to the comic past, Dante of its honky-tonk times.

For Klein the comic present absorbed him. He worked to acquire "the minutes"—the half hour or so a new comic needed in coffeehouses and clubs. He'd walk into the Improv and have in mind bits to do, old ones he figured needed sharpening, or new ones to flesh out.

He created material, even discarded some, routines with laughs he considered cheap. He had a bit on the immutable power of genes—a couple with doctored snub noses birthed an issue, as he put it, "bearing a remarkable resemblance to a parrot."

That bit went. So did one on a school principal known in P.S. 94 days as "strict."

> We used to call her strict. "She's strict." Bun in the back of her head. And Red Cross shoes. We used to say, "She's strict." I found out now that I'm a big person, they have names for peop—She is a dyke, ladies and gentlemen.

The "cheap shot," once a staple of the comedy that came out of vaudeville ("she was so fat/ugly/stupid that . . .") got the bad eye in smart quarters these days. A comic who took himself seriously avoided it or, in a few cases, took it to its far ends, the way a Terry Southern might on the written page, so that at its cadaverous extreme, bad taste was nudged to another dimension, instructing the queasy corners of our days.

Either way, the comic came to be thought of as more than a lowbrow stunt man, a change the times instigated. Personal and social politics were part of a new awareness for the under-thirty generation, the comic included.

The crowd Klein knocked around with in the Bronx had moved to bachelor flats downtown. In get-togethers, the guys still coveted laughs but now there were notes of radical politics and drug consciousness. No-Neck became a Marxist. So did one of the twins. Another of the gang got strung out on drugs.

The comics the boys from the Bronx knew were the fullacrap ones they'd caught in dial-switching transit on the TV. It made Klein careful. He did not want to be shrugged off by his own chums as inconsequential or irrelevant.

His ideas were undergoing change. Where once the grammatical flaws of blacks were a joke to him, they no longer were. He knew it was condescending. Women too were seen in more than one dimension. He'd evolve from calling them names ("dyke") to routines on chauvinist TV commercials. And for Klein, all of it'd happen at the Improv.

Night in, night out, he got laughs there. On the phone to his agency, William Morris, he got the stall. Polite evasions. Or patent nonsense. *Just talking to Otto Preminger about you.* Worse, none of the agents came to see him work. At least, not until Jack Rollins did. Then agents in numbers appeared—to forestall Klein's signing with a manager.

For Rollins and his partner, Charles Joffe, had clout in the business that'd force the agency to move on Klein's behalf, an effort its very structure argued against. Klein later saw it in absurdist terms. *Here they were—I'm paying ten percent—and they actually would do things against my interest. Not because*

they're evil men or anything. It's the bureaucracy. It's
business for them. They have to think of things that
make it easiest for them. To peddle a comic unknown
was no wisdom. Better to let him push on his own and
cash him in later.

Rollins was no clichéd schemer, talking out of the
side of his mouth. He was a tall, trim man with a civil
air, and an eye for finer things. Cigars, antiques, race-
horses: he could distinguish better/best. And so it
went with comics—Woody Allen, Cavett, Nichols and
May were his kind. And after that night, Klein was
too. *It's a way, man,* said Dangerfield.

Not that it changed his fortunes overnight. There
were still kinks to work out. The energy back of his
comic line was sometimes barbed. *Hostile* was a word
he heard a lot then. A shake-em-up imperative Lenny
Bruce bequeathed. There was a tutored note too that
was grating to some listeners. Klein, more informed
than most comics (B.A., History/Political Science),
used his store of data in the act, often in a spare
manner.

> Certain guys in history I feel sorry for.
> James Abram Garfield. A real lost soul.
> Do you know he was a good man? Eight
> times he was elected from Ohio. And he
> went to the Presidency, and he was assas-
> sinated. Shot by a disappointed office
> seeker, right?

> Don't they always say that same sentence?
> It's crazy. Every time you read his name—
> James Abram Garfield: "Shot by a disap-
> pointed office seeker." That's all they can
> think of what he did in his short office.
> You look at a child's milk container—
> Collection of the Presidents. It says,
> "George Washington, father of our coun-
> try." "Abraham Lincoln: Emancipation
> Proclamation."

> *"James Abram Garfield, shot by a disap-*

pointed office seeker." The man was swept under a rug.

You look in the Encyclopedia Britannica under "Garfield, James Abram." It says, *See Office seeker, Disappointed.*

Occasionally, though, he turned preachy, a flaw he had out of comic too. Simple questions sometimes brought labyrinthian answers. As a rule, he avoided the soap box. He was a bright, funny cat, at home in diverse areas—from baseball-card trivia to classical music to politics.

Rollins liked what he saw. To him, Klein had the comic eye. The line used in the trade was—*He thinks funny.* That wasn't all either. Up onstage, Klein was at ease. He could animate his material. It was where many new boys failed. Fear immobilized them. Their gestures were as disembodied as Nixon's. Klein had a knack for finding cartoon "action" to piggyback his words—and give all the more reason to laugh.

In the Improvisation Cafe, they laughed. Friedman's room celebrated new comics, not the norm in clubs at large. The clientele on 44th Street was lively and informed and occasionally contained a zany or two passing through the night. They were welcome.

There was, for instance, the married blonde from the Bronx whose alcoholic intake reduced coherent expression to a single thought. When drunk, she'd shout, "Kiss this," a setup for any comic drawing breath. By most standards the lady was daft. In the Improv, she had entertainment value.

Friedman did not mind an occasional bizarre interlude. Usually, he broke up comic stanzas with song and music talents, but he used fire-eaters, penny whistlers and exotic dancers as well. Once, a baton twirler too plump for her spangled outfit appeared, a sight that enticed bar regulars into the main room. She took their mock cheers for real and left the stage with tears of joy.

Another night, five strippers came in, each in hair dyed to an irregular shade. Without prompting, they got up to do their specialty, the night grinding to a halt when Friedman's Mrs. objected to one of them doing it with a customer's head between her knees.

Later, restaurateur Jim Downey stopped in and was told of it. Ushered over to meet the women, he said, "Ah, good evening, ladies. I'm Jim Downey. How are you tonight?" At that, one of them reached into her blouse and took out a breast. "Oh, hello, Jim," she said. "Have some."

The ghost of F-f-friar hovered over the room some nights. A touch of lunacy that prompted Dangerfield to joke, "You do well here, it means you haven't got an act."

Out of the Improv and into the fire: Klein began working.

In May of 1967 he was at the Bitter End for a hundred dollars a week as a prelim to a mentalist, Dr. Ireland, a strange taste for Bleecker Street.

It drew mink-coated ladies from the Grand Concourse who blinked in the cavernous dark and wondered, "Is this whe-ah the seance is?"

> Dr. Ireland. Wonderful working with him. Specializes in precognition. The ability to foretell events before they happen. He says God bless you, I sneeze. Pleasure working with him.

The good doctor was no laughing matter to the ladies. And neither, it turned out, was Klein. At least not then. The next week, with another headliner, he fared better.

In June, he did Mr. Kelly's in Chicago for five hundred a week. It was there a patron decreed, "You . . . thtink!" while he worked. Recalling it later in coffeehouses, Klein played it for laughs:

> "You thtink," he said. And I was cool, of course. I didn't blow it or anything . . . I-went-for-his-throat.

In effect, he had. *Where do you come off? . . . Who the hell do you . . .* and down the commode he'd gone.

Late summer, he was at Bill Hahn's, a Connecticut resort, where Hahn himself instructed in the spectator arts. "Now, you put your hands together and give him the biggest welcome you can." It did Klein no good. The middle-aged crowd was not attuned to his kind of humor.

No big thing. Ahead was an autumnal swing to the Coast with his first national TV appearance scheduled. Until then it was back to the Improv to spar with audiences there, trying new emotions on them or checking out old ones.

Some pieces he had were sure laughs when he hit pauses and punch lines in a prescribed way. It was a Klein that had worked times before. Not to say the bit was muzzled. Within it was space for him to flex, and find new ground. But a routine went wobbly without its sure laughs.

Some nights a line came out of the blue and was gone almost before he knew he'd said it. He'd try it the next night to see if it'd catch sparks. Long routines got started that way. It was why the Wollensak went with him. It gave him his every word in replay.

It was how he got material. He took his throwaway lines and built his act from them. He was simon-pure about it. He wanted only what was made and muddled on his own. More and more comics were like that —as distinguished from those who got laughs and were not sure why, the so-called "mechanics" who'd ask gag writers what the jokes meant. Short on wit, they had an instinct like the cat's for staying upright through any store-bought routine.

Others were hip to their own comic mechanisms. Dangerfield used a stopwatch on occasion to clock a joke. Time and tone: Rodney knew what he wanted. Klein did too. It was what he alone turned out, a method some claimed was madness. TV frisked a comic fast. It was unlike the days when George Burns and his Gracie toured with the same seventeen minutes for four years, never booked into a theater twice.

The market had shrunk since then. It was a thinning scene Klein was into. Late September 1967, he went on his first tour. It started in Washington, D.C., at the

155

CELLAR DOOR,

From the street it had the look of a Mulberry Street social club, its windows grayed over so the nonpaying public couldn't see in.

a small club in the Georgetown section of the capital.

A sign out front stated,

JOSH WHITE
$4.50 MINIMUM,

billing that slighted Klein. Contractually, he was entitled to a mention. But when he asked, he was told what he could do by the owner, a pompadoured fatty in his early twenties. "What is it with you," he asked, "an ego trip?"

There was little ego left after the first show. As he came down from the dressing room a flight up, he could hear a Joan Baez record that had stuck to a line—

Silver dagger, silver dagger, silver dagger,

it whined, an omen, it turned out, for an act about to be cut to shreds.

If Klein failed in some of his other paid gigs it was never in the stone silence he faced here. Within minutes, he was experiencing what comics refer to as "flop sweat," glandular chaos that was the telltale of panic. Icy beads of perspiration covered him. With the same material that had convulsed 44th Street crowds, he failed in Fat Charlie's room.

It left him to work out of fear, a state that Jack E. Leonard found his fun in. A rarity, that. Klein did what most comedians do: he rushed. Not consciously. For in the back of his mind was the caution to stay cool.

He came undone anyway. The big energy worked against him. The actorish strokes were choppy, frantic. He ran scared. "What the hell was that?" he heard a waiter say as he finished.

It was not just the failure that hurt. It was how the failure defined him. The help's brow-raised response to him was the measure of it. Neutral to him before he'd worked, they verged on rude after. From Fat Charlie on down, the chill was on. Klein did better that week at the Cellar Door but was not asked back for years.

On he went, jetting to Los Angeles, this time with Rollins along. He was there to do the first of a three-shot deal with.

THE DEAN MARTIN SHOW,

at escalating $2,000, $2,500 and $3,500 prices, top dollar for a TV unknown.

Arriving at the Beverly Hills Hotel, Klein found a bowl of fruit in his room with a note from the hotel—"Good luck on the Dean Martin Show." He had hardly put his bags down when NBC in Burbank phoned, and asked him to come by. He and Rollins taxied there.

The show's producer, Greg Garrison, wanted a look at Klein, a comic he'd booked sight unseen, relying on Rollins' say-so. They went to a Quonset structure a few blocks from the NBC lot. There, before Garrison and members of his staff, Klein was asked to do his act. For twenty minutes he did, standing in a bright tiled room, suffering silence again. Then he heard TAP TAP TAP TAP TAP, sounds made by fingers drumming on a desk top.

Q: You mean they wanted you to stop when they hit on wood?

KLEIN: No. I was through. And they applauded. That was their applause. . . . And it was like it had that dead sound.

Q: Why didn't they just clap?

KLEIN: Because they were nice guys, that's why.

Nice had nothing to do with it. Laughs were what counted, and Garrison hadn't heard many. Rollins argued it was the kind of chance Custer had had. In truth, Klein made out better. He got two thousand dollars to forget it, kid.

He didn't. Back at the hotel, he sank into a mood, sure that the Burbank mahatmas were right about him, he hadn't a ghost of a shot at TV. In a flash he saw hard nights to come, combats in smoky out-of-the-way rooms, a fast line to the bottom.

The TAP TAP TAP came back to him, casual dismissal that nagged and infuriated him. He saw the bowl of fruit with the note next to it, and stared at the walls wondering what next. In that mood he did a curious thing. With, as he put it, "that real childish but real human need," he phoned his parents in the Bronx.

The next day he found other solace. He wound up with an older woman of wealth, a tan shiny beauty also staying at the Beverly Hills, an acquaintance of a mutual friend.

In bed, she talked of fox hunt Sundays. And used amyl nitrates.

And he had himself an antidote.

He was not finished with LA either. He had the

TROUBADOUR

to do, an important room to the music-culture crowd. Even then it was an antenna to the times. Nineteen sixty-seven: something was going on. It was in the air. And in the Troubadour, Klein felt out of it in coat and tie. After opening night the tie went.

It got better. Troubadour crowds heard him out. He got his laughs. Even the owner, Doug Weston, told him he wasn't what he'd expected, the regular kinetic-frenetic comic. In spite of it, Klein learned two weeks later while in San Francisco at the

HUNGRY i,

that in truth Weston was far from sold. He'd told the agency he wasn't interested in picking up his option. On both coasts, Klein was running out of places to play.

And what he didn't kill, the business did. The hungry i, at one time a boom operation, fared so poorly with the jazz headliners Klein played with that owner Banducci asked out of the final week of the contract.

The entertainments were no longer so alive and well. In 1958, Henny's Roxy had ended its stage shows. Nearly a decade later, the room that had had Sahl, Bruce, Berman and Gregory was about to go under.

It put the kid comic in a bind. Booze crowds often didn't give a bleep what he had to say. And in rooms like the Troubadour, where hair was getting down to there, he was not quite right either.

It left Klein in limbo, more so as the Aquarian influence—drugs, sex, long hair—spread. The so-called psychedelic times widened the generation gap. With a comic that had the scruffy look, "You thtink" was, for all he knew, a political statement.

It came to less work for the muthas.

It made Budd Friedman a power broker in comedy.

He owned the audience. Without it, a comic could not find his sound.

If the freebies made a fat cat out of Budd, they could do right by the act too. For in 1967 the Improv was where TV talent-watchers went to inspect comic merchandise.

It was there the "Tonight Show" staff saw Klein and asked him on. TV legitimized comic unknowns. For Robert, it was a second chance. This time he meant to do it right.

The late-night talk format was TV's earliest starmaker, going back to Steve Allen and Jack Paar in the '50s. Johnny Carson arrived in October of 1962, and had been the midnight king since. A strong comic who enlivened lax moments with impromptu wit, Carson knew when to leave off. He gave fellow pros room to work and upped their laughs with the lines he fed. In tricky straits he was a cool number. He'd kept NBC on top at midnight. The show was the one comics wanted.

They were not alone. The program was a pop institution, really. For the public, it was magic time. All sorts of strange ones wrote or phoned, looking to be booked. There was a woman who grew grass in sculptured heads and kept calling to be on. A daring young man offered to jump out of a plane without a parachute if "Tonight" would film it.

For comics it was more cut-and-dried—a chance to get a career in orbit. It didn't happen as regularly as when the world and TV talks were newer. Just the same it *did* occur.

Rickles was an example. In the Casbar Lounge in Vegas, he became a local institution, the maximum needler who was best when he had other performers to bounce off. Rickles did not leave it to chance. He "merchandised." He'd go see other acts, and persuade them to come to the Casbar. *Please. I want you to see something I'm doing.*

What they saw was Rickles having the laughs on them. It made Don a smash in Vegas, but too risky for TV. The network men thought Rickles incapable of an expurgated act. It kept him a show biz rumor. Then Carson gave him a shot in 1965.

Rickles opened with

Hi, dum dum,

and, when Carson tried to answer, snapped,

Where does it say you butt in, dummy? I'm fed up with you already, you know that?

busting him up.

That's it, laugh it up. You're making fifty million dollars a year and your poor parents are back in Nebraska eating locusts for dinner.

Rickles went national after that.

For most comics, TV's effect was not so startling as it was with Don. Usually, it helped, but it took repeated successes on TV to gain stardom. To blow the follow-ups nullified a smash debut. TV was demanding of its new boys. That it could be a cruel comedown, J. J. Barry was prepared to testify.

BARRY: A guy I knew took a baseball bat to his car. He started destroying all the material things he had.

Q: Why?

BARRY: Because he'd had it. He was one of the first cats Jack Paar ever had on. Young unknown cats. A hit, and the next time [thumbs down gesture]. . . . And he didn't understand really what was going on and he went out and destroyed everything he owned.

TV-minded comics took no chances. When Jackie Mason was becoming a hot mockey act, he worked and worked at it before a TV shot. He'd call up owners of boîtes like the Blue Angel or Bon Soir. *How ya doin' tonight? Ya got forty, fifty people?* And off he'd go—five, six clubs a night to try out new material. Afterwards, he'd edit in his head: this was a laugh, that wasn't.

Klein worked that way too. He did the same five minutes over and over, making it a sleek beauty, capable of zero to sixty in seconds. *Don't save,* Rodney told him. *Be unmerciful. Powerhouse.*

In clubs, he did not parrot his act. He took alternate routes to the laughs, scheming them as he went. For TV, he was socketed in, an instant replay of the words and woozen weizen he'd worked out in Pip's in Sheepshead Bay, or at the Improvisation on 44th Street. He was a push-button act for the night, TV-tailored.

With TV, it was quick minutes and scram. A comic did not have the time to woo an audience with the cumulative rhythm of his act. The cafe or coffeehouse gave him up to an hour, long enough to live or die grandly.

On TV, he had five minutes or so, which suited some comics better than others. Shecky Greene for instance: The twenty-one-inch screen reduced him in more ways than one. The line on him was—*Shecky needs fifteen minutes just to say hello*. TV pinched his act. Greene was best when he bounced from a joke to pratfall to mimicry or song, building moment by moment a comic valentine. In a club, it played. On TV, it never got the time to, leaving Shecky to look like a sweaty hulk.

Most of them were better in clubs. TV was excerpt comedy, fragment of an act. Klein, with cafe time, was a stronger performer. Still, his act parsed. His routines were solid constructs. No surprise that when he did "The Tonight Show" in early 1968, he succeeded. He knew the bit up and down. He'd done it so many times it'd have run on automatic pilot. Carson had one word: *Whoooo.*

And?

And it helped. It got him bookings, money, more TV. What it didn't do was put him in front of his own kind. Too often he played to martini crowds he had to take care not to insult. A word, a weird notion: in hippie/hairy/Viet War times, it could queer it for him.

He monitored the act, and minded. There were times, moreover, when he felt like the medieval jester, a stooge for an hour. The "dance, boy" syndrome, he called it. Patrons picked spare rib remnants from their teeth, or belched and braayed, and looked at him absently. He was there. They were there. Let the show go on.

TV or not, he was hardly a household name, and where he did go in 1968/1969, it was with the feeling that the act was, as Woody Allen once said of his own, "for dogs with high pitched ears."

Something had to give.

The comics now were a breed apart from the Hanson's bunch. They had more on their minds.

They were college-bred, Kafka-read, TV'd/V.D.'d and nuclear heebie-jeebied, different jokers altogether. Many of them had baccalaureates to fall back on. For better or for worse, they had options.

Some of them didn't even act the part. Like Mike Preminger. Mustached, dark-eyed, he had a slow Bronx-broad sound that evoked an old gramophone fade. At Ithaca College in upstate New York, a room-

mate of his walked backwards when in his company
to avoid Preminger's dawdling pace.

> I used to have a younger brother. He's
> older now.

was the line Preminger did on it.

David Brenner was a tall thin Philadelphian with a
wraparound smile and a flair for boutique styles. For
years, he'd come into Budd Friedman's place as a
paying customer, sitting back and watching the comics.
At the time, he was a producer of TV documentaries,
earning up to thirty thousand dollars a year. In 1969,
Brenner abruptly decided to chuck it and become a
comic. When he told that to a TV executive, the man
doubled over. "Thanks," said Brenner. "That's my
first laugh."

It was not the reversal it appeared. Brenner's father
had been in vaudeville awhile and remained a cutup at
home. Once, when David's mother served indigestible
liver for dinner, the old man took his portion, fetched
hammer and nails and secured it to the bottom of his
shoe, trimming it to conform to the foot's shape.

In the Philadelphia school system, Brenner operated
with his daddy's flair. In his physics class, he was
given the first five minutes to tell jokes, under an
armistice that curbed him the rest of the class. Once,
in an auditorium used as a study hall, Brenner was
at the back carrying on when the teacher signaled
him forward. He came on roller skates, gliding the
length of the slanted floor.

Jimmie Walker was a product of a South Bronx
black ghetto, a high school dropout working as a
supermarket delivery boy on Manhattan's East Side,
snitching produce from orders. One time he was caught
at it by a five-year-old girl who told him, "You don't
have to steal. You coulda just asked."

Where Walker came from, it was the policy to take,
not ask. Jimmie himself had engineered a boyhood
raid on a candy factory and later on watermelons.
In his housing project, he'd knocked around with a
crowd so tough that even a game like hide-and-seek
was played for keeps. Walker remembered a lad who

paid dearly for being discovered. His pursuer unzipped his fly and peed on him, and pretended never to see him.

At the supermarket, Walker saw all that money could buy. The crammed shopping carts fellows his age could afford impressed him. He decided he could do with buying power himself. He got his high school diploma and then enrolled at City College in a SEEK program. Success in a speech class there sent him into uptown community centers to try comedy. He met opposition. *Get off, man. Get the fuck off. You ain't sayin' nothin', Jack.*

Eventually he drifted to a black cultural center in Harlem where the revolutionary Last Poets were. When he proposed comedy for their programs, they looked askance. "Two of the cats said, 'Hey, man, this guy's full of shit,'" Walker remembered. "'We don't have time for this shit, we deal in heavy revolutionary action. . . . This motherfucker . . . who is this dude?' But the other two guys . . . the other guys say, 'Hey man, fuck it . . . what can we lose? Let him get up there. Freebie. If he bombs, he bombs, fuck him.'"

On an inclement New Year's Eve, Walker opened with

> Boy it's raining so hard outside I saw Superman riding in a cab.

In his phrase, he "wiped them out," with jokes he'd taken off an album of black comic Clay Tyson.

There were harder times ahead for Walker and the others, all of whom started within months of each other in 1969. Some of them tried Village showcases, and regularly got the runaround. *Kinda pressed tonight. Sorry.* Those rooms deferred to singers, the worst of whom could do fifteen minutes off-key. When (and if) a comic got on, it was with the usual reminder: *Uh, look kid. Just do five minutes. Kinda tight tonight.*

If the Improv was the comics' room, it was so full up with them that new boys were left to sit and wonder if it was what they really wanted to do for a living. They waited in the bar area, or wandered into the main room to watch the other comics work.

With Dangerfield gone, Klein was up top of the roster, getting the prime time slots. He was there with his new Sony cassette recorder, still trying to come up with material. All the time he was thinking. At his apartment on West 103rd Street (a building Humphrey Bogart was raised in) were scraps in drawers, closets, old files on which he jotted ideas that came to him on the run. On cocktail napkins, lined legal stationery, torn corners of *The New York Times,* he'd scribble wherever he was.

At strange and unexpected times, concepts came to him. Lying on a beach—he'd think: *What a way this'd be to make a living.*

> What do you do?
> I sit in the sun.
> Really? What does it pay?

And suddenly his mind would be exploring. Supposition: An employment counselor offers this job. An outrageously easy, delightful job. No useful purpose to it, but a job nonetheless. Against this, he posed the unionist note:

> Sitting in the sun? I don't know. What are the hours? . . . Thirty-five a week? Well, my people have suffered many injuries. The sand blows. . . . We'll want beach umbrellas of course. What about rowdies?

He jotted it down but for one reason or another never did try to develop it.

One he did use originated in an afternoon of harmonica-playing. Klein was struck by how the instrument worked. *You give a harmonica to a child, you get the inhale-exhale symphony.*

He junked the line but considered the comic extension of the principle. It came out like this:

> I thought—what a hell of a nurse's aid. A guy is in the hospital, a nurse can put one of these in his mouth, hear how he's breathing, go away and play cards.

He illustrated what he meant musically. Arms at his side, he stared straight ahead and breathed into the harmonica, creating the musical equivalent of respiration.

> Any trouble—she hears right away.

His eyes got big, the music became irregular.

> And if he should happen to expire—love that word, *expire*. "I'm sorry, he expired yesterday." Is that dignity? You don't know if it's a man or a library card. "I'm sorry, he expired at four-fifteen." If he should happen to expire, at least it ends on a nice exhale, a major chord, very final sound.

HARMON-
ICA: Duh-duh duh-duh, daaaaaah.

Using his harmonica to illustrate, Klein proposed that death was a stylized affair. In Robert's world, the pompous man's came with the romantic flourish of a "William Tell Overture" that lapsed to the universal last gasp (duh-duh duh-duh, daaaaah). For "a funky cat," the end came with a primitive Sonny Terry sound, a gusty lament that ceded to the common expiring note.

Any and all ideas he tried out in Friedman's room. Klein was at home there, free to go to the kitchen and ask Louie for a cup of coffee or even a meal, carte blanche few other comics had.

Most of them Friedman treated, as one put it, "kinda wobbly." The same comics whose checks he'd pick up when dining out, he'd snarl at in his room, particularly if they blocked the doorway.

Sentiment never entered into Budd's operation. One

time, when a customer became unruly, Friedman began to drag him out. The man drunkenly babbled he knew Loretta Young, Loretta Young, Loretta Young. "So what?" Friedman said as he bounced him. "You think she's happy?"

He ran comics on and off the stage like a traffic cop, sometimes in the baseball idiom. "Gimme the right-hander," he'd say into the bar area (the "bullpen"). If he wasn't the Frazzini Brothers, he was no backslapper either. All business. It sometimes griped new guys, one of whom wrote a letter to *The New York Times*. It stated in part:

> *The first time I tried out for this club it was about 1:30 A.M. on a cold December night, and I went on after a nine-year-old girl tap dancer. I did about ten minutes of good material and after it was over, I went over to the club owner and asked how I did? He looked at me in the face and said, "Next time, do seven minutes."*

Friedman was nonplussed, claiming the comic was more entertaining on paper than onstage. He was not apologetic either about the use to which he put the comics. The only time he'd had pause was when a favorite of his, Richard Pryor, said he was mistreated on account of race. That night Friedman tossed in bed until he woke his wife. She advised him not to worry. "You should have told him," she said, "you take advantage of all performers, regardless of race, color or creed."

Preminger's line was:

> God came down here once. God came in the back door and asked to go on. And Budd said, "What do you do?" "Phenomenons and miracles." "Sorry, no magic shit."

It typified the once-over comics felt Friedman gave talent. And yet he was far from an ogre. Acts that moved up in the world found Budd out in the audience at theaters or clubs to watch them. A thorny sense of loyalty he had.

Budd was out to make money but he was open to what comics wanted to try. One night, he let Pryor, J. J. Barry and Martin Harvey Friedberg eat a meal onstage in silence. The three of them turned the meal into slapstick. They snatched food off each other's plates, licked the dishes. Finished, they crashed their plates to the floor. It brought Friedman on the run. "This is the way you treat my place?" he asked. And he proceeded to pull the tablecloth off of the table, sending what dishes remained flying. It knocked the crowd silly.

But there was a limit to what even Friedman would suffer. Lenny Schultz was a part-time comic who held down a regular job as a gym teacher. He was a sound-effects man, who liked to get far-out, particularly for comics standing around the bar. For them, he'd flash his *schwonce* and do shtick around it. One night for laughs, Schultz vomited on stage, emptying the place in seconds. Friedman suspended him for two weeks.

At least Lenny got on. It was more than new guys could boast. Often they were shut out, or bumped if a bigger name suddenly appeared. When Budd did put them on, it was, as Preminger said, "Like three-thirty, four in the morning. Who was there? People that didn't have a home or something. Or their papers had expired and they were leaving the country in the morning."

It was not easy on them. "Even though," said Preminger, "this is a place where new talent gets its chance, it's also a business, and Budd wants an audience to keep coming back. So he puts on who's best. Sometimes I'd stay away for a while because it was just depressing. Often, he'd say, 'Come in at ten and you'll start off the evening. Even if it's a small audience, at least you'll get on.' So I'd go in and once in a while get on at ten at night. But very often, I wouldn't get on. And I'd hang around and hang around and hang around and a lot of times I'd never get on.

"I'd sit alone in the back and watch. Or walk

around and get very down. And a lot of guys, the newer ones, would go for coffee afterwards. That was the highlight of the night—to go to another place for coffee afterwards. And we'd talk and bitch and moan, 'Oh, I coulda got on. I'm good enough to go on at least at two.' And that's what I really looked forward to, almost more than performing, was the hanging around with the other guys and going and having coffee.

"Most of the time it was Brenner, Walker, Steve Landesberg and sometimes Marvin Braverman. One or two others occasionally. We'd usually go to this coffee shop on Eighth Avenue and Forty-fifth Street. A lot of hookers in there on their break. Very little to say to us. I think that they could tell that we were comics and didn't have any money. And they wanted ten dollars and not a one-liner as payment.

"And Greeks too. It was a Greek place. Not Greek food but run by Greek people and a lot of Greeks came in there at three in the morning and it sounded like the muffled soundtrack of Z. A lot of, like, maybe waiters or dancers from Greek clubs along Eighth Avenue would come in there. There was one Greek guy who used to come in there and I don't know what he did for a living. But he had this giant case that could have had a whole housing project in it. And in it was a little kazoo. And he'd take it out and walk around playing it and making the sound of a duck with it. The first few weeks it was fun. But then I just couldn't take it . . . not at four in the morning. Anyway, we'd sit there some nights for hours and hours. Then go home and sleep all day."

As a teen-ager, Klein worked as a lifeguard in the Catskills at a place whose emcee had quit. Robert asked for and got the job, only to have the comic there come out and rag him. *Give a kick, the "kinder."*

Klein had the laughs later in a bit that mocked the Catskill comic and his predictable pap:

Hey, you look like a Jewish Mr. Clean!
. . . Hey! You two baldheaded men, ya

put your heads together, ya make an ass
of yourselves! But seriously . . . is that a
wart on your arm? Or is that your wife?

A resort owner told him the routine made him un-
employable in The Mountains, a distinction he rather
liked. For he wanted nothing to do with the toomler-
style comic. A new day/a new way in the '70s.

Bob Hope's politics were as out of favor with kid
comics as his style. Jimmie Walker, told by his draft
board he was underweight, was given a chance to
fatten up for the next examination. Up to the Bronx
Walker went to play basketball every day in the summer sun with a sweatshirt on. He beat the draft. So
did Klein. There were others as well. Preminger, in
the reserves, lost patience with a sergeant who
badgered him about the length of his hair. He knocked
the man down with a punch.

Hope was once timed at forty-four jokes a minute.
Now many comics were trying the living-room manner.
Simple things: Nobody, Woody Allen told a comic,
calls anyone ladies and gentlemen anymore. Comics
had been moving since Sahl/Bruce & Co. away from
the lickety-split whammo in-the-eye-and-fly old-school
approach. Something impersonal in it.

In fact, some of the new comics spoofed the old-
style guys. The '70s would see a Coast act, Steve
Simon, use flash cards with lines like

Take my wife, please

on them. If he failed to get a laugh, he'd dig into
his stack and pull out,

Are you an audience or oil painting?

and show it with a deadpan expression. He even had
a card that asked,

Did you hear the one about . . . ?

If an audience shouted "Yes," Simon dumped the rest
of his cards save for one. It said, "Thank you," and
off he'd go.

Albert Brooks, the son of a '30s Greek-dialect radio comic, Parkyakarkus (Harry Einstein), had been around comics since he was a boy. Cantor and Jessel came by the house. With Albert, familiarity bred contempt. As his friend Rob Reiner the actor recalled: "Joey Bishop had a gofer-type guy work for him. And we used to make jokes about him all the time. Because he used to send him on these errands. He was the kind of guy that when Joey would ask for a baloney sandwich, the guy would get up and start patting his pockets for his keys. You know, one of those guys. His reflex action—he'd start looking for his keys. And Joey used to sit out by the pool— he had a great tan. And he used to sit with a sun reflector, one of those tinfoil type of things. And Albert one day said, he told me, 'Ya hear Joey Bishop's reflector got broken, he's using the guy, he's having him dress up in a silver lamé suit and he's holding him up there.' "

The curly-haired Brooks at work was still the merry prankster, mocking bup bup's pretend charm and the minimal mind behind it. He'd come onto a dimly lit stage and stare at the audience while a tape of his voice played:

> My name's Brooks. Some call me a comedian. My job—make 'em laugh.

Invariably it did. And the prerecorded Brooks would say:

> You're beautiful. You're beautiful,

while his eyes flashed and panicked, wondering what to do next.

> Find another line of crap fast,

the voice advised him.

And so it went with Albert. He turned the old notions upside down: did five-minute routines on how to tell a joke, with Rube Goldberg-type diagrams; lined up friends onstage and ran up and down the row of them telling jokes to keep them laughing all at once like old vaudeville spinning tops; he even asked audiences to repeat after him—ha, ha, ha.

Brooks' "Famous School for Comedians" was his definitive word on the old-style mugs. It appeared in a periodical as the prospectus of an institute dedicated to making socko comics. Brooks, as the founder of the school, detailed the program.

Next to a photo of an instructor at a blackboard that listed various diseases was this:

> Since their lives are filled with making fun, many comedians feel a special responsibility for the serious side. This usually means working for a cause (which often takes the form of contributing their talent to the support of programs devoted to the elimination of disease). Here, the instructor is helping students choose what disease to work for in case they make it big.

On another blackboard were listed lines like *You're beautiful/You're a marvelous human/He's a real saint* —with the caption:

> Joke after joke can only end in one big barrel of laughs—and what good is that? To structure a routine, to give it a proper form and to build momentum, a comedian should inject an occasional heartfelt sentiment. This teacher is showing students what to say to convey sincerity.

On still another blackboard was written *The drum is your friend—don't be afraid of the noise*, and this notation:

> Working with a drummer can do wonders for a student's timing. The drum can suggest movement, such as walking, sitting or knocking on doors. Here, one of the older students uses it simply to "punch up" everyday jokes.

STUDENT: My wife is a very sweet, loving, kind and
gentle person. . . . If I didn't say that,
she'd kill me.

DRUM: Ra ta BOOM!

If the rim-shot comic was a joke to the new breed,
he was usually the only one a novice gag writer like
Richard Lewis could turn to for a piecework dollar.

Lewis, a longhair in his 20s, sat in the Stage Deli
one afternoon with Catskill comic Morty Gunty and
watched him spoon in matzoh ball soup while looking
over the jokes Lewis had written.

Mooorty! Comics came by, and greeted him. Smile.
Wink. And back to the pages of jokes Lewis had done
in between jobs he held at Herman's Sporting Goods
Store and the Museum of Modern Art. Sometimes,
comics stopped to talk shop with Gunty and he'd
introduce Lewis as "his writer," a phrase that made
Richard flinch. He wondered what he was doing
there.

At seven dollars a line it was hardly worth what
he felt. No kicks in it except for the time he'd taped
Gunty on TV—doing a routine that had a gag of
Lewis' in it. And what had Richard done then? When
it came to "his" punch line, he'd turned up the
volume so that the laughs were louder.

A closet case Lewis was, one of many to appear in
the '70s. After Woody Allen came the deluge of paper
comics, looking for more than the anonymous dollar
offered. They wanted better than a credit line. They
wanted the laughs.

For Lewis, it was not easy. Places to "try out" his
material were few. A night at the Improv as an onlooker sent him away, cowed by the talent there. To
the Village he went.

It was a far cry from the Bleecker/Macdougal
scene of the early '60s. Booked one night for a midnight slot at Feenjon's, Lewis arrived and found the
place empty. No one in the audience. "I stood up on
the stage," he said, "and there was a mirror parallel
to the stage so I could see me perform. Fucking crazy.
The guy from the place—'All right, Rich Lewis, you're

up.' Straight reading he gave it. And even he left. Went to take a crap or something. Didn't stay. And I was holding the mike looking at myself in the mirror and I just said—I don't know who I was talking to, I guess I was talking to my reflection—I said, 'I'm sorry folks. I can't go on with the show.' I put the mike back and walked out."

Another paper comic around the Village at the time was Ed Bluestone, a kid with a crooked smile and furry brows and an eye peeled for macabre twists. Bluestone was in the showcases even before Lewis, long enough to be thoroughly entertained by the weirdos in them. He was like that. As a schoolboy in East Orange, New Jersey, he used a detached air and sordid wit to make friends and influence people. If it denied a sensitive side, he let it be. Instead, he organized pools that paid off for the guess closest to the departure time of a dying prizefighter. Or made 4:00 A.M. phone calls to a teacher notorious for keeping students after: "The reason I am waking you is you wasted an hour of my time. So I'll go for an hour of yours." Click.

It was a knack that was prized by the bunch he ran with, one he used as routinely as a politician did double-talk. A few years later, sending a photo of his through the mail, he'd write:

> Here's the picture you asked for. The photographer's name is Don Greenhaus. Please give him credit if you use the picture. If you don't use the picture, I hope you'll devote some time in your book to a physical description of me, much the same as when Jacqueline Susann describes the handsome actor in one of her novels.
> Happy Yom Kippur,
> Ed

For a time, Bluestone wrote one-liners for other comics, a commerce he found tedious. He preferred to come up with gags that his hero, Woody Allen, might have used:

Knew a very sophisticated girl who used to try to drive with her legs crossed.

And how about the chiropodist who learned palmistry, and now reads feet?

Bluestone suffered the stage fright at first that Woody had. He was a flop even in showcases, rejection he was used to. As a kid in college, he tried his material on Alan Burke, the sharp-tongued TV inquisitor who'd had a run on national TV.

"See, one of my friends in college was a guy named Dave Burke, whose father was Alan Burke," Bluestone said. "And at the time I was just beginning to perform a little and he said come on over and do some stuff for his father. And . . . Burke, you would see him on television just abusing people. I mean what kind of guy can have a complete psychotic on his show and make fun of him? I used to love him.

"And I was really nervous going over there. I had never met a celebrity. And Burke was very much the same in person. I mean he wasn't only abrasive, but he would not have qualms about saying to wife and kids, 'Leave me alone with the young man now.' And he would sit there puffing those cigars and, you know, have this overbearing *force* and everything. Went in for some social amenities like expressing . . . 'A friend of my son is a friend of mine, but I don't go for any bullshit. . . . Watch your step. He had a way of keeping you off guard. And he said, 'Okay, let's hear it.

"And I got up there stuttering and stammering, trying to do, you know, takeoffs on the way Woody Allen worked, no style of my own. And afterwards, Burke gave me this scathing criticism, you know. Completely oblivious to the fact that he's talking to a terrified kid of twenty-one or whatever. Saying things like, 'The reason you're not funny is you have no identity as a person.' Something like that."

If Burke picked apart the person, others faulted the material. It was, some said, in bad taste. No question, Bluestone had random lines calculated to offend.

175

How do you make a dead baby float?

he'd ask.
Answer:

> You get a glass of root beer and two
> scoops of baby.

He sustained the morbid tone in routines of his. One
of them was a contingency plan for funerals of people
he didn't like:

> I'd started making up this revenge list,
> like people I'd like to get sooner or later.
> And the hang-up about doing this is that
> you're worried about them dying, and you
> won't get the chance. So I started to get
> different ways to be offensive at the fu-
> nerals. . . .

> Pass out baby pictures of the deceased.

> Shake the widow's hand with an elec-
> tric buzzer.

> Stand around the cemetery saying, "At
> least he'll no longer be tormented over
> being impotent."

> Tell the clergyman that the deceased
> was a vampire and ask if you can drive
> a stake through his heart.

> Show up at the cemetery masqueraded
> as the deceased.

> On the way home from the cemetery,
> tell the widow that you're not sure, but
> you think that you saw the body move.

> The day after the funeral, send the
> widow a candygram from the deceased.

They were ghoulish lines that took an oddball charm to succeed. Bluestone lacked it. Onstage, he had a darting uneasy eye. But had he the charm of Pinky Lee, it would not have changed things. To some, the material was in bad taste no matter what. Bluestone saw it in the grimaces of showcase proprietors he was often tempted to tell off. He didn't. There were too few places to go.

It was how it was for the comic starting out in the '70s. Empty rooms and imperious owners and deluded emcees who insisted their place was "happening." It was the case at the Champagne Gallery, where the bottle-swigging pianist who ran the show was always jabbering how "tight" it was, a claim the near-empty room plainly contradicted.

He was an ex-jazz artist with the Sugar Ray processed hair and Satchmo patois. At one time, he had made the keys jump. Now the hands didn't work, couldn't put the notes together. He'd bang, and hope for the best. All Bluestone hoped for—after walking around Village streets in thirty-degree weather—was that he could get on for a few minutes. Maybe if he could nail a laugh on a new line, the night would have some value.

In search of places to play, Bluestone got involved with a pert blond comedienne/impressionist, Daphne Davis. "An amazing person," he said. "Daphne knows nothing else but making it. The only thing I ever saw her show emotion towards were people not thinking she was good or her dogs—two spitzes, real white things with fluffy hair.

"Anyway, the big thing then was finding places to perform. Because I was pretty terrible to begin with. And Daphne would find limitless places, but unbelievable places. Like she'd look up in the *Village Voice* —it has things called poetry readings. They're in somebody's apartment and it's basically eight lonely people get together on a Tuesday night and bring their poetry. And we used to go to this woman's apartment down in some housing project . . . her name was Emily. And every Tuesday night, Emily had a poetry reading. Down in the East Village, near where Daphne lived. And we would go to Emily's house and there would be seven weird people, ten, fifteen weird people every Tuesday.

"Mostly the same ones. Once in a while a different one. And there was one woman who was really hot shit. She had had a poem published. So she would only come once a month. They had to bill her as a guest reader and everything. And she would read last. Like the main event. And she was really a nasty, bitter person, she never laughed at any of my jokes. And me and Daphne used to actually get up in the living room and start doing bits.

"And Daphne would go to a place where they didn't have shows. There was some Italian restaurant down in the Village. Nice place. Tablecloths. And like the owner used to have a guy who would get up three times a night, sing something out of an opera, which fits into an Italian restaurant. He was a waiter or something. And she would say, 'Look, you've got entertainment. You know what comedy is?' And the guy couldn't talk English. And the first thing you'd know she'd be up in this restaurant doing these bits, imitating W. C. Fields. It was amazing. People would look at us like we're nuts.

"Another place was a hip coffee shop that was also a commune. Across the street from the Fillmore— called the Figaro East. And the people that ran it also lived there in the basement in bunk beds like coolies. I mean the people in there were nursing seven million burned-out neurons from their acid days and their existence was hanging around this place night and day. And Daphne would get the guy to let us up to do jokes. And they tried. And we tried. But it didn't come off. Hell's Angels in the audience. It was nothing. Like jerking off.

"Am I conveying to you how bizarre all this was? At least for me. I mean, Daphne—very conscious of certain rules. Like if you do six thousand shows a year, it will pay off in some way. There is a god of comedians who keeps a checklist. Knows if you're working on that material, doing those shows. Knows when you get laughs. And when you don't. I mean, the two of us even went to hospitals to perform.

"It was set up by some woman. Woman who used

to run this thing was in a wheelchair. She had a hunch-back with a big mole on the hunch. And she used to sit in the wheelchair in a sequined gown and sing old Frank Sinatra songs. Like, 'They Can't Take That Away From Me' or 'Please Don't Talk About Me When I'm Gone,' and she'd be in this wheelchair, you know, she would do her numbers with a microphone and everything. A civilian she was, and for some reason she did hospital shows, and got money to do it. And she would invite us to come along to do something for free.

"I mean, you've got to picture this. Like, you know, you walk out there with your jokes. And you've got a bunch of people who are in a city hospital. And they're in bathrobes. They just had operations. They're in pain. I did it once. I was horrified. And Daphne would say, matter-of-factly, 'Well, hospital shows aren't the best but when you have no place else, you might as well do it.' "

Hard times for the new funnymen.

The club commerce of the postwar period was long past. In the '70s, money was a delayed proposition. To be a comic was a wager of time and trauma against what TV might later raise.

Comics budgeted. Brenner, who lived on 69th Street and 2nd Avenue, sometimes walked to and from the Improvisation at 44th Street and 9th Avenue, a half hour each way, to save the transit fare. In the Village, he'd leave with other comics to cut taxi costs. Some nights at the Improv, he'd catch a break. Hy the bread-man would come by just as Brenner was ready to leave for the night. Hy was crazy for show biz. Inside the bread van he had Polaroid shots of stars posing with him. He'd drive Brenner and other comics to their doors, and give them a loaf of bread.

Brenner took the pinch in stride. He was a paradigm of the work ethic; able to put in ten hours at a stretch on his tapes. The indifference of Friedman and the other bosses did not deter Brenner. He remained a marvel of good cheer and unswerving intent, a rarity among new comics. Most of them had doubts David never voiced. His words had the by-god fervor of Bill

Stern's. Nothing broke him. He'd have made a wonderful immigrant.

Preminger was more typical. He wasn't so quick to shrug off the lukewarm response crowds gave him. His voice was a problem. It was an inanimate bass, a few notches up from Smokey the Bear's. His energy was no help either. Onstage, he was a dirge.

In his one-bedroom flat off Central Park West, Preminger played back cassettes of his spots but they offered him no clue. All he heard were some funny lines played to silence. Dead end.

It was like that out of comedy too. No girls. Few amusements. One time the phone rang, wrong number, and he detained the caller anyway—held him on for fifteen minutes. It was a man just arrived in the country, calling about a job advertised in a foreign-language paper. Preminger's number had been mistakenly inserted in the paper's classifieds.

"I told him," he recalled, " 'Don't hang up. Maybe I can help you.' And I kept him on because it was the first person who had called me in three days." When the man said he'd call the paper to correct its error, Preminger told him not to bother, he'd take care of it. He didn't—he figured it'd be nice to have the phone ring.

It got to him after a while. Preminger, not yet thirty, had hairs turn gray. He felt depressed. Unable to afford a bona fide shrink, he went to a social psychologist. "I'd go for like an hour and I'd talk about not being able to come up with material when other guys were making people laugh, and I wasn't.

"A lot of my stuff will be . . . these are lines but they're truths to an extent. I had a teddy bear thing I did. About girls would come up to me and say, 'You look like a teddy bear,' which twice did happen to me. I'm sure it's happened to others. But I took it to the extent—

> I met a girl and she took me home. We went into bed and she made me sit up by her pillow all night. I said, "I'm not a teddy bear." And she gave me a big hug and a squeeze and my eyes popped out.

180

"All right, now a lot of those lines are really truths in a way. *Nothing terrible* happened to me. But nothing ever good happened to me. And one night, standing outside the Improv, a couple of the comics said to me, 'Why don't you be a shmuck onstage, a shlemiel?' And I said, 'But I don't want to do that image.' And it was like great hearing it coming out of my mouth. I said, I don't want to do that, I don't want to be the shmuck because I *was* the shmuck to an extent. I don't want to do that. I want to grow up. And if I want to grow up, I don't want to get up onstage and be the shmuck, though I'll deal with it here or there."

> I love singing. But I found out I couldn't at Yankee Stadium. Fifty thousand people stood up to sing the national anthem. The usher came down the aisle and told me to shut up . . . I was throwing the crowd off-key.

Or,

> Girls now say what they think. I was with one the other night. Two in the morning she told me to go to a sex clinic. Said I should ask for the emergency room.

Sometimes the very idea of repeating jokes in public struck Preminger as odd. *How can a grown person make a living going on the stage and saying,* 'She gave me a big hug and a squeeze and my eyes . . .' *I should be designing a bridge. And when I'm finished designing it, that night over a martini say something funny.* Going nowhere, Preminger left to join an improvisation group in Brooklyn, the Peep Show.

It was a way. Each comic had his own. Brenner found his on a rainy night in Brooklyn at Pip's. Weather limited the midnight crowd to a portion of the previous show's. To avoid repeating his act, Brenner heard himself ask, "Whaddaya want to talk about?"

The audience shouted out subjects, and Brenner voiced the first thought that came to mind. Some hit, some missed. At the time, he figured it was a way to get through a show. George Schultz told him otherwise. "You got it," he said. What he had was a way to find material.

A tricky one it was. It risked the tabu silence that Klein worried over even in the water breaks he took on stage. George Carlin solved it. He put the microphone to his larynx to give a drink's audible elements which he mugged to a laugh.

It took nerve to do it that way. Brenner had it when he worked in TV documentaries. To get answers, he'd used concealed tape recorders and threats when he had to. Once, he phoned a politician and told him he was in his office and had the camera trained on his empty seat. He intended to conduct an interview to it if the man's arse wasn't in it pronto.

One other thing about Brenner. He managed it without being cutthroat. He was often a help to other comics. Jimmie Walker, the ghetto comic: he told him a thing or two.

It went like this with Walker: Up on the stage, do a joke or two and

> God-damn. Noise in my set. I'm gonna
> have to come out there and cut somebody,

a line Redd Foxx used in the past.

If it got Jimmie his listeners back, too often it was just for a moment. Once he'd used up his variations on the "saver," it was *bzzz bzzz* all over.

It was a puzzle. Jimmie had the comic look, a big-lipped face with large twinkly eyes. A Jerry Lewis luminescence. At six-two, one hundred thirty pounds, he was a ditty-bop presence that promised a good time.

That it didn't always come Walker blamed on whitey, specifying it from stage. It was why Brenner sat him down for a talk. Out of it came the deblackenization of Jimmie Walker. It meant changing niggers and whites to "black folks" and "you all." And more.

"See, what would happen," said Walker, "was when I bombed, I'd say,

Henny Youngman: King of the one-liners. *Credit: Wide World Photos*

Milton Berle: "You heckled me twenty years ago. I never forget a suit." *Credit: Wide World Photos*

Jack Roy: A big man with a clipped street-tough sound and a hounded appearance. Roy worked the dives in the late '40s, retired and came back later as Rodney Dangerfield.

Lenny Bruce, circa 1950. He was a hack comic then. At the Strand Theater, Bruce wore a straw hat and did corny jokes.

Georgie Starr

Don Rickles: Not by design he ended up a comic viper in the '50s. It was his answer when all else failed.

Shecky Greene: In New Orleans, he was liable to do anything for a laugh. One night he ran down Bourbon Street in an ape suit. Here Greene, *center*, and comic Frankie Ray, *left*, appear with George McQueen at a benefit.

purple onion
Adam Keefe
Don Crawford
John Price, Piano AND Ron Crotty

Adam Keefe: It took almost twenty years of working the *toilets* before he got a break. The night of his nationwide TV debut, he had torn underwear and holes in his shoes.

Lord Buckley: "But I'm gonna put a cat on you was the sweetest gaaaaaawnest wailingest cat that ever stomped on this sweet-swingin' sphere. And they call this hyar cat . . . THE NAZ." *Credit: Courtesy of Dick Zalud*

Woody Allen: The logical and laughable extension of Herr Kafka himself. *Credit: Photograph by Damon Runyon, Jr. (Courtesy of Budd Friedman)*

Dick Gregory: "If Jesus Christ came back and was electrocuted, you'd all be walking with electric chairs around your neck."

Dick Davy: The white comic who scored big at the Apollo Theater in Harlem.

In the '60s, the Improvisation in Manhattan became a comic testing ground. Even old pros like the ex-Jack Roy (aka Rodney Dangerfield) tried routines there. *Credit: Photograph by Damon Runyon, Jr. (Courtesy of Budd Friedman)*

Young bloods like black comic Richard Pryor and J. J. Barry "worked out" at showcases too. *Credit: Photograph by Damon Runyon, Jr. (Courtesy of Budd Friedman)*

Michael Preminger

David Brenner

Jimmie Walker

Richard Lewis

Budd Friedman. *Credit: Photograph by Chris Shawn*

Ed Bluestone. *Credit: Photograph by Don Greenhaus*

Alan Bursky

Albert Brooks

Cheech and Chong: Nose-thumbing dragoons of the neocomic brigade.

George Carlin: The change from a short-haired wisecracker to real George—a hairy, sometimes contrary specimen of the Aquarian age. *Credit: Courtesy of Murray Becker*

Robert Klein: "The comeeee-dian, the comeeee-dian."

Bobby Baxter: "You start reliving the past, it makes you sick."

Bernie Travis: "Crushed, I was in Central Park and I cried for about an hour and a half."

Shelley Berman: 'I mean my life isn't over, but goddammit, it's hard."

David Frye: Politics made for strange bedfellows.

Lily Tomlin: She ditched two-fisted mannerisms for a silkier kinetic.

Jessica James (shown here with Jack Carter): "You start to look like one of those hood things on a '68 Chevy. You've got your chin out like this, you know, and it's like you're ready anywhere. People are only something to bounce your jokes off."

> Hey man, what's wrong with y'all? This
> stuff is dynamite shit. This works all the
> time.

And then I would talk about their being white.

> You're white. You don't understand
> what's going on here. You don't know
> what's happening—

do things like that. And you lost the people even
worse than you lost 'em with the material.

"So like Brenner said, 'Look man, what's your plan
of attack here? You want to be a social commentator
or you want to be a comedian. What's the plan? If you
want to do stand-up, man, you're gonna have to worry
about being funny rather than being hip with the social
comments and five thousand blacks died today in Bi-
afra and hey, what about you, what are you doing?' "

The times required strategy. By 1970, the racial
scene seemed bust, the sunshine rhetoric gone for
combustible phrases. Militancy/backlash were the
catchwords. Changes had occurred, shifts in the very
language of racial politics. Pigmeat Markham's use of
"colored" was a hankyhead sound for some. For de
Judge it was the anglo he was used to.

The concept of "blackness" was not the same either.
When Walker was growing up in the South Bronx, he
remembered the blackest dude among them being
kidded all the time. At night: *You there, man? Smile.*
His dark skin embarrassed the kid. By 1970, the
motto was Black Is Beautiful. Even "nigger" had lost
some of its sting. Blacks used it with reverse english
for effect. Whatever the word on race, it was no laughing matter by the late '60s.

Dick Davy found out. Even after he was the whitey
who scored at the Apollo, it was no breeze for him.
For one thing, he made lily-white crowds uneasy. In
places where he managed to win them over, it was, he
discovered, for the wrong reasons. Lingering in a club
after he'd finished his act, he'd do what manager
Steuer had warned against—talk the issues seriously
with the people.

"Guys," he said, "thought I was funny as hell— when they'd see how I really felt, they were pissed off. I found out that they didn't even realize I was putting down the things they believed in. They thought I was just a sweet funny kid. So Steuer was right. That I should just, like, disappear after a show. But I couldn't do it because I would be too lonely going back to my fucking hotel room. Some stupid . . . sermonette. The television ends too early in most of those towns, except in LA. They'd have used car ads with movies. So I'd hang around and I'd get in trouble."

He did better with black crowds except when he was booked into theaters on rock 'n' roll bills. The teen-agers had no use for him. At the Regal in Chicago, they threw popcorn boxes and candy wrappers at him and screamed, "Get the fucking whitey off the stage."

"And I found out later," Davy said, "that all comedians get food thrown on the stage, even if they're black. The kids don't want any interruptions. And certainly not from a white guy who's sitting on a stool. And not even moving around . . . Even the star of the show, a pretty good singer named Jerry Butler, the kids wouldn't listen to him, they'd walk out, they'd stand, they'd make a lot of noise, they wanted to hear dancing. Eight days, I got thirteen hundred dollars— that's a lot of money for doing five minutes of comedy. But I didn't even want to stick it out."

With the death of Dr. Martin Luther King in 1968, Davy's career came grinding to a halt. Suddenly he became a comic leper, a casualty of racial polarization. Frank Schiffman of the Apollo, who predicted he'd be a star, now wouldn't hire him. Black militant groups were applying pressure uptown.

"It just wasn't funny anymore," Davy said. "A white guy talking about race. In fact, *nothing* funny about race anymore. The only thing that's funny is . . . is like Flip Wilson. See, suddenly there's a big rush to give black comedians a push on television. To keep the black people from rioting, let's put them in commercials, let's put them on television. Let 'em see black faces now, so they won't burn up the town. But not controversial black faces. Not Dick Gregory. And if they wouldn't put Dick Gregory on, they certainly wouldn't put me on.

"No, let them see black faces talking about safe subjects. So that's Flip Wilson. I played places Flip Wilson played. And they all came up to me and said, 'You're much funnier than Flip Wilson. Flip Wilson bombed here.' Okay. Now Flip Wilson—I'm not saying he's not funny, but he benefited from this whole scare thing among the whites. Flip Wilson is making like he's a girl, talking this kind of . . . whatever he talks about. It's not inflammatory. It's not dangerous. Make him a big star. Cosby was the first. Bill Cosby was funny. He's really a very good actor and comedian. Cosby worked the Gaslight for almost a year. And he's the only guy, the only comedian I ever saw, get laughs down there. So he was good, you know. But what really boosted him was this desire to have more black faces on television. But not talking militant."

They were tricky times for the Afro-animated mind, more so for the Fetchit past the Negro came out of. To go to extremes was what black awareness summoned up in some of them. Richard Pryor went that way.

The first time he appeared on "The Tonight Show," Pryor was asked what his friends call him.

That skinny nigger,

he quipped, an ad lib that took a split second to topple to wild laughter.

Another night at a private party Friedman hosted at the Improv, Pryor casually upstaged a songstress he disliked by walking in on a number of hers totally naked, prompting one observer to say, "Well, there goes that myth."

Pryor was the crazy nigger nobody could figure, least of all the massahs in de cafes and supper clubs. Richard ignored the prevailing caution on race, and let fly with whatever was on his mind:

. . . like white people come out early. On Saturday night. And go home and leave it to the niggers.

That's great. When you think, we can all sit in the same club together, white and black . . . and-not-understand-each-other.

NEWSREEL
VOICE: It's amazing. It could only happen in Amurica.

I used to love getting arrested, though. In Peoria on Saturday night. 'Cause it was fun if you was in the lineup. That was like being in show business. 'Cause like all the ugly white girls couldn't get any, said niggers raped them.

COP: All right. Come on now. You wanna go down? You were down last week. You know what to do, don't you?

It was a lot of fun. Unless you got picked. That was your ass.

COP: All right. Break it up there. Alvin T. Johnson. Suspected of grand theft, auto. Step forward.

JOHNSON: (*high-pitched voice*): Uh, I'd like to say something about that. Uh, I thought that was my mother's car, man. I went downtown and my mother told me to pick the car up at one thirty and it was front of the bank and I took the car. I was about two blocks from home and I dug this white lady sitting next to me screaming and shit, I didn't know what was happening. I thought it was a stickup. In fact, I want to press charges against her. 'Cause she scratched my hand and shit and yelled loud in my ear, hurt mah ear an' everything. I have a medical report to prove that—

COP: You wan' an ass whuppin'?

He was unpredictable. Booked for the Ed Sullivan show, he chose not to appear, preferring to test out 16-millimeter movie equipment he'd just acquired. In a club in Chicago, he performed a set from under the piano and, when the owner asked what he was up to, he said he was "working something out." In Vegas, he got a quick exit after passing a salacious remark to a black femme superstar from stage.*

Jimmie Walker, who referred to him as "Wild Man" ("I mean, you ain't just talking about the average black guy. You're talking about the Wild Man. He's fuck-ing crazy") had seen him do lines to white women at the Improv that would haven gotten him a good whuppin' or worse on a street corner in Hattiesburg.

He could pin down ghetto types too, though—like the one who always got on him when Pryor came back to hometown Peoria to play the star. In a high nasal voice, it sounded like this: "Nigger, you ain't shit. You wasn't shit when you was here. I seen you do that shit . . . that's the same shit you doin' 'round the poolroom, nigger. It ain't nothing. . . . Lemme-have-a-dollar."

Pryor was an authentic character like Clay/Ali, which gave him license that mere mortals didn't command. And like yon Cassius, he was touched by a genius that often turned excess into art. It was why he could bait whitey and get away with it—and Walker couldn't. ("I swear," said Walker, "I never seen no shit like this guy, man. Unbelievable. Unfuckingbelievable.")

It was no act either with Pryor. He was Wild Man twenty-four hours a day, Super Fly high on smoke and snort and whiskey and wenches, sweets he sped through with a mix of paranoia/violence/and open-handedness (Walker had seen him routinely tip room service a hundred dollars). His combustible qualities and the frequency with which he made them public had squeezed the comic market on him but Pryor's gift kept him alive. More and more, though, he was

* At the Redd Foxx club in LA, he told the crowd, "Always like to get naked. Did that in Vegas. Got naked. Run through the casino nude. Jumped up on the twenty-one table. Said, 'Black jack!'"

using it in the movies, the only experience Pryor was reverential about.

In from the Coast, he'd call Walker and drag him over to Times Square, where they'd see one flick after another into the early hours of the day. In the movie houses, Pryor was in the ghetto tradition, dueling dialogue with the characters on screen.

As a movie pro, he held himself in check, though he retained the garish touches that made him the one and only unfuckingbelievable wild one.

Hired as a writer for the Mel Brooks movie *Blazing Saddles,* he appeared first day, warily eyed the other script men and sat down. In Caucasian company, he took out his cache of a white crystalline powder and offered it around. There were no takers. So he had a healthy snort of it and was ready for business.

At the Warner Bros. offices where the script was worked on, he'd order up a bottle of Courvoisier each day to ease him through the hours. As always, he kept his distance. To secretaries there, he played the stud blood at first but ended buying them trinkets as a friend, giving them on the run so as not to suffer thank-ya.

Even with cronies, he was that way. J. J. Barry said, "It's like knowing him and not knowing him. You know what I mean? 'Cause Richie was never specific. My relation to him was never specified. We'd hang out together, laugh together. Do some improvs together. Then he'd say, 'I'll see you.' And I wouldn't see him for four weeks. Then one night, he'd pop in. 'Hey, man, what's happening?' Like he saw me four minutes ago. I mean, I know he's out on the Coast. But I can't say, 'Drop me a line. Pick up the phone.' If I see him, I see him. . . .

"Oh, he did a great thing, man. I'll tell you an incident. My girl threw me a surprise party. I didn't even know Richie was in town. Somehow somebody told Richie, 'J. J.'s having a birthday party. It's in a loft in the Bowery.' So in the middle of the party, Richie walks in with an entourage—a dog, chick, two strange-looking guys. He walks in, he goes, 'Hey, baby. Heard it was your birthday.' Gave me a very expensive erotic book. Totally erotic book. Beautiful. Said happy birthday. Looked around, said, 'Too many whities here, man. Makes me nervous, man.' Dropped a little thing on me and said, 'I'll see you.' And walked."

Next to him, Jimmie Walker was propriety's child. He did not aim, in his term, "to fuck with the black/white thing," which he saw Pryor do—and with impunity he found hard to believe. Jimmie's avowed intent was to be more funny than fierce. Occasionally, he relapsed, affirming for the minor domos of agencies that he was still "militant."

It was an opinion Walker knew was not in his best interest. Voiced often enough, it took on the weight of fact, fact that could whack a career out of kilter. Walker's view was that he could get laughs in any room primates gathered—regardless of race/color/creed, an opinion not everyone shared.

"Like this guy from some dance studio used to come in the Improv," said Walker. "He says he wants to use comics. Fifty bucks for the night. You do twenty minutes and you go home. It's all old people at a dance studio on Ninety-sixth and Broadway. So Budd put all the comics one by one in there. He wouldn't put me in the room. Says, 'They're older people and they wouldn't really like you.' And everybody that went up there said just take the money and get the fuck out of there, man. There's nothing but old people there. Wow. You can't do nothing there.

"Guy came in the club one night. Saw me. Said, 'Geez, Budd, how come this guy has never been up there? I want him up next week.' So I went up there. Kilt the fucking crowd. Old people, man. People like seventy. Just have to be kind of cool there, not too much hip shit. Deal in stereotypes like

I'm thinking of moving to the suburbs.

Riverdale. Scarsdale. Get myself a house. With a black picket fence up front. Little white jockey sitting up there. Maybe for the front lawn, a fluorescent watermelon. Let my neighbors know I'm in de neighborhood.

189

"And the old ladies were . . . 'Man, we've had like thousands of comics here. But you've been the best one.' And this and that and that and this. This guy wanted me back the next week."

If agents made Walker out as a racial hotspur, comics knew better. Bluestone's line on him—he doesn't sit around dreaming of Sartre—suggested a practical side. It was CBS not PBS he was aiming for. He left the racial bolts to the heirs of Marcus Garvey. Jim wanted "in." And if it meant lightening up, shee-it, he'd give The Man what he wanted—and not look bad doing it. For Walker had the sinuous rhythms of the ghetto in his speech, the street kid's bop that put him on top of whatever it was he was saying:

> What's been happening uptown lately is there's been a lot of robberies, man, and what's been happening even worse is black people have been robbing black people, man. *We* robbing us.

> This leads me to the area of nonviolent crime. Now in violent crime we doing *damned* good. But in nooooonviolent crime—I mean when was the last time you seen a black embezzler . . . or a black man getting busted for juggling the bank books? I'd like to be walking down 125th Street one time and have a black brother lay a counterfeit one on me—with a picture of Booker T.

> Take a black holdup man. He ain't making no money. He ain't got enough money to ride a cab to work, he gotta ride a bus. He gotta stay in that dark damp alley, catching rheumatism in his knees. Suffocating 'cause he's got his wife's stocking over his head. Just to hit you in the head for four dollars. I mean, what's the use of having black brothers in the Supreme Court if we blacks can't make crimes classy enough to get there.

190

Not to say Walker still didn't blame whitey if the act sputtered. He did, more out of petulance than pointed racial feeling. It'd happen when Walker failed with a passing notion. He was not the mental acrobat a Cosby or Gregory was. With the random thought, syntax got scrambled and the laughs lost.

He didn't always face up to it either. Failure with a half-cocked idea still brought blah blah black. A moment later, he'd realize his mistake and try to pep up the crowd: *Yeah, yeah, it's all happening.* It wasn't. Deblackenization went on.

He was not the only one going through changes.

The frontispiece of the flyer said:

robert klein . . .

Inside was a color photo of him and this notation:

will make you laugh and sometimes think.

Klein spent two thousand dollars of his own money to have it printed, mailing it to 2,700 colleges. He figured it'd get him booked onto the campuses.

A reasonable assumption. Of the under-thirty comics only Steinberg and Pryor had done the amount of TV Klein had. Frost/Griffin/Mike Douglas/Carson/Cavett: Klein was a regular guest on those talks. If it got him more notice on the IRT Broadway local —*Hey, aren't you Robert Klein . . . ? I seen you on . . .*—it didn't make the phones ring at the West 57th Street suite of Rollins and Joffe. Buddy Morra, the man in that office who now managed Klein, was not deluged with nightclub offers.

What bookings Klein got were occasional one-nighters at up to a thousand dollars, so few in fact he was relying on still more TV and commercial voiceovers to sweeten his income. His schedule over the first half of 1970 read like this:

January   1   Dick Cavett Show
January 12   Voiceover, Drake's Cakes commercial
January 25   Ed Sullivan Show

February 3-9	Stage production of *Candide*/
	Corpus Christi, Texas
February 15	Ed Sullivan Show
February 24-	
March 1	Tom Jones Show/London
March 4	Dick Cavett Show
April 10	Voiceover, Red Rose Tea commercial
April 26	Ed Sullivan Show
April 29	Fairleigh Dickinson coffeehouse
May 5	Dick Cavett Show
May 19	Clay Cole Show
May 28	Club date

He was not having the effect on the public his old Second City mate Steinberg was. David had started at the Bitter End in 1968 and through television shots was the first under-thirty comic to acquire a following large enough to get him booked regularly at colleges, coffeehouses and large auditoriums.

The son of a Winnipeg, Canada, rabbi, he drew on his theological background in a series of Biblical routines that popularized him. Steinberg's Moses, advised by God to tell Pharaoh to let his people go, inquires who should he say sent him:

GOD: I am that I am.

MOSES: Aheh. Thanks for clearing that up.

The best Klein could do was a B'nai B'rith smoker or, at the other end of the spectrum, a small coffeehouse on a college campus. In 1970, he had yet to capture a substantial enough following to headline an important room.

In part, it may have been owing to the times. It was the height of the hippie/Viet War chaos in the nation. (In April, the Kent State killings would show how divided the U.S. was.) Klein's looks, scruffier than Steinberg's, were not calculated to win over disaffected Middle Americans.

He'd already received a letter that indicated what was on their collective mind. It called him a "Jew Commie Creep" and longed for the day

> . . . when magazines showed Sweet
> Freckled faced boys instead of Filth and
> Smut and Nakedness with Scum and Lice
> like you . . . those were the days when
> the American men of Christian Faith
> went to Wars instead of burning their
> draft cards and taking the Universities
> and Colleges because they were not Cow-
> ardly Scum whom use the Viet Nam War
> to hide behind, those were the days when
> real comedians were really funny with out
> using Sweet Little Faced Boys with Freck-
> les to poke fun at, and Little Old Ladies
> and men, because you Bums have no
> Talent of any kind, you are as funny as
> a Crutch.
>
> Give me those Good Old Days when men
> were men and Women were Decent and
> Respectable. Those were the Days mockie
> and will be again because I am the major-
> ity whom love freckle faced boys and
> men.

The political climate made people touchy about
what funnymen said. Just the season before, the
brothers Tom and Dick Smothers had been removed
from the airwaves by CBS for sociopolitical material
repeatedly deemed too "sensitive" by network ex-
ecutives. Their "Smothers Brothers Comedy Hour"
was one of CBS' top-ranking shows. Censorship
squabbles arose over what a few years later would
appear to be harmless material—a line like "Ronald
Reagan is a known heterosexual," or the use of the
name Mary Jane Roach (a marijuana pun).

(Indeed standards of taste changed. In the nine-
teenth century, Keith Circuit vaudeville houses had
signs that warned, "Don't say *slob* or *son of gun* or
Holy gee on stage unless you want to be cancelled
peremptorily.")

The provocation for the Jew-Commie-Creep tirade
Klein received was the lead-in of a routine of his on
substitute teaching:

I did not have the kind of kids in my class that we've all become used to over the years through the popular media. You know, that virtuous little freckle-faced kid with jam on his face. "Golly, Mrs. Dawson, can I mow your lawn?" The Norman Rockwell painting kid. I never had that kind of kid in my class.

I had the very large . . . formidable . . . threatening—I-had-murderers.

I had one child in my ninth grade class who had to take six months off from school for National Guard duty. He was going to junior high school on the GI bill. You know that type of kid? "Yeah, you and what army, Mr. Klein. Any time baby, outta school, in school, any time."

Robert hadn't the distance from his comic that a Hope or Berle did. His was a trick mirror of a New York weisenheimer, unmitigated by vaudeville silk. He worked with the foothold of a galento. In 1970 Anno Domini it was a hard way to go.

It meant that he did not "swing" on the cafe circuit. Klein's daily book was filled with notations of meetings aimed to cough up revenues in other arenas. Theater/movies/even commercials—Klein did them all.

I once faced a guy that I went to Yale Drama School with. He was auditioning me to be a talking toilet. To be the voice for a toilet. For Drano—one of those bathroom-bowl commercials. "I feel fresh and clean." Weird thing is—I wanted the job! And he actually asked me to play it a little sassier,

he told crowds at the Improvisation.

He still went to Friedman's room, all the time adding to his store of material. Some nights Dangerfield dropped by and caught a set of his, and remarked on the performing minutes he was acquiring. "Backing the truck in" was Rodney's phrase for it. It clocked out to more than two hours' worth.

On 44th Street, he was loose. He didn't think twice about what he said or whether it'd go. The Improv drew musicians, comics, political lefties, smartasses, New York crazies—his kind of crowd. He was loose in there:

> Budd Friedman built this place by selling White Cloverine brand salve door to door. Remember that? Back of the comic. "Win a camera! Win a nightclub!" Had a megaphone last week.

When not on 44th Street, he performed most often in TV studios. TV supported the comic habit, in Klein's case quite nicely. In the summer of 1970, CBS paid him twenty-eight thousand dollars to star in an eight-week summer variety show called "Comedy Tonight."

The laughs were taken care of—by a padlocked machine that had a keyboard an operator punched to dredge up ha ha of TV past. A macabre notion—the laugh tracks that shows used came from old audiences—people now dead and gone. TV called it "sweetening."

It was but one of many strange twists the summer run had for him. Several of them had to do with the slow-season budget. Figures appeared on screen without feet, sacrificed so the show needn't bring in a costly boom device. Shirts used on the program that were returned to Ohrbach's in "good shape" got a rebate. So on, so forth.

The show was fast forgotten, but not its star. TV still beckoned: Sullivan for $6,500, Flip Wilson for $7,500. *Hey, ain't you . . . I seen you on the TV . . . Steinberg, right?* No, he was Klein.

> robert klein
> · will make you laugh
> and sometimes think.

Not at the colleges. Of 2,700 flyers sent out, *not one* drew a response. A comic in TV limbo he was, too hip/too hairy for 1970 booze crowds, and address unknown with the shaggy young.

Something had to give.

It did with Carlin.

After "fright wig times" with Jack Burns, George went on his own, doing topical jokes and impressions:

> Barry Goldwater has definitely decided to be a candidate in '64. He will campaign in all thirteen states.

> Wilt Chamberlain is picketing the second floor of Woolworth's.

Back then, Carlin was short-haired and squeaky-clean, a period-piece wisecracker. He had the impish aspect of Mickey Rooney's kid brother.

The look belied the lad. In 1965, Carlin's manager, Murray Becker, got a call from the Chicago police force advising him that George was going to be busted for possession of marijuana. Forewarned, the comic beat it. And Becker bowed out as manager.

Carlin reappeared with an act that now drew on his earlier experience as a disk jockey. The result was Wonderful WINO *1750 on your dial, just above the police calls, kids*, a spoof on pop radio that included newscasts—

> Good evening, ladies and gentlemen. Once again, the little hand is on the four, the big hand is on the two, and it's time for the Six O'Clock Report. Well, the world breathes a little easier today, as five more nations have signed a nuclear test-ban treaty. Today's signers were Chad, Sierra Leone, Upper Volta, Monaco and Iceland. . . . In labor news, longshoremen walked off the piers today; rescue operations are continuing—

and featured regulars like sports announcer Biff Burns ("And quickly now, the basketball scores: 110-108, 126-114, 131-109. And here's a partial score: Boston 58") and the hippie dippie weatherman Al Sleet ("Hey baby, what's happening? Tonight's forecast is . . . dark").

The material made Carlin a hit on TV and in commercial rooms. *Time* magazine wrote him up. And as late as 1969, *Variety* reported him a "sock" in a forty-five-minute performance at the Holiday House in Pittsburgh. But like Klein, Carlin was caught up in the times. He was changing to real George: a hairy, sometimes contrary specimen of the Aquarian age, mind-mothered by chemical shazam. On LSD/pot he'd had a comedic vision, and it was not of him playing the foole. He wanted to (ooo-ooo-ooo) "say things."

It was not an easy time to speak out. At first he tried to appease the booze crowds he worked to. He wrote rhymed doggerel to squelch fear on his long hair but got nowhere. He still came up against the hard-line thinking.

Nothing new with George. He'd had people knock him as far back as 1961. At the Chicago Playboy that year, his JFK imitation prompted an onlooker, Joseph P. Kennedy, father of the President, to say: "I don't see anything funny in making fun of my son."

In late summer of 1970, there was an incident at the Frontier Hotel in Las Vegas. In a town where, as Carlin said, craps was the favorite pastime, he was joking about the word "shit." The scatological riff got him into a shoutout with an executive for the Hughes hotels, who objected to the use of the word. He called up to the stage for Carlin to stop. What George shouted back finished him in Vegas.

Months later, at the Playboy Club in Lake Geneva, Wisconsin, Carlin got into it with ringside patrons who didn't laugh. Carlin tried to win them over, and when he failed, he turned against the coat/tie crowd. The then entertainment director of the club, Sam Distefano, said, "George made a gesture with his finger and a remark. In so many words, he told the audience they were jerking themselves off." The club had to return 239 cover charges at five dollars apiece. Carlin's money was withheld, wages he went to see Hugh Hefner about.

Soon after, Carlin quit the cafe circuit. He went into hiding, surfacing months later with the look of the rock culture, whose comic he was fixing to be. In terms of cash dollars, it seemed suicidal. The under-thirty crowd did not put their coin of realm on comics.

Back then, Carlin's denouncement of Vegas loot for coffeehouse wages was like Marciano lining up Ridge-wood Grove for a title bout or Esther Williams doing aquatics in a bathtub. He did it anyway. Booked into the Bitter End for June 1971, he preceded the date with a test run in the Focus, an obscure coffeehouse on the city's Upper West Side. The place's owner, Larry Brezner, agreed to let George do all the time he wanted.

BREZNER: Carlin came down and the place was mobbed. There were two rooms. The up-stairs was the big performing room, which sat more people. Carlin came into the room and I couldn't believe it, 'cause his whole image was changed, and he was really strange . . . was heavily into grass and the whole number, you know. And Carlin was a wreck, nervouswise. I mean, for a guy who had done innumerable TV spots, coming into a small room where he knew he was a winner before he started, he was a wreck.

Q: How did he show it?

BREZNER: Well, he asked me not to let anybody talk to him. He was visibly shaking. His hands.

Q: Was he drinking, eating, smoking?

BREZNER: Well, he asked me if he could get some club soda. . . . I said, well, I didn't have any club soda around but I'd get him

some . . . and he got really desperate
. . . he said, "You don't understand, I
really need some club soda." I said okay.
I mean I would have gotten him anything at that point, he just filled up the
room. So I ran to the store around the
corner. Came out with a big bottle of
club soda, which he proceeded to drink
in about five minutes. He consumed the
whole bottle of club soda.

Q: Twenty-eight ounces?

BREZNER: Yeah. I was sure he was going to let out
an enormous belch onstage. I mean I
couldn't see how it was possible to drink
so much club soda. He was really a
wreck and I—

Q: Did people recognize him.

BREZNER: Nobody knew who he was. Everyone had
come there to see George Carlin. But
they had no idea it was him. I mean he
was just sitting there.

Q: What'd he look like?

BREZNER: He had long straight hair. It wasn't in a
ponytail. And he had a beard. He had
jeans on and a T-shirt. A colored T-shirt.
It was gray with some sort of tie-dye thing
in front. And people walked right by
him. I mean, nobody recognized him. He
looked like any freak hanging out in the
place.

Q: And what was he doing while he was sitting there?

BREZNER: Staring at his knees mainly. He was visibly shaking. There was no question.

Q: And?

BREZNER: Carlin came onstage and he was nervous, you can sense that from a comic . . . and when he's nervous he has a technique, which is using his body for laughs. He can do incredible things with his eyes. Ya know, he rolls his eyes in different directions and stuff. . . . He did a lot of that shtick just to warm up the audience.

Q: What else?

BREZNER: He used to twist his body around in really strange ways. I remember he was doing all those physical things before he got into any of his material . . . just to loosen up and relax. He then proceeded to do close to two hours of everything that he would be taking out to the public.

Q: A lot of new material?

BREZNER: Yeah.

Q: Any old?

BREZNER: He did. He went back to a few old pieces. Did a little bit of wonderful WINO. And all those old voices—he went back to them. But there was new stuff about drugs. And he did this poem called "Hair." And it was wonderful, the place went berserk. So he proved to himself he could relate to the kind of people he wanted to.

Of course, a coffeehouse on West 74th Street and Amsterdam Avenue was by no means a Gallup sampling of the populace, not even of the so-called psychedelic one.

A risky route Carlin was going. The change from cufflink comic to one in freak's drag was hard for entrepreneurs to figure. The Bitter End's Paul Colby was suspicious. It looked like blatant faddism to him, a chance to bank on a hippie-happy trend. But Carlin's management kept pitching, and Colby ended up giving George a shot on Bleecker Street.

In he came to score a modest success. Colby had a feeling it was tip of the iceberg. He booked him back for Christmas week 1971 and BOOM, the place was jammed second time around.

There was one other thing: Carlin had a record album due out at the first of the new year, and the hope was it'd put the word out on George in the circles he was moving.

No precedent for records booming the scruffy comics. Not just yet.

It took a Chicano and part-Chinaman to prove what a hot LP could be for kid comics.

The Chicano was Richard Marin, called "Cheech," son of an LA policeman. The part-Oriental was a bearded ex-rock musician, trucker and roofer named Tommy Chong. When they met, Chong owned a bar in Vancouver, British Columbia, out of which he ran an improvisional troupe with ex-topless dancers for female leads. Cheech joined up one night passing through.*

Cheech was a college graduate with a B.A. in English. Chong was a high school dropout. No matter: the two got on. And when the unit disbanded, Cheech and Chong took the material created in a saloon and headed for LA to do a comedy double.

In 1970, the year Carlin was going through changes, the two of them were just starting. They were so penny poor that

CHEECH: We didn't have shit one.

---

* Marin was on the lam from the military draft. On his return to the States, he learned that the courts had ruled the Selective Service's arbitrary reclassification of antiwar protestors illegal. In the interim, he'd broken a leg skiing in Canada. That—and a doctor's note—beat the draft second time around.

CHONG: So it's a matter of telling the landlord, look it's in the mail. Or not being there when he showed up. Or maybe going to the supermarket and nailing a steak or something to get by. You know, you walk by the meat counter and the thing jumps up and falls in your pocket. You know what I mean? I mean, what the hell, you don't realize it's there until you get out of the store. And I mean, all you came in for was some gum.

CHEECH: I had a really good scheme, did I tell ya about it? I used to go to the market and write down the names and addresses of all of the products that I dug, and then I'd write them form letters saying, "Dear Mr. Campbell's Soup: I found flies in your soup." And they would send me cases of the stuff, man. I had stuff coming every day.

Q: That literally happened?

CHEECH: Yeah.

Q: What were some of the—

CHEECH: I got a case of Bluestein Salad Dressing. The vice-president of Mayfair Market hand delivered three gourmet-cut steaks . . . . I got about four or five canned hams. All kinds of food. Whatever I dug.

Q: What did you say in the letters?

CHEECH: I found something in their product. I told Welch's grape juice I found a dime in their grape juice. He was the longest cat. It took him three months to give me a can of Welch's grape juice. But most of the other cats would send cases of

stuff. Seven-Up, Coca-Cola, Campbell's
Soup . . . I had a lot of soups.

In LA, the comics scuffled for jobs, often ending in
black clubs like Redd Foxx's, the York Club, PJ's,
places that still had a floor show rather than the
discotheque format the white clubs did. Strange joints
they were: Saturday nights at some of them, armed
guards were in the parking lot to see patrons made
it to their cars without a felonious hitch. Pimps, petty
thieves, Hollywood hustlers trafficked those places. A
tough clientele that made, in Chong's phrase, for
"some weird trips."

CHONG: One place was owned by gangsters, right?
They found a sucker that wanted to be
in the nightclub business, that had a lot
of bread. So they sold him the nightclub.
Then they proceeded to rip him off every
week. They'd rob his safe. They'd rob his
girl. They just . . . and they worked for
him too at the same time.

CHEECH: Another place, the Climax, chick came in
on a leash one time. Came with this real
black black dude. Blue-black—he was
dressed in white satin with a big white
satin hat and clothes and shoes and pants
and everything. And he had a chick with
a leash around her neck, man. And she
was dressed all in black. She was real
white with blond hair and had on a
black dress. Leading her around by this
dog collar. He was a pimp. And she
was—

Q: A hooker?

CHEECH: Yeah. Lotta those.

CHONG: At least she knew where she was at. All
she had to do was just follow the end of
the string.

CHEECH & CHONG:	(Laughter).
Q:	Any other stories?
CHEECH:	Yeah. We used to get blow jobs in the dressing room.
CHONG:	Not me. That's Cheech.
CHEECH:	Yeah, I got a couple of blow jobs. Wasn't bad.
Q:	How did it happen?
CHEECH:	Chick tell me, "I want to suck your joint, man."
Q:	That was it? That bald-faced?
CHEECH:	Yeah.

Chong's good fortune was fiscal. In changing apartments, he switched banks, which led to a clerical error —two thousand dollars to his favor. When Chong was informed he had that much money in his account, he told the teller it was, he suspected, a error. *I mean, ya know when you're flat-assed broke.* Advised there was no mistake, Chong shrugged and asked for five hundred dollars, came back two days later for one thousand dollars more. When the bank discovered its error, the money was gone. And so was Chong, who, it later turned out, was two dollars and fifty cents overdrawn.

So it went. Their lives read like ZAP comix tales, full of smokes and scams and water-bedded dollies. Chong, tattooed and bush-bearded, in his metal-rimmed glasses looked like a mad Marxist or a two-fisted biker. He was neither, more of an easy-timer in truth, a man at home wherever he put down. He had a slow sunny way with his days. Once married to a black woman, he now was separated from her

and living with another lady. He had three ___
two black and one white.

Cheech was a Chicano longhair with the ___
look of an Old West outlaw, and a bearing ___
gested he'd live up to it if necessary, swag____ ___
was muted by another side of him. While up in
Canada, he'd spent a year in Bragg Creek, Alberta, as
a potter's assistant. He worked twelve- to fifteen-hour
days as, in his term, the potter's "pack animal." It
earned him $1.50 an hour, enough to cover the rent
he paid for an electrified log cabin (no running water)
and an occasional meal out. The few free hours he
had he spent reading and meditating.

Leaving Bragg Creek, Cheech had a series of jobs
as a singer, cook and cab dispatcher before ending in
City Works, Chong's improvisational unit. City Works
—with its girls willing to work nude—was a big draw
in Vancouver, a favorite of hard-drinking hockey players, loggers and cowboys, who frequently got righteous
about the indelicate language used or, when jim-
beamed beyond their limits, the hippie look of the
actors—to the point of provoking fights.

Proprietor Chong was usually up to it. He was an
avid weight lifter who'd gone to Muscle Beach in
California for a year to satisfy, as he put it, "my
dream to work out with all the big guys." He was
on a first-name basis with most of the luminaries of
the Body Culture, and could tell a stranger the weird
times that were part of it. Like the homosexual who
paid cash dollar to a body-celeb for his used workout
apparel. And so on. When push came to shove, Chong
was handy. Cheech remembered how heads hit each
step of the flight of stairs on their way down.

The most memorable battle was one Chong had
with a logger who yanked a swatch of his hair out
as he fell down the steps. Chong helped him the rest
of the way with a deftly placed kick to the groin. Then
he took the logger's wallet and extracted money to
pay for eyeglasses broken in combat. Returning the
wallet, he kicked him in his backside and out onto
the street.

In LA, the fight was for the buck—twenty-five dollars a night in the black clubs, doing sex- and dope-

..ited material. They worked for free only at the .roubadour. "Hoot night," said Chong, "was a bitch, man. You had to line up ten in the morning and the box office opened at six p.m. The first six people lined up got to go on. So you'd get there in the morning and wait all day. Stand in line all day. There'd be guitar players and comedians. And man, we just sat around all day and bullshitted with each other and ate sunflower seeds. And people would walk up crunch crunch crunch, there would be like ten mounds of sunflower seeds all over the front. There was no other way. I mean you just couldn't get on any other way."

In LA, though, the Troubadour hoot was worth the wait. For the talent was eyed by variety potentates. In Cheech and Chong's case, it was Lou Adler who saw them. Adler, with his Midas touch was a record producer, figured Cheech and Chong as comics with solid gold potential. His idea was to parlay their spaced-out wit and his pop wisdom into the fast, fierce stardom for which the record industry had a genius. For the lovable pot-smoking crazies they played was an idea whose time had come.

They were not the first to bring the subject to the stage. Buckley had whoofed the weed in performance. And it was an inside joke when Keefe was in the Village. In the late '60s, that changed. The drug scene became part of the news fit to print. A drug culture came out of it. By 1971, it had an idiom and an import for a dude that the hip flask had had for his daddy.

Others made jokes on drugs, but with a detached air. It was where Cheech and Chong differed. Their Pedro and Man (as in "Hey, man") were the pot equivalent of Foster Brooks, drug not drink cartoons. It was what a smoke-reamed Dean 'n' Jerry might have done twenty years later, good impure fun.

It cast them as renegades, a billing fortunes were made out of in the rock world. The antihero was precisely what that crowd wanted. And Cheech and Chong were comics that needed no footnotes. Their catatonic configurations, the waltz of smoke-fucked potheads, were easy to "get." Audiences required no more than a goggle-eyed "Faar out, man" to convulse. No surprise they were a hot item with the teen sector. In the early going, the fourteen-to-sixteen age group had inundated FM stations with requests to hear cuts of Cheech and Chong albums. It started the action on them. The boys kept it going in concert.

How many of you don't smoke?

they'd ask.

And when a few hands went up,

CHONG (*drolly*): I wish I had your courage, man. I tried to quit.

Or,

How many smoke grass?

and when hundreds of hands shot up,

CHONG (*counting*): Six . . . that was a government survey.

In performance they worked out of a prop trunk, slipping in and out of assorted costumes, moving through a series of sketches. Most of them were dope-oriented, and done with a healthy respect for street idiom, which occasionally drove curious adults out of their seats and up the aisles.

Hey, that's ok. I have a four-year-old daughter who says I dress like a faggot. I taught her, though. I took away her lid,

Chong'd say, referring to dope quantity.

They were to the rogue vision what Danny Thomas was to god-bless. They were the princes of a new comic darkness, caricaturing the established order. An undercover narcotics agent is a dead giveaway by his misuse of drug-culture terms—"roofer" for reefer, "dud" for dude. POW Captain A. Ernest Whiteman, back from North Vietnam, is asked what effect his imprisonment had on him. He denies it had any—in a Chinese laundryman's accent.

Always it came back to drugs. That was the beat they worked best. They were its dilated eye, Stan and Ollie of pothead follies. Their ace lick was a TV take-off: "Let's Make a Dope Deal." In that one, Chong is a Harvard-educated "head" with a penchant for dropping acid in laundromats.

CHONG: I like to ride the dryer.

CHEECH: Isn't that dangerous?

CHONG: Not if you get a hold of yourself.

On the program, he is shown three doors, behind one of which is fifty pounds of Lebanese blond hash. Only after he decides to try for it rather than take the cash is he told that back of the other doors are narcotics agents.

Up in Canada, Cheech once made spare change dealing dope. *You'd score an ounce, two ounces, half a pound of hash and sell it.* It was penny ante next to what he was to earn with Chong for doing an act on it. With no TV, an album only, by late 1971 they were on their way to being a million-dollar proposition. If the networks didn't buy them, the counter-culture did. Platter power made them the biggest comic act in under-thirty America. Wherever they went, they got ovations that brought them back for encores. Even that tradition they kidded.

> We were gonna come back anyway. It's a cheap show biz trick we picked up in Vegas,

they'd say.

Vegas.
Robert Klein was there at the end of 1971, booked into the Hilton to open for Barbra Streisand—three weeks at five thousand dollars per.
In Vegas, big names—Cosby, King, Hackett, Greene, Rickles—made sixty-five to eighty thousand dollars a week. "And," said newspaper columnist Joe

Delaney, "I'm sure that until the government began checking it, most of the comedians got cash beyond their contractual amount. 'Cause, don't forget, if you're making fifty thousand a week and you can get ten thousand more in cash, that's like getting seventy-five thousand a week. And at one time, there was enough moving in the casinos to lay an extra ten thousand in cash, figuring the comedian's going to come in and blow some of it anyway."

Up at the top, comics dickered for "points"—a percentage of the casino's net—and sought multiyear contracts. Hackett was a vice-president at the Sahara. Others made do on five-figure weekly wages.

In the lounge, the pay was scaled down, and was money earned. It was a proving ground for a comic. At one time, most Vegas casinos had lounges in the shadows of the gambling pits. They were open to walk-in trade—at no admission charge. People came and went. To keep an audience, a comic had to work whirlwind—and with scenarios that made the patrons part of them. "Giving strokes," Peter Anthony called it.

Anthony was a lounge comic in a changed scene. Keno had absorbed the space once reserved for lounges. Most of so-called lounges now were enclosed "second" rooms. Only a few old-style lounges remained. Peter Anthony worked them with the helter-skelter he was educated to. He'd learned when he could say,

> You look like you bought those clothes
> from Jackman's of Warsaw.

and when he couldn't.

"It's a feel," he said. "A homing device. Above all, you learn to use what's out there. Like I look and see a big guy with tattoos:

> You an interior decorator?

I'll ask. And go from there with him. Somehow break the ice. Float to the back of the room. Get people involved. There's a guy with a 'stache and long hair, I'll say,

> Lemme make you feel right at home

and—*whhhhh*—I'll make like I'm puffing on a joint. Then go on to some other bit. Then I'll get back to him with another line. By the end of the show, I'll have him take a bow.

"I have created celebrities in this town, local celebrities. There was one guy that looked like the kind of kid that stole hubcaps, so I did some shtick on it. He came over after, said to me, 'Man, I don't steal hubcaps.' I said, 'Look, I'm just shticking. Don't take it seriously.' He winds up coming in two three times a week, and he got bugged one night 'cause I didn't mention he stole hubcaps. I created a monster.

"People like identity. And when you give strokes, which are honest strokes, it's okay. Sometimes you can't miss. A chick comes in with big bazooms, and has cleavage where you can almost see her navel. Now you're pretty sure she's not a nun off for the weekend. You feel the lines you can throw at her:

> Do you topple over much?

and you're off and running.

"Oh, sometimes it can be discouraging. I mean, I've had guys with vacuum cleaners coming through to clean up while I'm on. Guys turning tables over. But what I learned was—I set an attitude in my head, I don't mean Norman Vincent Peale. I set an attitude, that I'm an entertainer. No matter what. Guy comes in with a vacuum cleaner, I'll do time on him:

> Has anyone wondered what happened to the Crosley automobile? That's what they use the parts for.

Or,

> You wanna hear a success story? The guy with the vacuum used to own this place.

Anything, just to keep it movin'. Believe me, like some places you got people wandering in, falling asleep. Falling asleep while I'm working.

> A great place to work. This is where the buffalo come to die.

And the guy is out to the world. Zzzzz. And while he's sleeping I'll walk up to him and address him in conversational tones:

> Gee, man, is that what you think of my act?

Anything that'll make the crowd laugh. Say he doesn't wake up. I'll bend over and scream into his ear. And this guy'll jump out of his seat.

"Sometimes you get guys with cowboy boots on. I don't care what I'm doing. I see him walk in, BAP, right into 'Your Cheating Heart' or 'Home On the Range.' I'll do anything to get that guy.

> Moooooo,

Even that."

It was slapdash comedy—not Klein's kind at all. He was nobody's fool but his own. The summer of his TV show, he declined to wear an outfit that would have made him outlandishly plump, a "fat suit" to the trade.

It ran against comic tradition and, it turned out, Klein's too. For on Decatur Avenue in the Bronx, Klein had been more willing to stoop to conquer. The shlemiel was a stock character of his, one he no longer resorted to, out of a feeling for his trade that was not shared by Vegas, where taste ran to rim-shot dandies.

Back in the '50s, Wally Cox had fared so badly at the Dunes he was wheeled out to the airport on a stretcher to get the hotel off the hook. It stated the engagement was ended on account of "illness." In Vegas, Woody Allen was the weird apparent. To Jackie Gayle, a top lounge comic, he was like "that society kid, what's his name, George Plimpleton—an amateur doing an act."

A strange town. At every turn, its penny-vulgar soul was revealed. In Circus Circus' posh arcades was a machine with a live rabbit in it. Put a dollar bill in the slot and it'd spin a numbered wheel that ended with a prize coming down the chute. Another machine had a live chicken to bang on a miniature piano for a price.

Two dancers in a local revue reported being panty-napped—they claimed they were forced into a car and asked for their bloomers. The local response was ho hum. The revue was, after all, doing no business. To the Vegas ear, it had a bogus sound.

There'd been scandals. Booking directors at the hotels demanded kickbacks from performers, a practice some acts insisted still went on. *Ya quote me, though, and I'll deny it.* And there were sex extortions too. Jessica James, a lounge act in Vegas in the '60s, remembered one owner who chased her around his office with trousers at half-mast. It was a regular practice of his with girls who worked his place. The one who gave him a hard-on he intended to make a star. *I thought,* said Ms. James, *any minute now, he's going to trip over his own pants. But it didn't happen.*

As the story went, one girl finally did the trick.

JAMES: . . . and he made her a star. I mean it.

Q: What does she do?

JAMES: She's an actress. It's an interesting story. What happened was that he made her a star. And she married someone else. And then he wrecked her. He fixed it so she couldn't get a job in Hollywood. And also her husband.

Q: He had that power?

JAMES: He was a very, very powerful man.

One of many. Vegas was made in their image, toy town of pinky-ringed nabobs, where wink and stink were under chandeliers. And every corner of it was a cash strategy.

In the Hilton, where Klein was, stuffed animals were sold for a hundred and fifty dollars apiece in the lobby. It was easy to figure why. *It's approximately,* Klein estimated, *a hundred feet from where someone could win a couple hundred dollars on the roll of dice and grab one because he's drunk.*

In the casinos, Klein saw awe in the eyes of the people for swank that relied on flash in the main. Pop palatial. Even statues in lobbies, he sensed, were judged in terms of cold cash.

It made him uneasy to be there. It was another orbit to him from Upper Broadway with its Zabar's/streetcorner kiosks/Thalia. The values were fucked. In the twenty-four-hour click click of gambling wheels, amid the sinister velvet, Klein felt out of place, an alien in a trick town. It made him edgy, a mood that moved him to the brink of fear, whose bottom was failure. He worried he'd bomb.

He embroidered it in his mind. That happened with Klein. He seized panic by the lapels. He had the worrier's art down pat. Growing up in the Bronx, he succumbed to monster fear if faced by situations that might embarrass him. When chums of his gate-crashed a place, Klein was a reluctant party to it, ever wary of consequences.

Uger, the dentist-turned-comedy writer: "Sneaking into the Concord, something like that. Death to him at that time. A terrific fear of being embarrassed. I could never put that together with how outgoing he otherwise was. To this day, it's that way with him."

That scrupulous sense chastened him when he gave in to petty emotions. One night, he watched David Steinberg fail with an anecdote on a talk show, and initial pleasure changed to guilt for feeling it. Guilt was worry's adjunct. On Klein, it was a perfect fit. He brought it to his early affairs with women, some of whom he made Madonnas. He was a comic who could have been out of the pages of a Bellow or Malamud book, a Jew with full moral freight. And if Vegas was, in terms of a novel, a cunning plot twist, in real life it was an Excedrin headache.

The faces in the casino, with their tight parochial expressions, gave him a premonition of (hard) times to come. No rat-a-BOOM with him. He wasn't out of the baggy-pants school. His was a finer sound that he'd begun to suspect was limited in its audience. He was reconciled to it. The letters he got were encouraging. There was a literacy to most of them. And only a month before, a note had come down from Groucho, words from the maestro to cheer a comic soul:

> *Dear Bob,*
>
> *I address you as "Dear Bob" because first of all it's your name, and secondly, because you were so good hosting the "Tonight Show" last night. Your opening monologue was wonderful, in fact it was even hilarious, and I predict a GREAT future for you, and also a great past, for that matter.*
>
> *I have been watching you over the years, and being a master prognosticator, I predicted you were going to be a big star. And you are. Of course, the last one I said this about was Calvin Coolidge. . . .*

But Groucho was hardly the sum of the republic. Out there at the Hilton, he knew, would be people that'd discount him on sight. Months before Groucho wrote, a letter was forwarded to him from ABC-TV. It came just after he'd been guest host of an early-morning show on that station.

> *. . . we were shocked and amazed that ABC would allow such a sloppy and hippy character as Robert Klein on. He is actually dirty-looking with that despicable hair and untidy appearance. We do hope you'll get back to having clean-looking commentators and dispense with shady characters and hippies.*

The quick-hits of smoke Klein liked before he performed gave him the godfeel in the Improv and other places. In Vegas, it boomeranged, deepening funk. In that desert town, he went for a toke or few more than he usually did—at all hours of the day.

Its effect was obvious. Vegas-watchers caught it. The columnist Delaney used the word "strident"— and suspected that the comic gears were haywire well before Klein took stage. For there was an anger in him that reminded Delaney of Danny Thomas' "jack" story:

> You know, where the guy's car break down. On his way over to the neighbor to borrow the jack, he thinks of all the reasons why the guy might not loan him the jack, including the fact he didn't return the lawn mower two years ago. And so, finally, he gets to the guy's door and raps on the door and the guys says, "Hi Charlie, what can I do for you?" He says, "Screw you and your jack."

Robert fared as he figured, not well at all, making fancy dollars in the clink/clank of dishes and post-prandial dialogues that caused him to seethe. New Year's Eve was the worst. On one such night in Vegas past, two drunk women mounted stage to do a spastic tango while Judy Garland was on. For Klein, horns blared. Glasses clinked. *I could tell,* he said, *there was a different thing happening here, and the different thing was drunkenness.*

He thought it'd subside. It didn't. Balloons exploded. Garbled phrases were shouted. *Whaaaaa:* a man impersonated a brass section. And then a drunk shouted "Get off, get off." Klein did, but not before he cursed the man out from stage.

And when three weeks were done, he took the money and ran. Vegas was still contagious for the smarty-pants comic.

He had Vegas in common with Carlin.

What he didn't share were the spoils George hit on with the album.

Not that Klein had to plead poverty. He'd made

$66,000 in 1971, a figure he thought he could boost once he had a constituency.

Carlin—and Cheech and Chong—had shown the way. The 33⅓ recorded word. It was direct route.

Carlin's *FM/AM* was on its way to earning a gold record, signifying a million dollars' worth of net sales. It meant roughly four hundred thousand records, cassettes and cartridges sold at distributor's cost. Cheech and Chong's *Big Bambu* album would end up gold times over—more than a million copies *sold*.

No question: the record world was the new comic mint. The business magazine, *Forbes,* fixed 1972 gross revenues in entertainment in this order:

records and tapes	$ 2 billion
movies	1.3 billion
network television	1 billion
professional sports	540 million
Broadway	36 million

A comic with a gold record stood to earn up to a quarter of a million dollars in royalties. And an album put his name on the variety firmament as fast as a speeding *Billboard* bullet. In the record industry it could be a matter of weeks only. Klein felt it was no fad. He wanted a record of his own.

He put up his own money—hired a sound engineer to record him live at the Bitter End. And he diditthisfast—one month after the Las Vegas debacle. He paid also for studios to edit in, and musicians to back up songs on the album. Six thousand, one hundred seventy-eight dollars and forty-eight cents it cost him.

It was, as Dangerfield would say, "A way, man"—and not an easy one either. For Klein was back of the line now. Carlin/Cheech and Chong had capitalized the scene. It was moot whether the hard-rock world was up to another comic, particularly one without scallawag eminence. To be "baaad" was to be box office in that culture. And Klein hadn't the notoriety.

He was less the advocacy comic than Carlin or Cheech and Chong. George's patter sometimes had the crusader's stiff spine. Cheech and Chong were the first nose-thumbing dragoons of the neocomic brigade.

Klein was unremittingly Robert—more personal than partisan. If his material covered the same ground—sex, drugs and the idiocy of institutions—it was not so quick to choose up sides.

It made him (by contrast) more moderate to the culture's quick eye. He didn't do screaming say-yeah, or other affirming handstands. He was not so cavalier a figure. He was—what?—more regular.

A story Klein told on himself—a true one:

> I was in Boston playing a club. And, you know, like it was a lonely time. Nothing was happening. And I was in my hotel. Pouring rain out. I have to do my show across the street in two hours. Knock on the door. And there are two girls. Groupies, if I ever saw them. Long hair. Go, "Hey. Far out. What's your sign? What are you, a Sag? Where's your moon? On your cusp?" Whooo. You know, people go crazy. Is your moon on the cusp? What's your sign? Where are you? Ever get people that they guess twelve guesses? The last one—Aquarius? "I knew it. Long fingers."

> But anyway, two groupies. They immediately identified themselves as Boston's foremost groupies. I thought, oooo-A. They said they were nineteen. We're sitting and talking. And finally I said, "Got any eyes for . . .?" "Oh no, man. We love you. But we don't want to ball you. We just . . . We'd like if you could give us ten dollars to see *Gimme Shelter*."

> They got the ten dollars. You know, intimidated me. . . . But moving along very quickly . . .

It was an irony that Klein was outside the rock culture, looking in. For he was an early adherent of the big beat. He'd listened to radio back when Alan

Freed used Moondog as his tag, a name he gave up when a blind poet similarly called brought suit. In conversation with music freaks, Klein had a Toynbee command of the ebb and flow of rock history. He'd recall obscure groups from the '50s, the paleolithic period of that music.

He'd even indulged the rocker's "deludert" of being a recording star. At DeWitt Clinton High School in the Bronx, he was part of a group, the Teen Tones, he used to dream would tour the country in a limousine with the group's name emblazoned on its sides. The Teen Tones made it to "The Ted Mack Amateur Hour" and lost to a one-armed piano player.

A decade later, he did not have the standing he did when the Teen Tones worked out in school bathrooms to exploit the echoes there. Carlin was more readily the type. On the cover of *Class Clown,* his second album, was a warning that the record contained seven words not allowed on TV. It advised caution in listening—hearing them could warp mind, body and (it stated) "lose the war for the allies." On the record, Carlin eyed and aired gutter words in the sleuth's way. Cocksucker, he elaborated in concerts, was not a bad man but rather a good lady. So on, and so ——ing forth.

Carlin got in trouble when he did the routine in July 1972 at Milwaukee's Summerfest, a ten-day annual festival of music and performing arts on the Lake Michigan waterfront. He was arrested. Later, a parochial-school teacher in Springfield, Massachusetts, played the album for his class and was fired. He was notified in a letter from the district's prelate that school officials objected to the language on the record. It was to George's (if not the teacher's) good. Notoriety was negotiable.

The same album contained an acknowledgment of the mythical place Lenny Bruce had ("Special thanks to Leonard Schneider for taking all the chances"), one Carlin seemed drawn to. Some nights, he got on his high horse and did galloping riffs on the righteous cosmos whose orbits were, by George, in perfect alignment with his.

At Westbury, Long Island, not so long ago, he

came out and told a capacity crowd its suburban life was a forfeit on legitimacy, his hoarse voice full of the rigorism of the church he mocked.

Carlin had reason to be cool to the established order—nights that turned to "fright wig time." And more. Back in the early '60s when he was with Jack Burns, he was in Dallas to play the Gaslight Club. The afternoon the pair was to open, Carlin stopped at a laundry to pick up shirts he'd asked "rush service" on. The owner stooped behind the counter to get them, and stayed there. Out came a horde of police to slam George against the wall.

Carlin was detained as a suspect in an armed robbery. Partner Burns was rousted out of bed by Dallas' finest too. The basis of the law's suspicion was the discovery of a clipping in the pocket of one of Carlin's shirts. *Two men hold up automobile club in Chicago.* It took a while to convince the authorities that the reason for the clipping was on the other side—an item on the European Common Market.

George's brushes with the straight world in the late '60s came at a time of entrenched Babbittry. It coincided with the jesuschristing of Lenny Bruce. Carlin had wanted to play the Bruce role in the Broadway production *Lenny* but settled for the comic calling Lenny had had.

It was not the same this time around. Obscenity was no account. Carlin's case in Milwaukee was dismissed. In public, he talked of his use of drugs, and no lightning struck. It was as Carlin said: Lenny had taken the chances.

What George *had* done was re-route the laughs—a merchandising coup, designation that'd make Carlin blanch. For he meant to be more. He wanted to shock and shake. Not easy. For he worked mostly to denim crowds in sync with him. To them he was a funny focker. He'd been one since 1960. He had the slinky bones to hoodwink an audience. And he could, in the parlance, "think funny." He turned out the lines. While in limbo, he'd been a writer for Flip Wilson's show.

Still, he was beguiled by Lenny's hipster figure, a pose he liked to play at. He did at Westbury with an audience he put down as bourgeois, a quality he surmised from its address. It was cheap-think he blew thunder on. The closest he came to Lenny was in his shaman use of racial slurs. That night, he saw a cigarette smoker in the audience and cried, "He niggerlipped it . . . what's the matter? You never heard that? Nigger nigger nigger." Lenny did it when the word was a risk. Now it was tsk tsk.

Bruce once told an audience,

> I wasn't very funny tonight. Sometimes I'm not. I'm not a comedian, I'm Lenny Bruce,

words which taken one way were credo, another way license. In either case, they made Lenny complex.

Carlin went that way too. Half an hour before he was to do a concert at the University of Bridgeport, he skipped town, leaving his agent to say, "He was not in a funny mood, thus could not be funny on the stage." In the midwest, the comics Edmonds and Curley were rushed in at the last minute when Carlin backed out of a date. And when he did show up, he might not be altogether there. At the Capitol Theater in Passaic, New Jersey, in '73, George hadn't the snap and brio he usually did—whether because of whim or weed was anybody's guess. *Can't hear ya, man,* patrons shouted. Carlin made an effort to speak louder, then lapsed into a semi-audible mumble. When shouts recurred, he told them to get used to his unconventional usage of a microphone. That night he strayed from his material with disjointed patter that invariably wound back to the same query—*What was I talking about?* The audience indulged him.

It didn't at Westbury. Carlin's second night there, he had trouble. *Newsday,* the Long Island tabloid, reported:

> *You couldn't exactly blame the complaints about George Carlin's second show last night on the generation gap since some members of the Westbury Music Fair audience who did not mind*

the longhaired comedian's penchant for four-letter words complained that they could not hear them. But an estimated 100 patrons stormed out of the theater demanding refunds, and a number of others just stormed out.

Later, when a local VFW threatened to picket his return to Westbury, Carlin was less Bruce than beware. He canceled the performance, returning to California in his personal jet.

Cheech and Chong had their troubles too. In Miami, they were warned not to use "fuck" or its insidious cousin "motherfucker" onstage, or risk arrest. Four police officers were up front of the stage, their back to the comic pair. Once the performance started, the lawmen turned to watch, all but one of them laughing.

"I made up my mind," said Cheech, "to get him when we did *The Dogs*." *The Dogs* was the lads' finale. On their knees they went to play talking dogs:

What you been up to?

Running around chasing cars. Getting stoned on the exhaust.

You can get brain damage.

They sniffed and panted and acted canine, right down to the biological nitty gritty:

CHEECH: So we came to the part where we "pee." And we "peed" on him . . . on the cop who was really burned up. And I "peed" a long time on him and the other cops were just really falling out. And he was really getting mad. And everyone's howling. And then I went back and "peed" on him again.

One time we landed in Texas we were holding a lot of shit [marijuana] at the

221

time. And here comes these cops, uniformed cops. Came right on the plane as soon as it landed. And they said, "Are you Cheech and Chong?" "Yeah." "Come on with us." And took us out of the plane and we're going "Oh fuck, this is it." We get out and there's two more cops waiting. They go, "Come on, git in the car." And we go, what the fuck's going on . . .

They said, "Come on, you're late for the gig, we've got to get you to the thing." They turned on the siren. They took us to the gig, man.

Q: What do you do about that . . . carrying stuff?

CHONG: We don't. We don't need to get high that bad. It's not a priority.

CHEECH: Usually, if we want to get high, just ask "Anybody got a joint?" Get flooded. I mean, people throw joints onstage a lot.

CHONG: In Rochester, we brought up a lit one.

CHEECH: We've got high onstage before. If it flows. Some people are pretty obnoxious, and it doesn't. Another thing: a lot of people can't separate—

Q: The stage personality from the—

CHONG: Yeah, that . . . idiot I play on the stage. They say, "Wow, hey, there's Chong. Ha ha."

CHEECH: Sometimes they think we're permanently Pedro and Man. They think that's who we are. Offstage.

CHONG: And you can see that.

CHEECH: They do shit like . . . you know, like your parents used to spell in front of you. I mean, that's their mentality and we're looking at these motherfuckers, man. They think we can't see past our glasses.

Fellow pros thought even less of them, saying their material was stolen. The word was that much of it came from The Committee, an improvisation company out of San Francisco. Chong was matter-of-fact about the allegation. "We do their bits," he said. "We do a lot of their bits." But he qualified it with the assertion that it was changed and chonged in their hands.

To Coast comics, it was after the fact. But the fact, best as Cheech and Chong could make out, was they got five thousand dollars a night for concerts and their detractors got squat.

It paid to be up top of the rock world. To be a comic accessory was quite another thing.

Mike Preminger opened for a rock group and found that comedy was a new one on his audience:

I told a joke. Got a few laughs. Guy up front turned around, says, "Shhh, he's talking."

Edmonds and Curley, a team that toured the small-town college circuit, was underbilled to the rock group Three Dog Night.

JOEY
EDMONDS: And we'd just finished and—

THOM
CURLEY: And started to walk off and

POLICE: Right this way, right this way.

Entire gauntlet of these six officers on each side and a lieutenant leading them. Hup ho, hup ho, hup ho. And they got us offstage where the promoter was standing and he takes one look and says, "What are you doing with these guys? They're the fucking comics."

To do a comic prelim was no bargain. Albert Brooks had worked with Sly and the Family Stone. One night he got a phone call just prior to going onstage. It was Sly's manager, reporting his client en route by plane, only a couple of hours from touchdown. He asked could Albert hold the crowd. He'd have held the Alamo easier.

Brooks' solution for nights like those was the "big one," a word godsped, namely *shit*. Up against it, a comic had only to say the word into a microphone, Albert swore, to bring rock crowds to their knees. It was, he said, the stopper.

> *Shit* has saved my life. I know it sounds like a *National Inquirer* article, but it's true.

Albert advised stickup victims to use the word. He claimed the gunman would double up with laughter.

Brooks' routine was a wry allusion to the rock mob's collective wit. Klein noted it too when he said,

> Now—my obligatory drug material . . . *(drowsily):* "Far out, maaa-un. Far ooouuut,"

a knock on Cheech and Chong.

Those two, however, walked in where others feared to tread.

CHONG: It's none of that, "Louie, I can't go on. It's not my crowd. They'll kill me out there. They've got lights flashing. They're throwing frisbies." Cheech and Chong shut 'em up.

CHEECH: Like we were on the road. This was just after the record came out. And Doug Weston at the Troubadour had Donny

224

Hathaway. All-black audience. And they had some folk singer before him. And he would sing like this—[*archly*] "While riding on my horse one day . . ." And they booed him off the stage. It was hysterical. So Weston says, "Send for Cheech and Chong. They know how to control niggers, man." And he sent for us. But we had another gig. So when we got back, he had Bill Withers, who was another black act. So he sent for us.

Q: Any tough ones? How about the club in Boston that—

CHONG: It's rough. It's rough.

Q: Pimps at the bar?

CHEECH: And the cash register going ding ding every two seconds.

Q: So what do you do?

CHONG: Oh, do pimp jokes. Talk about 'em. I do a thing about how black guys hitchhike. "Hey, honky bitch, gimme a ride." And when they don't get the ride, calls her prejudiced.

CHEECH: See, like a lot of people, a lot a guys would do black humor, but they're afraid to. What are these black guys gonna think? If it's truthful, they're gonna laugh their asses off.

CHONG: Same hitchhiker, still hitching. A black guy. "Here comes my brother I know he'll give me a ride . . . Hey, brother . . . right on, baby." And the guy passes him. And the hitcher says, "You black motherfucker."

And the audience, AAAAH. They're over each other, spilling drinks.

CHEECH: Remember that one cat that got really upset talking about his hair in that club in Boston? He's sitting there.

CHONG: That was in P.J.'s.

CHEECH: No, that was Boston.

CHONG: Was it?

CHEECH: Yeah.

CHONG: (*remembering it*): "Say, use your comb, brother." Told him to take off his helmet.

CHEECH: He had the most far-out hairdo we ever saw. Going-every-which-way process. Yeah. Then we got everybody else on him. All the rest of the pimps go, "Yeah." Because you're articulating a lotta things everybody wants to say but they're too cool to.

It wasn't the comic who always had the last word, though. Richard Lewis, visiting friends in Ann Arbor, Michigan, was persuaded to stop in a local hangout called The Pretzel Bell and try his act out during the band's break.

He did—with little success. In fact, while he was on, a girl got up and walked out, returning with one of the band members. The musician walked up to the stage, reached into his pocket and came up with a switchblade knife. With it, he cut the microphone cord.

And then he sat down and french-kissed his girl until Lewis left stage.

Showcases/TV/and into the money.
On either coast, most comics went that way.

In LA, new boys ended up in the Comedy Store on Sunset Boulevard to work funny and free. They did it on the chance that the TV industry (all but gone from New York) would spot them.*

Out there, more novelty acts were seen. There was a comic who played plumbing fixtures. Another wore a turban and billed himself as the Milton Berle of Pakistan—Jackie Kahn.

KAHN   (to patron): Where are you from?

PATRON: LA.

KAHN: And you?

PATRON: Kankakee.

KAHN: Sucks.

PATRON: I—

---

* Not all acts needed TV to make it. Cheech and Chong were the most conspicuous proof. Another comedy team that did without it was Edmonds and Curley. They'd tried the tube but ended up technological victims. The problem was Thom Curley, a big disheveled cutup with mustache and long dark hair. His sound effects enlivened the act but confounded TV engineers, who frantically tinkered with dials to keep Curley and his partner Joey Edmonds at an acceptable sound level. The engineers managed to mute the wild piercing noises but—alas!—the laughs vanished too. Studio audiences whooped it up for them but on TV it sounded like Forest Lawn. Nothing. It drove Edmonds and Curley out onto the road. They played the budget-minded college circuit, booking in volume and often at reduced rates for neighboring schools that took them in tandem dates. It saved them road fatigue and gas money and kept them on the go. They'd speed from Grays Lake-Springfield-River Grove-Elgin-Lebanon in a blitz of mid-America. Lacking a name, they asked to be put wherever students congregated. It meant they'd suddenly appear in student unions, cafeterias, quadrangles and do their act—usually at midday. *Noon-ers* was the term. With Curley's sound effects, they got the crowd's attention. A hard grinding time it was but well worth it at sixty thousand dollars a year in spite of Big Mac rations, passing sex celebrations, Holiday Inns 'n' outs.

KAHN: In my country, they don't heckle. They're too busy eating rice . . . (*Gets laughs.*) You like the shit jokes?

Sammy Shore ran the room. He was a comic who sometimes played Vegas. In the '50s, he'd teamed with Shecky Greene briefly. He moved comics the way Ralph Williams did cars—fast and with an eye to profit.

Comics knew there was money to be made if they hit it big. *Variety* reported that Carlin pulled "a strong $40,027" in five performances at New York's Palace Theater in 1972. Cheech and Chong had struck it rich too.

On the way up, though, it was hard to find places to play in LA as in New York. What Bluestone/Lewis/Walker and Co. suffered in tight markets, Barry Warnoker did too in California.

Warnoker was a comic/writer, a tall stocky kid with dark harpo curls who'd teamed with Steve Simon to start, a partnership that produced a memorable routine or two. As "Dick Carver & Son," they were "moils," specialists in circumcisions.

In the bit, the elder instructed the kid in the cutting art, using a doll to practice on.

Trim the side, and take a little off the top,

he'd say. Or,

Change your grip. And choke up a little.

They did "Dick Carver & Son" to an all-Japanese audience one night, and played to silence.

Another night, they were offered ten dollars to appear at a raunch bar in San Fernando Valley. Silence again. The reason was simple. Stag films flickered on all four walls while they worked. No sound tracks/only fuck flashes.

They directed their act to the films—and still failed to elicit a laugh with their running commentary. Soon they were standing there doing intermittent rim shots in phonetics . . . Ba-DUMBA . . . Ba-DUMBA.

Nothing. Too embarrassed to ask for their money, they left, laughing all the way home.

On his own, Warnoker fared no better. In fact, one club owner advised, "Keep your day job, man." One night, he went to a black club in Inglewood. "And I began," he said, "to do the jokes, and they'd say, 'No, no, ya gotta get dirty.' People talk to you there. They're not awed by the fact you're a performer. I'd do a joke. 'Nah. That's a white joke. Do some dirty stuff.' Started ad libbing. All the dirties I'd ever heard. Worst or best, they laughed."

> Two gays meet in a restaurant. One says, "I'll be frank." Other says, "No, let me."

Ba-DUMBA.
"Now they were on my side.

> There was a prostitute who took her eye out. And the guy screwed her in the eye. Loved it. After, he says, "How can I get in touch with you?" "I'll keep an eye out for you," she says.

And they kept laughing. I did dirty until I couldn't remember any more."

There was no winning for Warnoker. He made more money writing gags for Vegas comics than performing his own. He got a job at the San Francisco Playboy but little else. Unable to be the act he wanted, he was a dropout by 1974. LA comics heard he'd joined a commune for a few weeks, then moved on to work at a mental hospital in Louisiana.

He'd given up the star-trek—for the time being at least. Without a reputation, it was hard for a comic. With it, the laughs came easier. Buddy Hackett put it nicely on a night the audience was a trifle slow:

> Don't forget. I'm sold out. *You're* on trial,

he quipped in his puckish way.

It was to get that stellar edge that comics aspired.

Star-lust: Budd Friedman saw it all the time—and not just with budding pros.

Through his door came blokes of all shapes and sizes looking to be stars, the most uncommon of them the late Eddie Carmel, the circus giant Diane Arbus had photographed.

"Eddie Carmel," he said, "fancied himself a stand-up comic. So he used to come by here with a few funny little things he did. Well, one night, Jack Rollins was getting ready to leave just as Eddie Carmel was about to go on. So Eddie stood in the narrow corridor leading to the door, physically blocked it. No way Jack could get out. And Eddie said in his deep deep voice, 'Mister Rollins, please sit down. I'm going on very soon.'" The manager obliged.

Ed Bluestone once saw a Bowery bum walk in off the street on hoot night at Folk City and demand to go on.

Q: Really a Bowery guy?

BLUE-
STONE: Well, yeah. Old overcoat with puke on it. Whiskers and disheveled hair. And torn shirt. And the guy was big too. Six-four. Really big 'n' strong.

Q: Young?

BLUE-
STONE: Oh, maybe forty. And he comes on and he says to the emcee he's a comedian. He wants to go on. Emcee says, "We're ending the show now." Guy says fuck you. Guy picks up the microphone and he starts talking to this empty room. And the bar-keeper, who is not afraid of anybody, gets up and says to the guy, "Get the fuck out of here." And the guy says, "I'm entertaining." And the barkeeper tried to grab the microphone out of his hand, but he can't. And the two of them have the microphone and they're onstage struggling over it.

Right out of Nathanael West it was. So was the response to the school for comedians Albert Brooks had devised, a put-on that included Komedy Korner answers to student questions.

Q: Do the Jewish people dominate the field of comedy?

A: Don't be a shmuck.

Brooks' manager, Herb Nanas, said the article had brought mail asking for further details, correspondence from folks that took it for real. *I was funny in Sheboygan. I would love to go to your school.* Now you know they read this fucking thing, and didn't realize it was satirical. My god, it's scary.

Stardom could be had any number of ways. Albert Brooks himself was proof of it. He was the Garbo of the new comics, appearing infrequently in public. He did not want the hopscotch schedule. He was content to do TV shots and a very occasional coffeehouse/club, and wait for his star to rise.

If it made manager Nanas' 15 percent short numbers, Albert was unconcerned. The money—his and Herb's—would come. He had faith. He told people, and meant it, that he was funny since the age of three. If he was, no question the influence of his father-the-radio-comic was there. Parkyakarkus was a man who had stood in movie houses to sing along with the flicker or, in a restaurant, risen to say, "I want your attention, all of you, this boy [Albert] is not eating his vegetables."

Carl Reiner had seen Albert do a spoof on Houdini when he was sixteen. It was Houdini as a total incompetent. The kind of Houdini who couldn't remove his hands from his pockets. Reiner laughed, and later when Johnny Carson asked him who the funniest men he knew were, Reiner said Mel Brooks was one, and a kid named Albert Einstein (Albert's given name) was the other. At the time, Albert Brooks was still in high school.

Reiner's son, Rob, claimed Albert needed no showcases to know if a routine would work. He spoke it aloud in an empty room and, if it struck him funny, the next time he'd do it coast-to-coast.

Brooks was a patrician, Prince Albert of the coffee-house circuit. When he did a date, he took it and Albert seriously. At the Bijou, Albert asked management who was to carry his case of props onstage. To his chagrin, Albert Brooks was the one. Nights he performed there, he holed up in his dressing room, and, if he heard footsteps outside, he'd throw the door open and ask, AM I ON?! AM I ON?!

Q: What interests does Albert have?

ROB
REINER: Nothing. He's into nothing.

HERB
NANAS,
MGR: Albert Brooks has no interests in life.

It was the initial response of two who knew him well, both of whom extenuated it for fear, no doubt, that Brooks would come off as the Strangelove of comics. So Albert, it was noted, liked cars and stereos. And he was "into the future," the technology to come.

Mostly he was into the comedy. Brooks' was unlike any around, a spoofing conceptual approach. Only Albert could make a routine out of a confession that he'd run out of material. Seated in an easy chair, he told the audience of the pressure to keep turning out "bits" and the impasse comics occasionally come to. There was his record company, which felt appearances on TV would prime the album, the cover of which he unabashedly displayed. In the name of honesty, Brooks declined to foist inferior material on the public. He was not a comic, he allowed, who'd do just anything for a laugh. He could, of course, smash a pie in his face if he wanted cheap giggles. Why look—and he did. And so it went, right down to the trousers he dropped to display boxer shorts and knobby knees. In mood lighting reminiscent of a Jimmy Durante exit, he went off, to return when the Muse was working.

No, Brooks was not the routine comic soul. He was

a jingling skull. In Albert ran a fine paranoiac edge, able to imagine assassins in audiences he played down South, or perfidious intentions in police officers that crossed his tracks. He was wound tight. AM I ON?! AM I ON?!

"When we were kids," said Rob Reiner, "he used to ask me about his hair all the time. 'How does my hair look? My hair all right?' 'Albert, your hair is fine.' It looks the same all the time. He has the curly kinky hair. 'Looks fine, Albert.' He said, 'No, but really. Tell me, is it OK, because I've been picking at one spot, it's a bald spot.' He used to pick his hair as a little kid.

"Very nervous, very insecure as a kid. And very paranoid. But he seems to have grown out of that. Used to eat a lot. Eats a lot now. But he'll eat like . . . in one night, he'll devour the entire output of the West Coast Hershey division. And then he won't eat for three, four days.

"He's uncanny. We were up in the hills, on the outskirts of Los Angeles. And we got absolutely lost, we didn't know where the hell we were. I mean, we were really lost. We didn't know how to get back down to the freeway, nutin'. Anyway, passed by a meadow. There was one cow. A lone cow grazing in a meadow. And we drove by about twenty feet. Albert stopped the car, backed up and stood in front of the cow. And said, 'Excuse me.' Cow kept its head in the grass, and kept eating. He said louder, 'Excuse me.' Cow picked its head up, looked straight into Albert's eyes. He said, 'Could you tell me how to get back to LA?' And the cow . . . weirdest thing, the cow went like that, just like it was flicking a fly off its shoulder. But he gave it a head nod in the direction over one shoulder. And Albert said, 'Thank you.' And just drove on. We're driving along. I said, 'Albert—' He says, 'Don't worry. He knows. He lives around here. He knows how to get back.' I said, 'You can't go by a cow.' And it turned out to be the right way."

With his own career, Brooks was not so casual. "Very concerned," said Reiner. "He'll check the *TV Guide* listing to see who's opposite him the night he's on the Carson show. Or if he's on Flip Wilson or something. Just because he cares. He's very concerned about how he's presented and what can combat him. I remember once *The Wizard of Oz* was on opposite a re-run of something . . . oh, "The Dick Van Dyke Show." He [Alebrt] was on Van Dyke, played a part on it. And *The Wizard of Oz* was on. Albert says, 'Nobody watches *The Wizard of Oz* anymore. I mean, how could they watch *The Wizard of Oz?* It's on the hundredth time.' I said, 'Albert, there are more people who are going to watch *The Wizard of Oz* than a Dick Van Dyke re-run.' He said, 'I don't see how you can say that.' He's very protective of his own stuff, very protective."

If Brooks eyed stardom on his terms, Alan Bursky, it seemed, would have it on any terms. On the Coast, he was the *enfant terrible* of comedy or, as he put it, "sorta a legend."

The legend was secondhand Sammy Glick. Bursky (nee Achilles Sambursky) was, it was thought, the youngest stand-up to appear on Carson. He went on billed as eighteen. In fact, he was nineteen at the time, younger at that than any other comic to appear there. He'd falsified age for the edge he figured it'd give him, a minor transgression by Bursky's lights. The pint-sized (5'4", 125 lbs.) comic, in his hurry to get to the top, had pilfered and pimped and otherwise brazened his way.

When gag writer Ed Monaghan first saw him at the Comedy Store, Bursky was the parking-lot attendant there, allowed inside only for the few minutes allotted him each night onstage. He used the time to do other comics' jokes, thievery that earned him the enmity of most comics there.

If the room was hostile to him when he was on, Bursky never backed down, pluck that made a fan of Monaghan. It was why when Alan asked to work with him, Monaghan agreed—with stipulations. "I said, 'Look, now you have to follow orders. These are professionals at this club. Now they know . . . they know now I'm working with you. And now they're going to be watching. So when it's raw material, I don't want you to do it there. I want you to do it somewhere where we're hidden. We get a tape, we edit. Then you go up there.'"

Bursky agreed, and then went straight to the Comedy Store to try out his new material, the height of folly to Monaghan. He told the kid to get lost, that was it.

Without Monaghan, Bursky was in a bad way for material. He did what he had to. He befriended other gag writers, and even offered to get them girls in return for jokes. Several of them took him up on it and, had the gags been as fine as the girls were, it is likely Monaghan never would have heard from Bursky again.

It was not the case. And soon Alan was on the phone to Monaghan, asking him to reconsider. Three months straight, he called every night. He finally "got" to Monaghan. "He was charming me," Monaghan said. "I don't know if it's the son I don't have or whatever the hell. But he was getting to me. So finally he called up and said, 'I want an appointment and I don't want no bullshit. This is a business appointment.' So I said okay.

"He came over. Sat down. Three months had passed. He said, 'I have to have you. I have a feeling that we'll make it together.' So he said, 'I'll do this for you. Forty percent of me for life, or I'll kill any one person that you name.' And he's like . . . intense. And I fell on the floor. I damn near threw up. I thought that was so funny . . . but of course that's the game. The charm is on and off as he turns it on and off. So I said, 'All right. We'll try it one more time.'"

Bursky was not new to the biz. He'd started as a child performer out of Far Rockaway, Long Island, doing magic at birthday parties for thirty-five dollars a show. Eleven at the time, he worked the greater metropolitan area, one night assisting the magician, Amazing Randi, at a Park Avenue party the Duke and Duchess of Windsor attended.

Growing up, he had Legg-Perthes, a disease that deforms bone tissue in the thigh joint. It hospitalized him from age two to four, kept him on crutches from age five to eight. Afterward,

Q: Kids picked on you?

BURSKY: Yeah, but I used to whack them with the crutch.

Q: Really?

BURSKY: Yeah, some lady tried to take my mother to court to have crutches taken away from me because they were like weapons, she said. I hit her kid in the head. I was sitting down one day, eating grapes. And he came over and took them out of my lap. I picked up the crutch and went *voom*. I've been violent like that ever since, ya know. I once hit somebody in the head. When I was about fifteen, some really big kid started picking on me, I was carrying a sawed-off broom handle . . . ya know, like a little billy club. I was going to make a magic trick out of it. And I was holding it in my hand, and he was really picking on me. And I got scared, I thought he was going to hurt me. So I took it and whacked it across his face. And I think broke his nose.

Q: Why did he pick on you?

BURSKY: I was small. I was always the smallest kid in the class. Smallest kid in the neighborhood.

Q: What about the crutches?

BURSKY: I wasn't on crutches by this time. This was like when I was fifteen. But I was . . . always kinda the neighborhood oddball. I didn't play football. I collected comedy albums. I used to run off to the city by myself . . . and learn magic tricks. I really didn't have many friends. Maybe one or two. I was just the neighborhood

oddball. I'm the kid everybody made faggot stories about, you know. I'm the one
girls would call up and complain about
their boyfriends. Girls I would like. "Oh,
my boyfriend's such a monster, why can't
he be more like you?" I'd say I don't
wanna hear it. Click.

Even then, he was into hustles. With card tricks,
he'd get pizza slices, or maybe suits cleaned. In the
neighborhood, he'd do three-card sleight of hand *bet
the queen. Where's the queen?*, earning lunch money
and an occasional beating from sore losers.

In the summers, he'd stake out an empty lot near
the beach in Far Rockaway, and wave cars in. He'd
get a quick sum, and run. From a magic book, he
discovered how to make lockpicks. He fashioned one
in a shop class and went car door to door scooping
tape decks. "I even tried once to mug an old lady,"
he said. "I'll never forget that. I swear to God. I was
standing around with a friend of mine. I said, 'Your
money or your life.' And she didn't hear well. She
said, 'Who do you like?' I said, 'Forget it, lady.'"

At sixteen, Bursky bought a Woody Allen album,
and became hooked on comedy. He saw the ex-
vaudevillian Billy Glason's ad in a trade paper, and
went up to his place to buy gag files. Soon he was
making the rounds of showcases—the African Room,
the King's Pub. He even tried The Improvisation.
Friedman booted him out on account of his age. When
he performed, it was with Woody Allen's material,
which he knew by heart.

Q: What did people say to you about the
material?

BURSKY: "Gee, that's the most original material,
the funniest I ever heard in my whole
life."

Q: And what did you say?

BURSKY: "Thank you."

He was not content to do just Woody. When he moved to the Coast, he borrowed wholesale. At the Bitter End West, he was caught in the act. The act was, it turned out, David Brenner's. A comic friend of Brenner's was there, recorded it and played it for him long distance.

Brenner threatened to incapacitate Bursky when he met him later. He was not the first. "They have threatened him with physical violence," said Monaghan, "on a number of occasions. I know he has been thrown against the wall. And there was one guy looking for him to give him the beating of his life. So Alan gave him back the joke he had stolen. His logic was that it was the only good joke the kid had, and he wasn't going to make it on one joke."

When he got up to perform at the Comedy Store, comics were in waiting. But Bursky was quick on his feet. When a stout gay comic heckled him, he said,

> He's one of the few guys I know who carries monogrammed kneepads,

to which the poor fellow could only say,

> You tacky litle mother.

Comics credited Bursky with having a quick wit. Some thought he was better as an insult comic than he was with lines. Indeed, he changed onstage. Off it, his face was dead space, a sallow inert mask. It brightened in performance.

He remained a Woody Allen fan. In his room in his parents' apartment in Sherman Oaks, Bursky had movie posters and clips and photos of the owlish comic. He managed to meet him too.

> To a great guy and a credit to his race,

Allen had written on a poster of *Take the Money and Run*. On an 8x10 photo, Woody penned this:

> To my idol and inspiration from your protégé.

238

If Woody did not mind him, other comics did. The LA clan considered him a pesty hanger-on. It was not unwitting. Bursky claimed he did it to see what he could learn from other comics. Whatever his reason, he did not take hints well. When other comics told him to beat it, he stuck around.

Bursky was that way. He did what he had to— and lived with it, feeling no need to mitigate.

Q: Is it true you got material by getting writers women?

BURSKY: Oh, I always used to go to waitresses, right? At [Cafe] Brightwater or some place. Used to say, "Look, I got a cousin. He's a comedy writer. Writes for Johnny Carson. Makes a lot of money. Would you like to go out with him?" "Sure."

So I used to call up the comedy writer and say, "Look, I've got a cousin. A beautiful girl. She's a waitress. She'll go out with you." He goes, "Really?" "Yeah, just write me a few jokes and I'll fix you up with her."

When Bursky did his first "Tonight" shot, he suffered jitters the night before he was to go on. It was Brenner who helped him, a gesture that made him the Bernard Baruch of comics. Recalled Monaghan: "David gave him a tremendous amount of good advice, which blew my mind. I'm not accustomed to that among comics. I mean, David really took time and worked with him. See, the night before the Carson show, Alan did the routine in the Comedy Store with the attitude of *fuck you* and the thing bombed. It died. And so he was ready to quit the business.

"And so David said, 'You little shit.' And just grabbed him. And said, 'Now look, you didn't work the material. You didn't wait. You didn't do your pauses.' And held his head together. And really, I don't know him very well, just through Bursky, but it was a tremendous thing to do. Because most of them won't help each other."

When Alan was a parking attendant at the Comedy Store, he'd try to persuade agents and managers coming there that their best comic bet was to sign him. None of them paid him any mind. The day after the Carson shot, some of those agents were on the phone to him.

Success did not spoil Alan Bursky. He remained the same teen kong. One of his first acts was to draw up a list of fifty-three people he intended to "get." It was not all he did. When an agent sought to sign him, he told him to book a job out of town for another of Monaghan's comics so he could have the writer to himself. The agent did and Bursky signed with another one.

When a friend from New York came out, it was like the old days.

BURSKY: We went out and knocked off vending machines on the street.

Q: Like what kind? Newspapers?

BURSKY: Yeah, and things like that.

Don't be a comic, Ben Klein used to say when Robert smarted off as a kid, an admonition he ultimately chose to ignore.

He'd made his wise guy pay.

The boy who'd interrupt his mother's friends to confide that he'd been breast-fed—*Oh, what a mouth on that one*—now kidded around for fun and profit both, though if asked to be funny at family functions —*Do the dentist bit*—he'd beg off, considering it an insult to be on call. Unprovoked, he'd riff in company, monitoring what he said for future use.

Since 1967 he'd made a living being funny. In that time, he'd learned his business. He knew how to do an act and more. He could make it sound as if he'd just thought of it. He had tricks/techniques/call them what you want. Sometimes, he'd get a sly smile, as if a phrase had just occurred to him. It made whatever followed *feel* spontaneous. Certain pauses were, with Klein, calculated too. In a routine on the tribulations of teenage sex, he'd say,

> When I was sixteen, seventeen, I used to hang outside the drugstore, trying to work up courage to buy contraceptives. Padding my order.

KLEIN: *(to pharmacist):* Could I have four bathing caps, a tube of toothpaste and a-pack-of-*hhrrmmmms* . . . ? *(Shrugging.)* No, it's for my brother. He gave me a note.

> I would have *paid* a guy to do it for me. He could have made a fortune. A kind of . . .

—and here he'd wrinkle his face to suggest he was searching for the term—

> contraceptive purchasing agent.

Always that phrase, preceded by the ruminant pause. And when he said it, he used the microphone in a special way. He'd put it close to his mouth and empty "contraceptive purchasing agent" into it, giving it electronic italics. He did it with many phrases, talking them into the mike so they'd balloon from it. It stoked the laugh.

The techniques, though, were in service of a pulsing rhythm, one that made the insider's cognition beside the point. The rhythm seduced the knowing ear, and made it function on the comic beat. It was that way with any capable comic—and with material as disparate as Henny's or Lenny's. Rhythm was the magic, eureka in the bones. Some had it. Some didn't. It was the bedrock of style. At the Improv, Klein's influence could be heard in other comics. Consciously or not, they let him in their acts. Occasionally, Klein's girl friend, dancer/operatic singer Brenda Boozer, sounded like him when she was joking—words were stretched and shimmied in his sound.

Time in the clubs had given him the knack for dispatching hecklers. He rued the tradition, though. At a club in Boston, when he found the pimps' act had precedence over his, he skipped out early rather than shout over the commerce at the bar.

Like most comics he had prepared lines:

> The guy woke up this morning, said, "I think I'll go bug the Jew comic at [name of club]." Either that or hijack a plane. Take the TWA and fly it to the desert.

At the Bitter End (1972), he came across a fan of his who wanted to get in the act, a gray-haired man who'd obviously been into his cups.

> They told me it'll never happen. It's an ice cream joint. What's gonna happen? They said they serve frap-pays. A little chocolate soda. Coffee. Nothing heavy. The only thing I can figure is . . . you look like the kind of fellow who works well with your hands . . . airplane glue is the closest I could come.

The man, name Marty, was intent on turning the night into Abbott and Costello. Klein begrudgingly took him on, just before doing a song improvisation.

KLEIN: *(mock whisper):* Have they arrived yet with the . . . the Good Humor man . . . Who's got the thorazine? Put it in his frappe, will ya? Uh, the name of the song is—

MARTY: Uh, Bob, I'll give you oo-wahs in the background.

KLEIN: My enthusiasm is somewhat diminished for that idea, Marty. You've proved yourself to be a tremendous drag so far and uh—

MARTY: I have oo-wahs ready, in case.

THIRD
PARTY: You've got a case.

KLEIN: You've got a case alright. A good healthy case he's got. What is your profession, Marty?

MARTY: Mainly, I do dooo-wahs. I'm a professional for Capitol Records. Like for the Chiffons. They're dead now but I do a . . .

KLEIN: That's an appropriate job doing doo-wahs for dead people. 'Cause you're partially dead yourself. I don't know if anybody told you that. (*Audience laughs.*)

MARTY: I do all three voices.

KLEIN: I know. Go to someone else's show.

THIRD
PARTY: You're a shmuck.

MARTY: Hey, Bob let's get that guy later . . . after the show.

KLEIN: Marty, he called you a shmuck for one very simple reason. (*Laughter.*) I'm not sure if you know what that reason is. He called you a shmuck bec—You pick one, Marty.

A) You're a nice guy.
B) You're an intellectual.
C) You're rude.
D) You're a shmuck.

The next morning Klein got a telegram from him:

YOU WERE BEAUTIFUL LAST
NIGHT AS USUAL. I WOKE UP ON
THE WOODLAWN STATION EARLY
THIS A-M.

Marty was one of many fans of his. And if their
number was dwarfed by some other comics' followers,
they were (to judge by the mail-pull Klein got) a
bright lot.

There was, of course, a percentage of extremist mail
in the large manila envelopes where Klein kept his
correspondence. It came from people who offered to
help him gain an afterlife ("for as He, Himself said,
'I am the door: by me if any man enter in, he shall
be saved' ") and from those who feared they were
losing hold of their present one.

> *I desperately need help, someone to reach
> out to. I want to live but I don't feel I
> can any longer. Going on 28, I never
> really lived, I just existed from day to
> day, inhaling and exhaling. A woman
> whom no one ever gave a damn about
> and has been kept a prisoner in a home
> filled with domineering people and a lot
> of hatred.*
> *Please, Bob, I'd just like to talk to you.
> My phone is . . .*

If most of it was more normal, it asked nonetheless
to be handled with care. Much of it was in lady's
hand. And not a few averred to getting-together some
time, in the shrinking prose of apologia.

He used to answer the post, wanting to oblige, to
please. It Ms-fired mostly, brought more candid re-
plies, often with a lonelyhearts note he hadn't bar-
gained for. He responded selectively now. The strokes
were in the jokes.

Up top of the act, Klein liked to let the crowd know
it was not word for word what he'd said before. He
usually did it by periscoping the place. If he worked

a revolving stage in Westbury, Long Island, he'd come out and say,

> If you stay here, do an act, you actually gain six months of life,

then bend over, reach for the floor and announce:

> I feel like the tone arm on a record player.

At Fairleigh Dickinson, he kidded the academic standing of the school:

> It's in Lovejoy's College Guide. "Will accept you from the top hundred and six percent of your class. If you can reach the bursar with twenty dollars, you can come."

It was a comedic hullo. A comic once told him of the time he'd worked a joint filled with sailors. He was sinking fast when he happened to mention the name of a ship. After that, he was okay. He called out ships all night to nonstop cheers.

Klein modified the approach. Dangerfield taught him—"Know who these people are." Klein would try to. He'd ask around, hoping for a fact or two about them he could use in an "inside" line.

It helped but only for the night. Klein's long-term comic was still in trouble in 1972. Vegas had wised him up on that score. His calendar at the beginning of the year caught him in transition—resort dates at Kutscher's/Downingtown Inn/Mt. Airy Lodge against the coffeehouse kind: Bitter End/My Father's Place/The Bijou Cafe.

Without a name in the rock world, he was often the low end of the bill. At the C. W. Post campus, the attraction was Sha Na Na, not him. Sha: a rock group that affected the greaser look of the '50s, doing the do-wop of a day long past. It drew rough trade, none too eager for comic relief.

"The emcee goes out," Klein remembered, "and they don't quiet down. Kid from the school: 'Atten-

245

tion, please.' Nothing. 'Let's go. We're not gonna have a show less you . . .' Somebody yells out, FUCK YOU. Guy says, 'WELL, FUCK YOU TOO.' Now this is just before I'm going on. I said, oh shit."

To change it, he was doing college dates, usually for less money. If he got a thousand dollars at Downingtown Inn, he was lucky to earn half of that on the campuses. It was the price he paid for 33⅓ anonymity. In a few instances, he even worked for free on the chance it'd lead to college bookings.

He did it on the West Coast when the concert department of CMA found he was Robert-who? to college buyers out there. Doug Weston, owner of LA's key room, the Troubadour, knew the name but in a bad way. Since '67, he told agents he was not inKleined to have him back. For CMA's sake, Robert agreed to do a no-pay guest shot at the Troubadour, hoping to sway Weston in the bargain.

He had qualms about "auditioning" but he did it back East too—for a conference of college talent buyers at Grossinger's. Not only did he work for free but he kept his act to twenty-five minutes—under a twenty-dollar-a-minute penalty for exceeding the limit. Staggered lights signaled the time remaining. The stipulation applied to all acts. Klein was one of the few acts there with major TV exposure.

It was hardly what he had in mind the night he sat down at the Avery. It chafed even more when he was told the emcee, comic Chris Rush, already had used a bit similar to one of his. In that, Robert spoke of the euphemisms parents had for private parts, a baby-talk biology at odds with adult experience:

> I submit—the world ain't like that. When you grow up, the doctor is not going to examine you and say, "I'm afraid it's your poo poo, Bob. I'm going to have to perform a poo-pooectomy. You have Blue Cross? Fine."

> The draft board, they do not go, "Everybody line up. Show your tu tu to the sergeant. I said, tu tu, soldier. Not poo poo.

246

Poo poo's Monday morning oh-six hundred."

Rush claimed his bit dealt with bodily functions,
not parts, a distinction Klein dismissed. Coming off
the stage twenty-five minutes later he was muttering,
"Fucking idiot. I could have used that poo poo tu tu."
Aggravation.

The $6,178.48 Klein invested was a hedge against
more of it. He'd sunk the money into recording his
act, and distilled six and a half hours to forty-five
minutes of tape. Soon after, he found a buyer for it,
a Coast record company, Signpost. It agreed to print
the album, but calls to its office to finalize the contract invariably found the boss there busy, giving
Klein a portent of what would be once the record was
out. If Signpost didn't care, who then?

Neil Bogart was who.

Bogart was co-president of Buddah Records. He'd
become a rock mogul while in his twenties with what
the industry referred to as bubble-gum music. It was
a teeny bopper sound (circa 1967) typified by the
song "Yummy Yummy Yummy" (he-had-love-in-his-
tummy). It was Bogart's answer to the six-figure ad-
vances acid rock groups were paid at the time. He
produced bubble-gum smashes for $1500/$2000 ad-
vances.

Before that he'd been a singer under the name Neil
Scott. When he was seventeen he'd had a "semi hit"
called "Bobby" about a dying girl revived by the bedside appearance of her sweetheart. Another song of his
was on a boy's confession to his priest. Bogart, who is
Jewish, researched it by spending three days in St.
Patrick's Cathedral "to get a feel." The record flopped.

Bogart made out better on the executive end. He
and Buddah had a series of hits, including a comedy
album, David Frye's *Richard Nixon, Superstar*. Bogart, it turned out, was a fan of Klein's. When he
learned the deal with Signpost was tottering, he arranged a new one. He put Klein's manager, Buddy
Morra, on to Brut, the toiletries division of Fabergé.
Brut had an entertainment subsidiary with its own rec-

ord label. Morra negotiated a new and better deal than the one with Signpost. The advance was twenty-five thousand dollars. And Buddah was to distribute the album.

Robert Klein: Child of the '50s it was called. The hope was that the nostalgia craze the country was in the midst of would run the album up the charts. The '50s theme recurred in the material on the record, and its cover shot. It was a photo of Klein in a bedroom made up to resemble the one he'd had back then. In it were '50s memorabilia: baseball cards, erector set, Kingston Trio album, football helmet, cap gun, a satin Yankee jacket, actual photos of the short-haired Klein himself. It even had a DeWitt Clinton pennant that Buddah tried to obtain from the school. Clinton authorities refused unless they could hear the album first. The pennant ended coming from a Bronx sporting goods store.

On the back cover were more mementos of the '50s: a tattered copy of *Catcher in the Rye,* a Tootsie Roll wrapper, civil defense dogtags (Klein, R.M. 3525 Decatur Avenue) a jackknife and a coaster with the famed Marilyn Monroe nude. Sunflower seeds were placed over nipples so as not to offend merchandisers.

With the record, he was ready to take his 33⅓ word on the road, and see what it'd fetch. What it came to was playing catch-up in the neocomic trade. As one of its early, prolific and literate voices, Klein was yet to get the turnout he wanted. Out of the old comedy and into the new: jumping-off point for a tour to promote the LP came at the

BITTER END

in late February 1973.

The Bitter End remained a name to conjure with.* The red brick wall that Peter, Paul, and Mary popularized on an early album cover was still there. So was the club's precarious location—just beneath several floors of apartments. From time to time residents still

---

* A year later—with the advent of a nearby club, the Bottom Line, and a change in management—it wasn't.

phoned the police about the noise. It made the Bitter End's Paul Colby wary of amplified musicians. Colby was a cryptic man given to blue work shirts and denims and thirty-dollar Stetsons. An ex-music publisher, furniture designer, artist, he was more relaxed out of the club. In it he had the dark eye, particularly for raucous rock. "You trying to put me out of business?" he'd ask musicians who played loudly.

For Klein the Bitter End was the closest thing to his comic turf. He'd been there in '64 to play the hootenanies, and could still recall other hopefuls knocking around then. Like David Frye, who'd belly up to the men's room mirror to snarl "You dirty rat" at it. Or Richie Havens, who'd do his soulful sound for busking money.

On Bleecker Street, long lines of people queued up to see Klein. A New York crowd it was—hard-core fans who'd leave flowers, or cigars (Casa de Rey, *formerly made in Havana*) before the show, and come by after for hullo. In the city, he was a winner. Marty the heckler was back—this year the gray-haired fan was sober and silent. One night, two girls sent a note. WE TEACH YIDDISH AND POSE FOR PORNO. *Hold all calls,* Klein kidded, closing the door behind him.

Another night, a letter was waiting for him from a mother in Little Neck, New York. She wanted to fix him up with her daughter, a twenty-six-year-old

> . . . *who has been seeing this "creep" for about 2½ years. I keep saying to her— "Why can't you find a fellow like Robert Klein?"*

She assured him they'd have much in common.

Since he'd last been at the Bitter End, the dressing area had undergone alterations. What remained unchanged was the men's room, toilet facilities he swore no human hand dared touch:

> I'm the Ralph Nader of men's rooms. And that's the Corvair of New York City. If they ever call back a toilet, that's number one.

The laughs came in rips at the Bitter End. It was the blood jolt the Knicks got on 33rd Street, or James Brown at the Apollo. The room was a small one, its seats like church pews in a three-sided arrangement. When laughs came, they were like thunder in a phone booth.

It had an effect on Klein, nudging his energy up a notch or two. In the five nights he was there, he was often reluctant to leave stage. For late shows in particular, he'd exceed the fifty-minute hour he usually did. The laughs were quick-hit, as if the crowd was in sync with him and wanted to propel him to the next bit of fun. One night a contingent began to sway side to side to the song finale Klein did.

> Hold it. I'm getting nauseous,

he quipped.

He was loose up there. One performance he did Rod McKuen—syrupy phrases in the talk/song the poet used, the scratchy voice against the backup sound pianist Phil Galdston provided. And afterward he told the audience:

> He had nodes implanted in his voice. Transplanted from Andy Devine in 1948. You didn't know about that, did you? Then Andy Devine became Dennis Day. No one knew all these things were happening. They were in conspiracy.

Even with Colby, he kidded. He played the temperamental star:

> Colby (*backstage*): Time to go on.
> Klein: Not till Soviet Jewry are released.

At the Bitter End, Klein's urban material went over big. He did a comedic Cook's tour through Manhattan island. On 57th Street, there was the panhandler who looked like Khrushchev and wore a woolen hat and

> had a bit that was *unbeatable*. How can you pass an old man going

—here he bent over from the waist and yowled:

> "P'LEEEAASSE, P'LEEEAASSE.
> *MANGE.* P'LEASE."

> Gave him a quarter, half, dollar bill.
> I would have written him checks, any-
> thing. One night he blew his bit . . . I saw
> him loading his belongings into a Buick
> Electra behind the New York Athletic
> Club.

> I felt like such a shmuck. I really did. I
> said, "Hey, *P'lease,* come here." I didn't
> know what to call him.

> I was working at NBC in Burbank, Cali-
> fornia. I come out to the parking lot.
> There's a guy in front of my car going,
> "P'LEEEAASSE." . . . It's-a-franchise.

> He sells P'LEEEAASSE kits. For failures.

> *Failure:* I'm nothing now, honey, but in
>   ten days after my pls, pliz,
>   please, pleese, P'LEEEAASSE—

> His wife gives a quarter. "Oh, it's you,
> you son of a . . ."

He took his audience on late-night shopping at
Smiler's, the twenty-four-hour grocery chain, each
branch of which came with a hostile West Indian sandwich man. YOU WAHNT LETTUCE, MON? A cast
of thousands in there, some of them solid-looking cit-
izens until it came to ordering:

> "Give me three thousand Yankee Doo-
> dles, four thousand Hershey bars and a
> pack of Camels."

It was then a fellow noticed the sweet-toothed late-
nighter scratching his junkie face.

Klein caught the bittersweet spirit of the city for those stuck on the place, a tribe of survivors—from the high- to the low-life form.

> I don't know. I like people that hold on in the misery and the adversity of the city. You ever see a guy fishing at 125th Street and the Hudson River . . . ? That is *patience.*
>
> I mean, supposing he did catch something. Could you imagine what kind of bullyock sick monster fish that'd be? Come out of the water, BOOM—

He tilted his eyes up, became big-jawed.

Sick
Monster
Fish: Get that goddamn hook out of my mouth. What . . . does that tickle, you moron? (*Snatches boldly.*) Gimme that bait, you son of a bitch. Twenty years dodging tugboats, I'm gonna fall for that hook, you rube?

Dangerfield was there Klein's last night. Rodney and he were not as tight as before. Back in the late '60s, they had traveled around together. An odd couple in the eyes of some. *Do you bother him, hanging around?* Ben Klein would ask. Rodney's cronies wondered too. Klein was a new one on them—with the politics, Bach and whatnot.

He and Dangerfield got on though. Down to Jersey, up to the Cape they went, Rodney at the wheel, using words the way a man on the lam would fix up a satchel, jamming it full and fast. Klein was left with the slack corners of the conversation. He did not mind. Dangerfield's line was lively, even in its recurring funks. *It's all bullshit, man.* Dit dit dit. He had the heart. He felt life and fought it and knew it some too, in his own idiosyncratic way.

Behind a wheel, he went full tilt also, charging

through traffic as if Upper Broadway were on speed-way regulations. More than once he'd had accidents. Sometimes, Klein worried over the way he endangered his old bones. He felt himself occasionally inverting the customary roles—the kid fussing after the fogy.

It changed. They got busy, saw each other less. Some sore points developed. Why'd-he-say-this? What'd-he-mean-by-that? *It's all bullshit. It's all cock,* was, Klein claimed, Rodney's way of shouldering past conversation. One night, Klein stopped in at Dangerfield's place after long-time-no-see. Rodney began talking. Two and a half hours he went without asking Klein what he'd been up to. When Robert remarked on the oversight, Rodney begged off. *Hey whaddaya want from me, man?*

Now when they got together, their conversation came with shadows. It was a friendship that looked over its shoulder. That last night at the Bitter End, Dangerfield remarked on the time Klein did on stage. *Long set, man. Long one.* What'd he mean by that? Klein wondered.

If the Bitter End promoted intimacy,

MY FATHER'S PLACE

in Roslyn, Long Island, did not. It was a long deep room, a bowling alley converted to a club. Built like a German beer hall, it had rows of tables with red cloths covering them. Hard drinks were served.

The club's rotund proprietor, Michael Epstein, brought Klein on as

> . . . a comic who's a favorite here. Just cut an album for Brut—the guys that make cologne and dildoes.

It made Klein a comic the crowd could be at home with. Any man mentioned in the same breath with dildoes couldn't be all bad.

Out in Roslyn, Klein's energy was not as super-volted as it was on Bleecker Street. The audience did not give him the oomph it did in the city.

Klein worked his comic anyway, making it snap

253

to the moment. If he did not usually look to provoke scenarios, he did not avoid them either. Once on a TV show, he'd followed a six-year-old organist name of Lucky Peterson, and said,

> Lucky Peterson. He's too much. If you think he's something, you should see his wife backstage.

In Roslyn, he worked that way too. When the mike loosened and slid down, in Vegas parlance he "did time" on it:

> Is this mike impotent, or am I growing?

> Alice: Did I have a cookie?

In another routine Klein pointed out the dilemma a handshake posed. Where once it was a uniform gesture, it no longer was. The youth culture had its own "hip" clasp, one that in collision with the conventional handshake led, he said, to permanent deformity.

> Ya ever see a freak walk around like this?

he asked, curling his thumb back irreversibly.

> It's not from hitching. It's from the period of transition,

he said.

To explore the technicalities of "handshake conflict," Klein used a female demonstrator in the routine. *We'll be passing our hands around shortly so you can look closely.* That night, to draw her closer to the microphone, he put his arm on her shoulder. Immediately, she nuzzled against him. He took the laugh she got and upped it, singing Johnny Mathis lyrics while cheek to cheek with her. As she pressed up against him, he asked the familiar '50s question:

> Wanna get pinned?

Performing was just part of the push. Promotion figured too. He was previewed, reviewed and TViewed in every city he went. Buddah got to work lining up the rock journalists to have Klein defined for the record-buying public. *Rolling Stone/Rock/The Boston Phoenix/L.A. Free Press.* Dit dit dit: The answers offered times before came smooth-tonguing down again, often with the same images winking like jewels for this interrogator and the next, offered with no hint of boredom. He'd answer straight out.

The calendar was crammed with appointments aimed at putting the word out on The Product, as Buddah personnel referred to the record *cum* poster package that was *Child of the 50's.* In New York, the FM radio stations were giving it air play. Buddah had made a special edition of the album with "obscenities" bleeped out for the convenience of disk jockeys. WNEW-FM, a leading Manhattan rock station, was playing cuts from the album in the early days of March with regularity. At Rollins and Joffe, it was the station the office's audio system was tuned to, giving secretary Rita Donovan (unaccustomed to rock) a severe earache. She much preferred the soft strings heard before the album was released.

To pump The Product, Klein got into his green Mercedes on a gray morning in March, and drove to Philadelphia to talk it up on a midday taping of "The Mike Douglas Show." Standing back of the closed partition, he got into a three-point football stance and, as he heard his introduction, said, "Begin smile." Beaming and erect as the curtain parted, he emerged, did his minutes, and got back into the car for a short ride to Cherry Hill, New Jersey, where

KAL RUDMAN,

the record tipster, lived.

Rudman was a plump man with a mild demeanor that belied a sharkish ego. Out of his split-level house on Hilltop Court, Rudman wrote "Money Music," a column that appeared in *Record World* magazine, and he edited the *Friday Morning Quarterback,* a tip sheet considered important in the music business. He also did promotion work for record companies. Simply put, it meant that sometimes the tip sheet (subscribed to by broadcast and music-business people) touted the records Rudman was hired to push.

In his spacious den, Rudman ran the afternoon like a ringmaster. Up to answer a phone. Back down to hold forth on the state of 33⅓, addressing Klein, Morra and a Buddah promotion man, Buck Reingold.

On hand too was Rudman's twelve-year-old son, Mitchell, a junior sharpie who informed Klein, "I have some ego-shattering news for you. I just called a friend to tell him you're here and he doesn't know who you are." Said Klein: "I am a household word . . . like Clint Hartung."

Back and forth it went, the senior Rudman talking in the bop prosody he favored—*Mort Sahl, when he was hot, was kicking ass and taking names*—then zeroing in on Klein. Who-when-where he wanted. Klein gave it to him in a flash bio that occasionally resorted to his own routines to cover a question. Finally Rudman said, "Let's talk about the album."

KLEIN: (*with mocking innocence*): What album is that? (*Laughter.*) Should I leave the room?

REIN-
GOLD: He's going to be the biggest comedian ever.

RUDMAN: He better be . . . as bad as you guys need the money.

Rudman and Reingold went off to confer. On their return, Kal did a (first-person) singular riff with a splatter of jive phrases: *You gotta carry the bag, bob 'n' weave, shuck 'n' jive . . . forty-three years old, man, in my head, I'm eighteen . . . I'm Peter Pan . . . sprinkle stardust Bill Withers "sprinkle stardust on me" . . . it's like pro football . . . boxing . . . the difference is the blood doesn't show.*

Kal finished strong, sent them off with the disk jockey dit dit he did back in 19 and 59 in Camden, New Jersey.

> Uh-uh uh-uh uh-uh, don't touch that ra-
> dio dial, cats, it's your Uncle Kal, your
> big-beat pal, smokin' in from the blue-
> denim pad, like a dungaree den—deep
> deep deep *deep* in the dingy dungeons of
> WCAM. We do-da-do play more riff rock
> and boss beltin' bebop than any rock jock
> on radio.

A virtuoso performance.

Said Reingold: "Sometimes you have to take five steps backwards to go six steps forward."

That night Klein opened at the

MAIN POINT

in Bryn Mawr, Pennsylvania. In his dressing room was a balloon mobile with a card attached: *Hi, Robert!* A sign on a wall said, *Smoking—tobacco only please.*

The Main Point was situated just down the road from Bryn Mawr College. It drew a smart set if graffiti were any indication. A lavatory sampling:

> *Pray for atheism.*
>
> *Are there really urinals in the Vatican?/
> Only for communion.*
>
> *Eat it raw (that is an organic joke).*
>
> *Nostalgia just isn't what it used to be.*
>
> *Fatty Arbuckle lives.*
>
> *The nicest thing you can do for an enemy
> is merely to be his friend/*(Another hand-
> writing) *Catchy but what does it mean?*
> (A third signatory) *See you in him and
> him in you.*

Opening night, while he was on, Klein heard an alarm ONK ONK ONK, a deep gravelly sound from the streets.

he said.

The closest he came to a bomb was a few days later at the Main Point. Early show/Saturday night. He drew a crowd whose laughs were not the full-blown beauties he was used to. It showed. He lost his silk. He phumphed. His nerve ends gave him away. Time and again, he went to a colored bandana to mop his brow. At least a dozen times he used it.

He became more wordy. When laughs were slow, he'd cut a routine short and try another. The beat was gone. The stitching showed. He drifted to the onstage piano, and leaned against it.

Empty the house. A new audience in. He went at it again. This time he had a crowd that was with him. High-octane laughs. It made his comic jump. Words spilled out and never hedged. Quicksilver-smooth his line was. He worked stride's distance from the piano, and not once went to the bandana.

So it went in the comic trade. Fortunes turned, not always so rapidly to be sure. When Klein was at the

CELLAR DOOR

in 1967, in Washington, D.C., it was to experience the first "flop sweat" of his career. Back then, he referred to himself as the pseudonymous *$4.50* of Josh White's billing.

Times changed. Fat Charlie, the *wunderkind* owner, was gone. Word was he was a street musician in London, getting by. And now Klein came in as a headliner, re-routed as a dungaree comic.

If no one knew him in 1967, it was not the case now. On his arrival, Klein found a gift waiting for him. It was a red-white-and-blue knitted coverall for the genitalia that came with a note: "Warmest wishes for your every comfort in the coldest weather." No name was signed.

Less anonymous was the D.C.-area promotion man for Buddah. Bernie Block was the name, a peppery man in a toupee and monochromatic pants and shirts outfits, the Miami Beach lobby look. The fortyish

Block talked in a black dialect that lapsed to the Balti-morean vowels on occasion. Words like Coca-Cola were run up through the nasal passage and emerged pinched.

It was Block who chauffeured Klein to radio/TV shows to promote the album. Its success, he said, was guaranteed. He intended to swing his weight behind it. *Ahm gonna bust yaw album,* Bernie swore. How he proposed to do it he never mentioned. It was beside the point. He was a few laughs.

Whether meticulously brushing his toupee as he whirled through capital traffic, or remarking on the street action, Bernie had the boyo's flair that was back of legitimate comic pros. In him it was tied to sales techniques.

Lines: Block's best came when he told how he'd solved his boy's limited Talmudic gift in having him bar mitzvahed:

> I asked the rabbi could we have the ser-
> vice lip-synced.

Klein got one off in the dressing room, when a leggy beauty inquired after the British rock musician who opened the show. "Know where Colin is?" she asked.

> Lower intestine,

said Robert.

It went well at the Cellar Door. He left there with $2,238 for a short week's work. (Other returns: Bitter End: $3,147.80/My Father's Place $1,500/Main Point $1,500.) It was not Vegas dollar. But if he was working for less, he was enjoying it more. And the coffeehouses were one phase of the commerce only. There were college and concert dates where one night's haul could double the take of a week in Roslyn, Long Island.

Not to mention the record. In every city, he was booked on radio/TV shows to talk up the album. *Robert Klein: Child of the 50's.* Brut. Sell. Sell. Sell. He sold *begin smile* and wondered would it amount to anything. Early ripples were promising. New Jersey reordered a thousand more albums, New York three thousand extra. Korvette's this, Sam Goody's that. No surprise: he was strong in New York. It was out of it he was not so sure of.

Klein had an image: an attache case with an 8x10 glossy in it, a photo of him. In his mind, it stood for each and every comic. *You're selling you, man. They don't like you, ain't no way to hide it.*

Where he went, the 8x10 Klein was with him, a rough-hewn face with large Borgnine teeth, clefted chin, long dark hair. It was a Klein divined by the listening/looking public as a literate comic cat, one able to take nuances of human experience and make them funny in the playback. At that "Klein," he was fine.

Another story he was when out of comic. Getting laughs was a flash taste that begged another. Klein got his in whisps to the deep. *Can't imagine anyone going through life with no highs,* he said.

Some days he got into moods. The eye and mouth that enlivened his expression crumpled, so his face was the retreat of a stooped psyche, too weary to assert what was best in it. Often it led a life of its own back of whatever words came out him, an unkempt visitor in the mind's parlor.

With strangers, he managed to put the bright face on, even while in a gray funk of his own. It was etiquette, and more. He liked to be liked. He'd do verbal somersaults as easily as Scrooge did humbug.

It was what propelled him (and others) as a comic. To be locked in to chug-a-lug laughs was a good time. And Klein, typical of working pros, was wary of losing any part of it. Nights when laughs came, he was aware of even one soul holding out on him. In the hour before he was to go on again, he'd chart that point—the bit, the phrase—that finally convulsed the bastard.

There came a night some time later when an attractive blonde in a front-row seat sat deadpan through a Klein performance that had the rest of the audience bent over. He began by eyeing her, trying to fathom why, and ended by doing lines to her on the chance he could get her by direct dialing. She was, it turned out, French, and limited in her English, a fact which, when relayed to Klein, made him feel better.

One night at the Bijou in Philadelphia, a woman caught his eye in performance and silently mouthed I LOVE YOU, so startling him that he looked away, lest he lose the fine humming line he had going at the time. Laughs, man. They were what cranked the comic.

And to get them, Klein was Thomas Alva with his act. He had a routine on diseases that exploit guilt in commercials. A forlorn man faces the camera, holds out a hand and says, "I have one kidney. Gimme a dollar." A funny premise but too close to reality (he found). So, to nail the laughs . . .

> Hello, I have no kidneys. I'm gonna die next week. This is my family. Gimme a dollar. That's "Kidney," Box 816, Radio City Station. . . .

One night a fellow approached Klein and said his mother had died of kidney disease and he found the bit in "bad taste." That he went to the lengths to explain why he did the routine was typical of Klein's dealings with people. He was aware of others, even in eluding them. To a medical student (and a fan of his) who invited him to stop by his flat, he did a panicky "take" and said, "Can't stand the sight of blood, Doc," letting him down gently.

He was the function of his tension. The comic face made the best of it, though angst was always beneath the surface. It had been as long as he could remember, back to the pinched quarters in the Bronx, where words were rat-a-tat against the oy-vay ways of an inimical world. The unsparing view was taken. If Robert reported a 95 test score, pappa Ben wondered where the other five points were.* Life was seen as an adversary system. *I remember,* said Klein, *exchanges between my father and mother and the landlord:*

---

* A query that might come with a wink, though. For Pater Klein had the comic touch too—whether trading quips with cronies in New York's garment center or doing slapstick with young son Robert in Aunt Anna's parlor on Pelham Parkway.

"Drop dead."

"You first."

"No, you. Then we get the apartment."

"You'll have to roll us outa here."

"I hope it's tomorrow."

The landlord was the enemy, Mac.

A month after he was through at the Cellar Door, Klein was to marry Brenda Boozer, an easygoing Southern girl whose nature was more tranquil than his. Indeed, early in the relationship, Ms. Boozer spent a day with the Kleins and returned afterward to the Riverside Drive apartment she shared with Robert. *I'd never been with people like this. Such nervous people, such tense people.* "Hello, dahling, get-in-the-car, get-in-the-car . . . Benny, watch-the-car, watch-the-car/I'm watching, I'm watching./Go-ahead-then. No, Benny . . ." *You couldn't believe it.*

With Klein, anxiety turned in at times and immobilized him, the mood occupying him like a suit several sizes too large. "See everything with Robert—and this what I see in his parents too—everything is on a dynamic level which is very high," said Brenda Boozer. "Nothing is simplified. Everything is overcomplicated."

Q: Can you particularize?

She did: If, in that mood, Klein had petty chores to do—return phone calls/take the car to the garage—he'd make them epic in scope, mind-boggling their simple execution. When he finally undertook them, he was okay. It was in monster forethought the trouble began.

MS.
BOOZER: It's like he was complaining about people in his dressing room. How can he get his head together to do another show? How

can he do it? Be by himself. Listen to his tapes. Just be quiet a minute. People aren't sensitive to that. You have to help them along. And Robert—he says, "Ya, that's a pretty good idea." But see, when you do that, you're facing the reality that in ten minutes you have to go on and that it does exist. But not sending them out is like it's not really going to happen. You know what I'm saying?

Klein beat around the countryside, booming his comic, drumming up business. To the Quiet Knight in Chicago. The Bijou in Philadelphia. Passim's in Cambridge, Massachusetts. W-this W-that. The strategy was paying. The calendar was filling with the dates he wanted. Busy busy: it was when he was happiest. It made his cash outlay for the album a smart investment.*

By late April he'd been hard at it for two months. Days before he was to be married, he was scheduled to make still another appearance, this one for a Manhattan cable-TV station. A limousine was sent for him.

Klein came onto the street. He was weary-looking. His face had the puffy quality it got when he was fatigued. He climbed into the limousine, plumped himself into the soft leather seat and sighed. Then he raised up a second and asked to change seats with the passenger next to him. He nodded to the rearview mirror up front of him. It was angled so he could see himself. Klein didn't want to.

---

* Earnings 1973: more than $150,000.

263

Part Three

Old Pop came undone.

This was just after WWII.

The wife died. He took up with a young Spanish dancer. It was the end of the ocarina man in the amateurs.

For when he came by, it was in store-bought suits the dancer insisted on. "What can I do?" he complained. "She won't let me wear my uniform."

It blew the act. Pop in a Botany Bay looked like a reformed derelict and not the Spirit of '76. In the bars, he became just another guy.

And so it went with comics too.

Vaughn Meader once mimicked President John F. Kennedy for a living. An album he made, *First Family,* sold 4.5 million copies.

With Kennedy's assassination, Meader's career destructed. In those days, he drank too much and was querulous when he did. One night a man he belabored put an end to it. He looked up from the bar, studied

Vaughn up and down and said, "I thought you were dead." Meader slinked off.

For those alive in it, the gag racket was a tonic.

Old comics were as spry as any men this side of Bernarr MacFadden. Youngman kidded,

> I'm sixty-six and it takes me all night to do what I used to do all night,

but in public places he carried miniature currency and trick gadgets that could be bought in Times Square novelty stores.

And he still did the jokes. There he was in the 1973–74 Manhattan telephone directory

Youngman Henny   77 W55 - - - - - - - LT 1-7755
ready to go to work if the money was right. In Manhattan, Youngman manned Dial-a-Joke. Ring up 999-3838 in April 1974, and prerecorded Henny was on the line—some days with a laugh track no less.

Over at *The New York Times* was a long blue folder rubber-stamped ADVANCE OBIT and bulging with clips for Berle, Milton. But the lead paragraph on it was a long way off to judge by the way Berle carried on. His schedule was crammed with working dates.

At any age, it was exhilarating to be on. Often when comics were together, even informally, the one doing jokes stood.

M
E

was what it came to.

Harry Morton was familiar with it. He was an ex-Catskill comic who knocked around with (and sometimes did business for) top pros, people like Morey Amsterdam, Phil Foster, Corbett Monica, Jan Murray, Buddy Hackett. He'd had comics over his house for dinner and seen them stare at their image in the window and talk to it the entire evening.

Q: You've seen this?

MORTON: Absolutely. I don't make these things up. They'll walk in and it gets darker and a pane of glass . . . if they see their reflection . . . the whole night will be spent looking into their reflection . . . playing to it.

Being on was a comic rite. Not a new one, either. George Burns remembered an afternoon in a Broadway restaurant when a comic name of Harry Rose began to scream, "I know where it is, I know where it is," and bolted from his table, out onto the avenue. Rose ran, drawing a crowd. He covered several blocks before he stopped, opened a trash can, removed a straw hat, put it on and said, "That's where it was."

A semi-evil genius at the comic prank was Pat McCormick, a gagwriter pal of Jonathan Winters. During an earthquake in LA, McCormick picked up the phone while the city shuddered and dialed a comic to say,

The God Is Dead rally has been canceled,

and hung up.

To celebrate the baptism of his baby boy, McCormick had chums of his over for a sit-down dinner. After drinks, he disappeared a moment, returning with a silver platter that he set down on the table, revealing the wee McCormick surrounded by carrot and onion trimmings. Taking hold of the infant's member, he asked, "Who wants the Pope's nose?"

At a wake for his mother, a hearty woman who was a great fan of McCormick's diabolic schemes, Pat sent her out in style. The afternoon began routinely with a viewing of the body. Then the mourners —mostly comedy people—retreated to folding chairs, and sat quietly. Not for long. One of them remarked in the voice of John Wayne. McCormick came back as Clark Gable. Someone else as Walter Brennan. Soon, full-scale "bits" were going.

The sound of footsteps was heard. Chuck McCann,

the comic, looking mournful, muttering the solemn phrases . . . *Sorry . . . my condolences* . . . incredulous at the laughter his sentiments provoked. Ten minutes later, he was in on the giggles too.

Finally, new footsteps. A straight couple. Friends of the mother's. This time, the group exercised restraint. McCormick ushered the couple to the casket, stood a moment back of them and dropped his pants.

With the kid comics it was not so antic.

What they did was to detour conversations. The crunch for material was behind it.

Material was more crucial in the age of electronic comics. It was why Steinberg lost some of the glitter that made him a *New York Times Sunday Magazine* subject a few seasons back. On TV, he was ditto David, same material again and again.

It was what kept the wheels turning. "Always looking for premises," said Richard Lewis, "And I mean it's hard to breathe sometimes. I mean, it's hard to live. How can I describe this now? Always looking for something comedic is a defense from really being yourself. And if you have trouble being yourself, that's an easy out—to find humor in the situation. It's hard to really stay straight. If I do now, it's because I know how important it is. You see a lot of the old comics going, dah-dah-dah . . . yadda yadda yadda—turning into that kind of monster. And it would be . . . I mean, it's a nightmare to me to think that I would ever be that way. So I make an effort now.

"It's like all of a sudden, I hear something said. And it clicks in my mind. I get a connection and a premise. I'm certain there's a twinkle in my eye and I sort of, my whole energy level goes up a notch. And I'm still myself but I'm not as relaxed. Even with comedian friends of mine, most of whom are pretty real and nice and not performing . . . when we're talking or they're talking to other people and something comes up, I *know*, man, when I see that twinkle in their eyes, they are on to a premise and they are not just dealing person to person. They are, in a sense, performing and seeing how it goes over.

"See, coming up with a line is a great feeling. It's

an absolutely fantastic feeling. And when I'm with people, I just want to relax a little and not think of comedy. But if I come up with a premise, I try to leave the room and go to the john and take out my pad and scribble it down. Because I really don't like doing it in a social situation.

"Most guys carry pads. In fact, today when I was coming here, I said, 'Gee, I'm gonna be interviewed. I'll be driving in. Will there be any time between driving? Maybe I'll think of something while I'm sitting there or when I'm driving home.' So I brought my pad.

"It's tough because if I'm driving on the West Side Highway, I can't pull over. I get my pad out and jot it down as I'm driving. Because it'd be painful to forget it. And sometimes you lose ideas because you can't decipher them. And it's very painful. In fact, I call people up. It's been embarrassing. Went to a party, and I scribbled down something quickly, and I couldn't read it. And I went absolutely wild. And I call them up and say, 'By the way, when I was talking about . . .'

"The first time I was turned on to the pad was with Morty Gunty. He was driving around New York. And I was talking. And he thought of something while I was talking. At that point, it didn't piss me off. Because I sort of had no claims to anything. He was the comic. And I was just rapping. But it was funny because he pulled down his visor. And he had a pad there with a little pencil. One of those Statue of Liberty pads that you buy like for a quarter with a funny little pencil. And he'd . . . he was jotting it down while he was driving. And I thought that he was really bizarre. He told me that he had pads in every room of his house. He said he had pads wherever he went. Gee, what a way to live . . . and not long after, I followed suit.

"Brenner too. He's a basic pad comic. He always writes things down. I find though like . . . it's weird when I'm standing with some of the comics at the Improv, there's a very tough moment when we're all bullshitting and . . . we build on each other's

269

stuff and get ideas and you have to figure out did it come from you or another guy.

"One time, we were talking and I noticed something funny. I forget exactly what it was. But I immediately got out my pad. And all the other comics were talking. And as soon as I got out my pad . . . silence. They all got uptight. They all thought they missed something."

Few old comics needed pads.

They were not in the business of creating jokes.

Telling them was their work. And at that, they were at ease anywhere. Berle, in the Improvisation one night, ended on stage, wondering, as he put it, "if this is an audition and I don't know it."

Thoroughly modern Miltie he wasn't. But he was quick. When the phone rang and he quipped,

>I'm canceled!

he was the perfect foole.

The jokes he had were good, bad, borrowed and bought, most of them the passing thought of gag men, a group often in need of help after working with comics. It happened to Marty Farrell, who landed on a psychiatric couch after almost a decade as a gag writer. What put Farrell under was a comic who insisted Marty's jokes were not up to par and demanded his money back—under threat of having both of Farrell's legs broken.

While in college, Jim Mulholland was hired as a gagwriter for "The Tonight Show," a welcome reprieve from working with stand-ups. One time, he went to see a ventriloquist-comic to finalize a fifty-dollar-a-week-deal. When Mulholland quoted the price, the man began to hem and haw. Finally, he went to the box where the dummy was kept.

VENTRIL-
  OQUIST: Bruce, this kid wants fifty dollars a week to work.

  BRUCE: What's the matter with twenty-five a week? I mean, the kid's only seventeen.

VENTRIL-
OQUIST: You think so, Bruce?

Comics rarely regarded the gag men as equals. Long before he wrote for teen comic Alan Bursky, Ed Monaghan had his trouble with Slappy White.

MON-
AGHAN: Never paid me. Tipped me. I made fifteen thousand a year, at least. Year in, year out. But it was all in tips. I was never paid for anything. He would not pay me. Money would come in the mail. I would go to Vegas where he was performing and he would . . . in front of people give me five hundred dollars. But it would never be for pay. I said, "You have to stop that. I'll work on a percentage. I'll work by the minute, I'll work whatever you want. But it has to be pay." And he couldn't do it.

Q: What was his thing?

MON-
AGHAN: He had been tipped all his life. And now he was a star and it was his turn to tip somebody. And he tipped everybody.

Q: How do you mean, "tipped"?

MON-
AGHAN: He was black . . . or is black—that doesn't change. And that's how he was always paid. He was a waiter. He was everything. So that's how he paid everybody. And I said, "No. I can't."

Q: So, in other words, he'd walk up and—

MON-
AGHAN: Yeah.

271

Q: He wanted people to see?

MON-
AGHAN: Yeah. And in front of Duke Ellington I told him to shove it up his ass. And he said, "You really hurt me." I said, "Good. I got through once. Don't ever do it again." But of course, it lasted for about a month. And he was back at it. So we don't work together anymore.

Of course, gag men were not all simon-pure. There were hacks who lifted jokes off TV or out of books, and altered them. "Switches" was the expression.

Occasionally, there was a madcap among them. Like Pat McCormick. McCormick, who was the size of a regulation pro basketball forward (6-6), could be walking on Park Avenue and see two old biddies coming toward him. Spying dog flomp at the curb, he'd hunker over it and nod to the aghast ladies.

McCormick was the exception. Most gag men kept to the shadows. They resisted identity, which suited comics concerned for their own. "Alan King," said a writer once in his employ, "always used to say, 'Hello, boys,' *Boys* is very often a word that you suffer with as a comedy writer. And I remember meeting him one morning as he was coming into the office. I passed him in the corridor and I said, 'Good morning, Alan.' He said, 'Good morning, boys.' And I was alone. And that's where his head was at. I just about collapsed."

Frank Darling had ego but a matter-of-fact kind— the snap of the competent pro. The frenzy of the comic in quest was not part of it.

Back in Korea, he'd been Frank D'Amore, a comic endorsed by Matthew Ridgway and the Eighth Army. Now he went by Frank Darling, club-date comic.

Dark-haired, trim, he had the look of a crooner. But it was his way with a gag that got him paydays. He was Rubber Man at it, a comic for any occasion— from the archdiocese benefit to the smoker where the stripper was raffled off for after.

272

Darling, forty-one, worked around. Summer of 1973, he was out to Lake Tahoe, Nevada, for eight hundred dollars a week, then back to New York to do the one-nighters at seventy-five to two hundred. Not Henny-ante exactly, but it was a living. Darling had a split-level house out in Wantagh, Long Island, with a swimming pool and two cars (Chevrolet/Chrysler) in the garage.

In the mid-'50s, he worked in the Northwest— Spokane, Yakima, Lewiston—and at each stop he went around and befriended the townies . . . *Yeah, I'm at the Elks Club, whyn't you come over.* He didn't do it anymore. No need to. Darling could size up a mob and figure it on the fly.

DARLING: I know what to do and where. Say a stag —a guy getting married. Fourteen guys in Bayonne, New Jersey.

Q: You literally did that?

DARLING: Oh, sure. Yeah. It's a show done in the back of a bar after they've served a Polish sausage thing. And you find out who the guy is who's getting married and you make friends with the guy. You have a couple of drinks, you stand up at the end of the table and tell him to go fuck himself and tell a bunch of jokes. They scream laughing. You get your dough and leave.

Q: Couldn't be much money?

DARLING: No. They tell you it's a lightweight one before you even go.

Q: Why would you take it?

DARLING: Because it's a Monday night. Or it's Wednesday. And I'm not doing anything but watching television. So I jump on my wheels and go over there, stand up and tell some jokes . . . and leave. Eat their dinner, you dig? And it's that kind of thing.

Q: What other—

DARLING: Geez, I worked mortician things. Twenty morticians got together and they wanted to hear some stories. Or a restaurant in Netcong, New Jersey. Served special meals. You call and tell them what you want. And two days early, they'd start preparing it. Right? And so I'd show up there and smoke a cigar and do an after-dinner speech for a bunch of guys that get together once a month to have a French dinner, you know. And they just want to hear some light jokes, not even dirty. They didn't even have to be dirty. They just want to hear some jokes that they hadn't heard before . . . like after-dinner talk.

Whatever the gig, Darling was up or down to it. Working a stag in New Haven, he'd be brassy with carnival roustabouts trying to shout him down. At a Sylvania convention, he'd be smooth in the tux, a cuff-link comic with a smile-on. He knew what he was doing. The strokes were in the jokes.

Just after the Russians sent up their sputnik, Darling appeared at an Air Force base the very day a missile exploded on a pad there. That night, a champagne cork popped loudly during his act. "That," said Darling, "is the first thing the Air Force has got up in ages." To a roar.

He knew what to do and where. *I'm the doctor*, he'd say. Once he played to a Jewish organization. Members asked whether he was a *landsman*. Sephardic, he told them.

With the Italians, he was a paisono whose father came to America in 1922, worked hard and was caught in the crash of 1929.

274

Truck hit his pushcart.

For the veterans, he was a Marine paratrooper with the whimsical rank of carpenter's mate first class.

> See, when the boys got ready to leave the plane, it was my job to hammer at their fingers until they let loose.

Put Darling in front of a group of Shriners in Albany, New York, and he'd have a joke to needle the Catholics. Supposition: Cardinal Spellman dies and goes up to heaven. He's greeted by St. Peter, who asks his name.

SPELL-
MAN: Spellman.

ST.
PETER: What did you do on earth?

SPELL-
MAN: Cardinal. Cardinal Spellman. Was in all the papers in New York. I work for you people.

ST.
PETER: Oh, I didn't know that. You worked for us? . . . Excuse me, I had you under real estate.

Mostly one-nighters they were, a string of jobs up and down the eastern seaboard, requiring 1001 comic faces. Darling had them. He was at ease in the changing scenes, a man who made out. A pro. It was why when Budd Friedman caught him one night and invited him by the Improv, Darling passed. "I know my act," he said. "I don't have to go anywhere to learn it. I'm just not famous. That's all."

Nothing fancy with him. Material he got a number of ways. The little Jewish lady down the street— *Hey, Frankie. I hoid a vundaful*—was a source. His wife, Nadine, wrote lines. There were jokes up for grabs—stock material. And there was the old switch number. Take a joke and run.

Sometimes, Darling saw cartoons in magazines, and he made them into lines. Newspapers too were a source, sparking funny thoughts or just there for the taking. The columns Earl Wilson or Leonard Lyons wrote had occasional one-liners.

Money was the nub for the club-date comic. It was not the 10 percent cut here. Whatever the agent could put in his pocket, he did.

Darling once did a show at the Hotel New Yorker for a hundred and seventy-five dollars and afterward the treasurer of the company throwing it told him he was worth the thirteen hundred dollars paid. *I just about shit, you know. I swallowed . . . gllllll.*

It was why club-date comics clued each other to jobs where no agent was involved. Darling was put on to stags that way. A comic who doubled as a TV kids'-show ventriloquist asked him to fill in at a stag for him. After that, Darling began telling dirty jokes regularly, earning seventy-five to a hundred and fifty dollars at the bashes of firemen and police and fraternal orders.

He was comic relief to strippers who had their erotic specialties. Like knotting a tie around their pelvis and having its owner undo it with his teeth. And so on.

Oddest of the acts that did jokes at stags was Marie Alvarez, stage name of a sweet-faced woman out of the Brighton Beach section of Brooklyn. She was a Jewish lady in her seventies with a shock of white hair and the Old World in her speech. Old biddy by day, she was a raunch comic by night: with a blond curly wig on, she was transformed, animated. She became, in her expression, "one hell of an act."

The act was novelty. Marie, looking like Harpo's kid sister, came out and

> What do you get when you mate an elephant and a hooker? A two-thousand-pound broad who fucks for peanuts.
>
> What do you get when you mate an IBM

machine and a hooker? A fucking know-it-all.

She did jokes in a delivery more that of the yenta than of the vaudevillian she claimed she once was.

She started to do stags in the early '40s. Second time was for an opera singer-turned-agent. Alvarez piled into a car with her and four strippers. Off they went to a country club in Westchester County. Marie did the jokes. The strips came on in G-strings. And for a finale, the agent sang "God Bless America" while the girls strode naked through the room.

"There was," she said, "a girl ahead of me started doing dirty jokes. Marge Taylor. And then there was Dave Vine. I heard him use fancy words, you know. He'd say,

> You want to get fucked tonight? Cash so 'n' so's checks.

"That's where I got the idea. Used to pick up dirty jokes. Now there's nobody living who has the amount of material that I've got.

"To me, it was nothing to get up and do dirty jokes. Even when I was a kid, I used to love to shock people. I never forget, I could hardly speak English. I come from Germany. And living in New Jersey, the kids were all a pain in the neck. They used to make fun of me, you know, my German accent. I'll never forget. I stood there and I said, 'Oh shit.' And the next day I was called in by the school board."

She was Little Girl Blue still. If Belle Barth put the leer in the line, Alvarez wrapped a ribbon around it. It was an act that could have played the Continental Baths. For thirty years now, Miss Alvarez had been on bump 'n' grind bills. And at age seventy-six, she was still at it.

On a night not so long ago, Alvarez was booked for the Sayre Woods (N.J.) Elks Club. She got in her car and tooled down the Jersey Turnpike to a rendezvous off Exit 11 where she was to meet the agent for the job, a man who, to hear it from Marie, was the direct descendant of Ebenezer Scrooge. *Lissen,*

Berger. I'm only getting sixty dollars. So you pay for gas, huh? On the way there, she profiled the strippers for that night, getting a twinkle in her eyes as she talked.

Mood changed when she discovered she'd gone too far down the pike. Trying to correct it, she made the wrong cutoff, and soon she was calling down curses on the agent who'd set the night up. *That rotten no good cheap conniving !**!*%#. He couldn't just give me the address. Sixty bucks, that cheating lying !**!*%#$. He should only . . .* and the speedometer edged up past 65.

No suasions could calm her. She was leaning forward at the wheel, fire in her eye. Then she quieted a second and told her passenger she'd refund gas money if the night didn't pan out. And *zhoom*, up the Jersey T she sped. *That rotten no good . . .*

Alas! she was not too late. The agent was there. He was a lean sideburned slick with the seedy look of a second string race-car driver. He was waiting in one car with his wife, a silicone-made glory. The other strippers were in a second auto. The caravan rolled into the night, bound for Sayre Woods.

Once there, Alvarez huddled with an Elk to get names to work into the act, names that fit certain jokes she figured to do. *Which one of you !**!\$s is a good talker?* As she conferred, the strippers figured their end. *Who's going to finish?/Oh, not me. I don't have the tits for it./What do you mean? It's not my strong point either.* And then back to more mundane matters.

The agent's wife (A Christ cross in her cleavage) was first, coming out in a panty frame only. Her husband was to whisk her away to the Bronx for another shot that night. Here she worked on a raised stage in the center of the room. The room was rectangular, smoky and low-ceilinged. Around the stage were tables, chairs and Elks of all ages, a few hundred of them. Some quaffed pitcher beer.

The stripper came on to recorded music and live remarks. And soon she was bouncing on her ass and over, spreading/jiggling/jumping, shaking silicone beauties at the Elks, using her breasts like pinwheels.

Up on her feet, standing wide-legged, she teased her lips with slow tongue, showed a pleased smile, and peek-a-booed here/there until she ran out of time and places. Hoorah. Good-bye, Joisey. Hello Bronx.

A rush on the beer to slake the salt of sex. And then direct from Brighton Beach, up a three-step stairway (with a helping hand) came Alvarez in a cotton-candy-pink party dress and matching shoes. The cherub smile was on her. She carried a purse.

She started in a serious vein, spoke of tight economic times and suggested a hedge against inflation.

> If you want to get your pencils ready . . . Now Cott Beverage—it's on the American Exchange . . . about twelve dollars a share. They're merging with Barton Candy. Gonna put out a lollypop. Call it Cott Suckers.

A throaty roar filled the room. *Hey Ma-rie!/Shutup, you bastard./Whooaaa.* Big grins all around. Alvarez gripped the mike and leaned forward the instant a remark was made and zapped its source. *Hey, you with the beard. You got a face that looks like a snatch./WHOOOAAA.* And she did it as Shirley Temple would have had had she been programmed for stags.

The change in her was marked. In her apartment earlier that day, she'd dragged. Now she had a fierce energy, bolt of last resort in it. *Hey, mustache. You look like a Spanish pimp.* It was a game to her, and she enjoyed it immensely. The profanity meant nothing but laughs to her on nights like these.

It was another thing when she appeared at a bungalow colony in the mountains. She remembered the codger who'd met her. "Meez Alvarez," he said, "the committee vants you should go to town." She asked about the children there and was told: "Never mind! Becky's ten years old, she understands everything." It made her uneasy.

As liberated as she was, the porno hit *The Devil in Miss Jones* disgusted her when she saw it in Brighton Beach. *What crap.* Another time, she worked a private party for an Orthodox Jewish doctor. "A bunch of Jews in yarmulkes," she said. "The food was brought in special. They had strippers there. And in front of his friends and relations, the doctor spread the stripper's legs and went down on her. Garbage."

Sayre Woods was what she was used to—Mother Marie the caper comic.

> The Second World War, I joined the WACs. They gonna send me overseas. Doctor gave me a physical and says, "Gu-what-a-canal."

> Then I was going to join the Waves. But I was very disillusioned. I found out the twenty-one-inch Admiral was only a television set.

> I'll tell you though. I feel like the girl who was raped on Essex Street and thought it was Grand.

Her line wasn't taut as Henny's but she was charming enough to keep the Elks hollering up to her. *Hey Moms!/Now, now, boys. I got room enough for all of you*—and she did a suggestive bit of shake.

When their interest flagged, she put strokes in the jokes. *Charley so 'n' so, where are you? I hear you're a good speaker.*

> Great diction. I'm not kidding. He's supposed to be smooth as clay. Not Henry Clay, but the kind they make piss pots out of.

WHOAA.

She kept them hopping. She had to peek at a list to get the names in, but in Jersey the strokes didn't have to be silk. Just get the *!**!#%ing* name right. At the end, she was cracking the whip.

> Black guy meets a Jewish genie. Genie says he can have any wish he wants.

Black guy says, "I wanna be between a white gal's legs." ZAP—the genie makes him a tampax.

Black guy says, "There's always strings attached with you Jews."

All riiiiight, all riiiiight. She came off to cheers after twenty minutes.

For Alvarez, the stags were a way. Not the only one, though. She had a card:

They're genuine
The laughs you get when

MARIE ALVAREZ

acts as
Comedy Waitress and
Story Teller
Perfect Entertainment for Private Parties
and Banquets

Nights like those she'd put on an apron and serve drinks and insult the guests until the host let on who she was. Then Alvarez performed.

One time, a group that took an outing each week embarked on a mystery trip. Into the bus they climbed. And

ALVAREZ: I'm standing there at the Marine Parkway. You know the Marine Parkway? And I had a car. And the bus driver comes by. And I hold up the hand. And he says, "You in trouble, lady?" I said, "Yes, take me to the nearest gas station." I'm all dressed up, you know. Jewelry and all. "My car broke down. Take me to the nearest gas station." He says, "Here you are." I say, "No, no, I told you a Mobil station." "Well," he says, "I've got to take these people to a place by twelve." I say, "I don't give a fuck what time they've got to be there." So then I start telling my jokes. The bus stops. That's the mystery.

Q: The mystery trip?

ALVAREZ: That's right. The mystery trip.

No mystery what the work did for her. It kept her going. "Before my husband died in 1950," she said, "I started getting seventy-five, hundred-dollar jobs, but after he died, it was the only thing to preserve my sanity. I took any job that came along, twenty dollars, twenty-five. If it hadn't been for the club dates, I wouldn't be alive now, tell you the truth."

At seventy-six, she was alive and well and still a hell of an act.

For a certain cut of kid laughs were a way to come to terms with his world.

Errh errh errh, Fat Jack had said to drown out the jeers, and primed it to become the ultimate needle of his day.*

The star comic was one who made his own spooked senses into magic mug, a face, in Mr. Eliot's term, to meet the faces. It was a gift of con, charm and the sweet frauds of personality, which didn't change what was there to begin with. If comic stars ended insecure, paranoid and blah, it was in the works.

Shecky Greene was, by most accounts, hail-fellow, a lively and generous spirit. Bobby Baxter once stood on a Chicago street corner with him and other comics years ago, passing the time. As the bunch of them kibitzed, an older woman in threadbare dress came by, asking a handout.

"And we all tried to ignore her," Baxter said. "All but Shecky. He goes through his pockets and says, 'Gee, I don't have any money. Here, take this.' And he took his wristwatch off and gave it to her. I looked in amazement."

He was that way onstage too. Back then he'd drop

---

* Before he passed away in spring 1973.

in at the Vine Gardens to nose around, and stay to do a guest shot—with a vigor most men reserve for wages. A great and pure energy he had, used to incite the clamor that made him greene with envy if it wasn't just for him. So said Sammy Shore, his first partner. Shore remembered the outsized charm—*He'll give you an arm, he's a warm guy . . . but—*

SHORE: Very moody. Very moody.

Q: When you were with him?

SHORE: Yeah, we used to fight a lot.

Q: Over what?

SHORE: I dunno. What was I doing out there. Or if I got more laughs than he did. Or just . . . who knows? We were just kids. It was the normal thing of a comedy team working together. Then after, he wasn't satisfied enough when we finished our show, he'd go back in an hour later and do an hour by himself.

Q: What possessed him?

SHORE: Just the drive. He just had to get up in front of those people.

Q: Then?

SHORE: Then I'd go up and fool around a little bit.

A striking image: a comic who'd double back on his partner to get the last laugh. It spoke of an uncommon need to be noticed, wanted, and warmed to.

And back then, Shecky was not even sure he wanted to be a comic. He wavered. When he did turn up at a club, he'd often get sick to the stomach anticipating the performance. He was considering dropping out of the biz when he got an offer to go to

New Orleans. He was about to tell the man no when he heard him say Sammy Shore was down there. It rang a bell. If Shore could do it, by Christ Shecky could too.

It was altogether like him. With Greene, emotion was the trigger of calculations large and small. He was a man of spirit, a trait that likely made him suspect of Shore. Shore kept his song in a pocket. He was a wiry man, gaunt, square-jawed—more remote a person.

Greene was impetuous. When Frankie Ray handled business for Shecky, Greene used to insist that the only reason Ed Sullivan didn't have him back on the show was Ray never called. Not so. Ray phoned and found that Sullivan was down on Greene. Shecky wouldn't hear of it.

Disguising his voice as Ray's, he called Sullivan and got a cheery hullo. It changed when he asked about Shecky Greene's next appearance. Sullivan's answer was a series of obscenities. *I wouldn't use that bleepedy bleep bleep.*

If Greene was mercurial, it cost him no pain until his first wife, a part-Indian, left him. Embittered, Greene began to drink in excess, which led to a series of noisy and violent episodes that recreated Greene in his own image—not as the hurt and betrayed spouse but as a rollicking night character. A Behan in baggy pants.

The Vegas lounge act Jessica James was with him on a night he drove his black Cadillac through the door of the Sands Hotel—at the time being remodeled —and into the casino, and exited to take an Olympic-style dive across a craps table.

It was typical of him at that time. As Miss James recalled: "He was so mad at his ex. So mad but he was really heartbroken. It came out in anger. And his whole act proceeded to be around her."

On stage, he turned wilder, made that way by wench hurt and whiskey. Booze put the dark glint in him. Shecky—who stands five feet nine inches and has a blocklike upper torso—was suddenly the combustible comic, a Nagurski of the gag trade, informing it with wit and Vesuvian fury.

There are those who swear it was vintage Shecky,

comedic ecstasy in the agony. No question it was gripping stuff—Mr. Greene's Dipso-Dervish Laugh Machine, an act with the whisper of riot, a voyeuristic confection, one he often kicked off with references to his ex-wife.

JESSICA
JAMES: He was very funny. But he got a little crazier. He got almost a little bit too much. When he would get drunk—which is something he never did before his wife left him, he was not a drinking man— I mean, it was like Dr. Jekyll and Mr. Hyde. I worked with him before—while he was married to her. And he was like pleasant. Sweet and adorable. But after she left him, he became like a sweaty Lon Chaney, you know. It's like he'd get up on the stage. And he'd . . . repeat himself about her and go on and on and on. And he would go on for hours on that stage. Longer than any . . . like his musicians would keep playing him off because the time was up. He wouldn't get off. And he literally tore the Riviera stage apart. He didn't like it. They said that they were going to build him a stage at the Riviera Hotel. And they didn't do it. He didn't like the stage they had there. And it took them too long to remodel the stage. So he started ripping the whole place apart.

Q: What'd he do? Pull up boards? Pull down chandeliers?

JAMES: Right.

Q: Did he pull down drapes?

JAMES: Right. He did that. All of that. He pulled down chandeliers, he pulled down drapes.

Q: How could he pull down chandeliers?

JAMES: Could reach up and pull 'em. Are you kidding? He'd get up on the piano. You've seen his act, haven't you? Well, how is he? I mean, he's not passive, is he? Well, when he gets mad . . . Have you ever seen him mad? Well, he was mad. And he was like a little insane bull is what he was. He would literally go and knock his head against the wall. He ripped the whole back of the Riviera stage apart and the front.

Q: When you say the musicians played him off—how long would he do?

JAMES: I've seen Shecky do two and a half hours on the stage. I mean, you know, that's ridiculous. Well, the man was fainting from being tired. And he didn't know it. Wringing wet besides—throwing water all over himself.

Q: What?

JAMES: Throwing water all over himself, taking pitchers of water.

Q: Throwing?

JAMES: Oh ya. Throwing it at himself. You know, he threw water all over himself.

Q: People ever walk out on him?

JAMES: Never. Nobody ever left when Shecky was on.

Q: Can you recall—

JAMES: He would run along the bar . . . on top of the bar . . . I'm thinking of the Riviera Hotel. He would just take off and run down on top of the bar. And of course, everybody's drinks were on the bar. And he'd merrily go jumping down this bar. Step on drinks. Slip and slide. Pick up the ice scooper which was about that big with a long handle and he'd put it on his head, march back and forth, salute, like a little tin soldier.

Once he was done, he took the act to the streets, usually with a few belts of liquor in him. In the Cadillac, he careened through the nights to challenge the gods—a Wallenda at the wheel. One time, he drove through the fountains at Caesars Palace, screaming, "No spray wax." Other times he was in trouble with the vehicular police of the city of Vegas.

On his own feet, Greene was as erratic. In a horse-race parlor in Vegas one night, he got boisterous. Asked to button his yap, he didn't, and soon found himself in an alley with several ex-hitmen from Chicago as company. It took a few words from a newsman to spare Shecky a beating, a favor Greene repaid by knocking him into a wall with a forearm blow and skipping out without a word of thanks. He did not remember it happening the next day.

Sammy Shore got it too. In Vegas with Elvis Presley *and of course I was the toast of the town. . . being in front of Presley and doing a great job* . . . it was weeks before he looked up old partner Greene. He found him—in the lobby of the Riviera where he ended up on the bottom of his pants, listening to Shecky say, "Three weeks ya been here and ya didn't even come over to see me."

Greene's rage put Riviera management at tippy-toe caution. Bobby Baxter, there once as Shecky's guest, informed the maître d' that the room was too cold. The maître d' agreed, but he said, "If it gets hot in here, if he thinks it's warm, he'll yell and he'll scream and he'll tear up the drapes, he'll rip the whole place apart."

The wonder of it is that Greene stayed in one piece through stormy years that ended in a second marriage —this one to a Polynesian dancer. In Florida with Sinatra, Greene mouthed off to the wrong man—one of Frank's "boys," a cousin (it turned out) of Al Capone—and suffered a bloody beating. More often, he didn't have a hair mussed when he was on a binge. Those who knew him figured he meant well. Not so with Buddy Hackett, a man cold sober when up to no good. He had the bullyboy's ease, a distinction the very look of him argued against. The bulbed nose, the crooked mouth, the cherub's cheeks: it was the best of comic faces—and, it seemed, a masterpiece of illusion.

For Hackett was a man whose name provoked obscenity-filled denunciations, many of which had "off-the-record" tagged to them the moment after they were uttered—and by comics who otherwise stood by their words.

Buddy's history was one of random goddamn that made them worry he'd want his pound of flesh per paragraph in the future. It kept them on guard in talking of him. But the tales told under anonymity were of a kind with those that on-the-record narrators spoke.

An intriguing portrait it was. As Las Vegas comics went, Buddy was considered brighter than most. He'd tried a hand at poetry, was versed in medical affairs, was a shrewd businessman. There were sides to him, and the columnist Joe Delaney claimed to have seen them.

DELANEY: Onstage, I find that I can predict Buddy . . . offstage I can't and we've been out socially quite a few times. And he could say fuck you as easily as he could say thank you.

Q: To anybody?

DELANEY: How they strike him. How will that person react if I say, "Fuck you"? He's very disarming. So he doesn't get punched in the nose too many times, if at all.

Q: Does he literally say to somebody, "Fuck you"?

DELANEY: Yeah.

Q: In what context?

DELANEY: A lady came over for an autograph. "How would you like to perform a unilateral act?" She said, "I don't know what you mean?" He said, "How about, go fuck yourself. Is that clear enough?" She said [*huffily*], "Well!" He said, "Then give me the piece of paper and I'll sign." I really feel—

Q: Head games he's playing?

DELANEY: Yeah, really. I think so. I think he knows he has the power to move people now if he wants to.

Q: Enjoys playing with them?

DELANEY: Except I don't think he's a tamperer in that sense.

Q: What do you mean, "tamperer"?

DELANEY: I think that if he felt that that lady to whom he said, "Go perform a unilateral act," was truly hurt, then he would try to make amends . . . you know what I'm saying? I don't think he's a hurtful man. . . .

He really, he really is a very gentle sensitive man . . . I remember once sitting with him and I described some Zen haiku. And I looked up and he's crying. Now this wasn't a put-on cry, because it's only the two of us sitting in the dressing room drinking and it's about four o'clock in the morning and I'm into Zen.

Q: What were you describing?

DELANEY: I was describing like two classic Zen poems . . . one about

> bullfrog
> lily pad
> old pond in the moonlight
> splash

and why that moment *splash* rather than the next moment or the moment before and

> butterfly on the bell
> village steeple in the sunlight
> one second till noon

which is really the Oriental equivalent of for whom the bell tolls. And he was so moved because I told him I had used that butterfly on the bell/village steeple in the sunlight/one second till noon to describe John F. Kennedy's assassination. Because we don't know . . . that we're the butterfly just when the guy down below will pull the clapper, and the concussion will send us doing Marcel Marceau to the ground. . . . And I looked over at Buddy and he was crying. And I realized that without trying to reach him, I had touched him. And he was touchable.

Q: Did he say anything?

DELANEY: No. He had another drink and we never even discussed it. Because I felt that he didn't want to. So I respected that. I backed off.

A man capable of jumping words to the nerve ends was at the least a flexed and oiled intelligence. If whiskey or late-night funk fingered the emotion in them, still it took working wit to perceive the possibilities.

But Hackett's reputation among Vegas-watchers as a high-powered intelligence was inflated. His own flirtation with poetry was a giveaway. Onstage, he did verse that was the worse of saccharine slops—*Life's mellowed to the acme of its time,* so on, so forth. It suffered the thrombosis Massah McKuen's poesy did, a surfeit of sugar-shit in the works.

Hackett's use of it—the swiftness with which he swung from toilet jokes to dithyrambs and back—was mind-numbing. He'd truck it in as the kind of pace-changer that often passed in the variety field as diversity. *Hey, de guy is talented.* It was just the quasi-poetic fix to make middlebrow audiences there for laughs feel culture-fucked in the bargain.

One moment, Hackett was on his knee before a gray-haired lady, doing weighted-down elegiac verse he'd written for his deceased mother, the next moment he was using her proxy in an old-bones hump joke. *Whaddayasay soldier, you ready to go with me? You hold her and I'll* . . . Weird mulligan it was, one other Vegas comics did too.

Rickles: Let alone, his insult act was a mad catharsis, an evil beauty like the black widow's web. But Don reneged. He went from

> You're a Jew. You gotta be. Or with that
> nose, you're a Buick

to chintz sentiments like *I am no rabbi, priest or reverend* . . . *I stand here and speak of all faiths* in a blah-blah blink. It was the slovenly shorthand that politicians used, palaver that short-circuited thought.

Shecky Greene's act had it too. With him, it wasn't the afterthought it was with a Hackett or Rickles. He was the kind of amiable bighearted lug William Saroyan might have created and in whom blarney was a tune. Shecky used it the way a saloon crazy did. Besides, he was able to kid himself.

> No, no, I'm not Danny Thomas,

he said one night, when a *pro patria* remark of his

brought applause. Thomas: slick prince of sanctimonious blather.

Not that Greene never stretched his heartfelt rhyme beyond its binds. One night he brought his wife (#2) onstage to sing a love song to her for the finale, a moment that had the B-movie's cheap sentiment to it. At bottom, of course, it was a question of an individual's variety RH or, to put it less delicately, just what mix of shit and shucks he was up to.

As for Hackett, give him this: He was a master at being Buddy. With a crook of brow, or an inflection, he could extract the laughs. Or, if he wanted, he'd wring tears with the verse he wrote.

But transcribe Hackett, let pure words do where puckish good will did, and it left scatological hodgepodge. It was where a Hackett—as potent a performer as he was—and a Lenny Bruce differed. The bound volume of Bruce's routines reflected a mind wrestling with its smoke. It was why, nearly a decade after his death, Lenny mattered.

Hackett was Charley Brown of poop and pinkystink jokes. Moving in and out of an audience, he worked mostly to women, using tits 'n' ass for his starting point. He liked his ladies well hung. Let him see one and he'd do time on her with the coyness Marie Alvarez affected. *Will you stop pointin' them at me?*

Around his running commentary, he ran his jokes, most of them scatological. The toilet was his *sine qua non*. He called it "man's best friend." He was the Ahab of stools. In his act were Vegas toilets built near slot machines whose payoff was soft-ply paper. There were Beverly Hills toilets that brought plumbers, he said, that looked like fops out of *Gentleman's Quarterly*, right down to the weskit. *At foist, I thought it was Alan King.* There were stuffed toilets. Army toilets. All God's toilets.

And through it all, good-golly postured as Rabelaisian. Buddy would ask ladies to say doity words in public. *You don't wanna say dat? I don't know why, Marlene. It's not really a bad word. It comes from anterior superior spine. A.S.S. It's a medical abbreviation.* He was constantly asking ringsiders—"You don't mind my saying dat, do you?" What was to mind? It was yesterday's news. With Bruce, raw idiom sought the double-barreled laugh, fun with some fire in it.

A curious relation he had with Lenny. He knew him in New York back in the '40s. When Bruce came out to the Coast later, Hackett was already in the movies, one of the first of the bunch to "make it." He and Bruce knocked around. Hackett got him a job as a scriptwriter and helped him with money.

Later, when Bruce started to get high on drugs, he gave Hackett the brush a few times, which Buddy apparently did not forget. When Lenny died, Hackett declined the wired request for money most of the big names in the comic colony got and heeded.*

Some time after, Hackett met Sally Marr. She was with Bruce's daughter, Kitty. Are you still stripping? he asked Sally, aware she'd been a dancer/comedienne. He knew her from when she and Lenny had had a fifth-floor walk-up on Livingston Street in Brooklyn. The Hanson's days.

With Hackett, the injury he gave was often premeditated. If he'd timed his laughs to impair Shecky Greene before he was a star, Greene was not the first comic he'd done it to. And when he said *scwoo you's* to the boys in Hanson's, it was not out of character either.

GEORGE
SCHULTZ: Soon as he made it . . . could see—he was like a prick. He could be very nice. Then turn on you. Like when I opened Pip's. And he was working at Town and Country, which was a big night club in those days. Ben Macsic's Town and Country. Eleven years ago.

Q: In Brooklyn?

SCHULTZ: Yeah. It's not in existence any more. Judy Garland used to work there. He was a star there and I just opened. And so I

---

* Curiously, it was the show-biz types that Lenny always was putting down who came through with money at his death. Milton Berle was very generous. Sammy Davis too.

called him up and told him it would be
good for me if he could come down, you
know. . . . He said Saturday. Two three
shows . . . came down . . . brought the
whole show. . . And sweated up. Came
in . . . people thrilled. Buddy Hackett
. . . a great thing to do, right?

Q: This is around 1963?

SCHULTZ: Sixty-two. So then a week later, I go in a
restaurant, and he's there eating. "There's
Georgie Starr, who used to be my friend."
He was mad at me. Why, I don't know.
. . . Then I meet him the next time in the
city. Doesn't know what to do for me.
"Come to the Concord with me . . . let's
do this . . . let's do that." He's a nut . . .
he's a twisted head . . . he's really distorted. He's mean . . . mean guy. Not
nice. . . . He's crazy.

Q: Mood changes?

SCHULTZ: Yeah. I don't like him. We go to Vegas,
I told Rodney I don't want to go to his
dressing room. I just can't stand him. Joe
Ancis feels the same way. Top prick.
Really is.

He kept an eye peeled when he worked, wary of
distractions. His position at the Sahara put waiters at
caution. In Vegas, he was known to throw his weight
around. *Literally,* said Jessica James. *When he walks,
if you don't get out of the way, he'll push you.*

When New York radio station WNEW held an
anniversary party at the old Madison Square Garden,
Hackett appeared, advising the disk jockey who introduced him not to allude to his weight loss, he wanted
to do jokes on it when he got out there. The deejay
ignored him and mentioned it and, later at a party,
Hackett grabbed him by the lapels and bounced him

against a wall again and again. *Told you not to do it.*
THUD. *I told you not to do it.* THUD.

A guy who'd run with comics put it this way: "If
they ain't a little crazy, they ain't funny. Gotta be one
to be the other."

The crazy the man meant was the kink that converted anger and/or imbalance to unabated strength.
It was what second-rate comics missed. Without it,
they were pale virtuosos of technique—that term
again, *mechanics*. Like Léger figures—all nuts and
bolts. Nothing of the idiosyncratic marrows.

A comic in control of his spooked force was a
one-r, an original, transmitting some bent piece of the
source. The failed comic was an approximation of a
funnyman, a guesswork of exteriors, a comic by the
numbers. Without mothering pulse, he was a cargo of
pat answers. A victim of duller obsessions.

No such charge was likely to be leveled against
Rodney Dangerfield. In him the dark eye that instructed his "no-respect" lines was the one that informed his cosmos. Rodney was on a first-name basis
with the dreads.

He'd been tested. Past age forty, he came back to
the business and scored. In the money, he was not out
of his senses. *What's it all mean, man. It's all cock.*
In Houston in 1967 for a gig, it was, he reported, entirely to his liking. The food was fine. The sun shone.
The girls were beauties. The jokes got laughs.

> So tell me—WHY AM I SO DE-
> PRESSED?

he asked by post.

He'd opened a club—every comic's camelot. *Dangerfield* (1118 First Ave., New York) was his own
joint. In it was a dressing room he repaired to after
his nightly turns, a place barred to strangers. It was
paneled and carpeted and had chairs, couch, TV and
table.

Rodney liked to lounge in there in a terry cloth
robe, working on the jokes. The TV would be on—a
movie or Carson—and he'd scribble the lines. Some
nights, George Schultz or Joe Ancis knocked and was

buzzed in. Cronies from the joke-jamming days on Avenue N in Brooklyn.

Ancis was still in siding, was high eloquence at it, capable of chameleon art, changing accents and politics according to the room he was in. It got him the quick buck and time to spare. Joe asked no more of it.

Once in a while, he'd go on the comic tear, but not often. No drive. If he'd lost the old impulse, he kept what was back of it, the woeful air of a philosopher prince. *Oh, man. Everything's a drag. Everything's an effort. Can't make it. Got to get dressed. Got to go out. Go to work. I've had it, you know?*

What Ancis proposed was to have a baby carriage designed, large enough to accommodate his person. In this, he proposed to be wheeled about by a hired hand while he reclined on pillows embroidered *Sweet Baby* and *I don't want to be a big boy*. It was a switch on the millionaire he'd played years back. *I'm too rich to walk,* he'd say, demanding chums tote him about.

The hip ennui in favor with Rodney's bunch Joe conveyed with the master's touch. He was practically rabbinical. Once, asked why he'd fathered a second child, he shrugged and said, "Eh . . . to break it up . . . a new face."

Schultz had other expertise. Comics came to him to sound him out on new routines. He had a knack for enlivening material. Preminger would take the D train out to Sheepshead Bay to check out his routine when he had a TV shot coming. Brenner paid him a percentage. With Rodney, it was contract work. Schultz knew the flawed line and how to doctor it.

George and Joe jogged cobwebbed memories— places and people and bizarre figures from a long-gone past. Hanson's was out of business. Brooklyn was changed. And time ticked its nagging stitch. *Oh man, I'm almost fifty. Such a drag.*

The look back was more encouraging than straight ahead. It restored the sweet note of a gone horizon. Take The Doctor. Back then, he was a dynamo of sex, an express machine that ran and ran. Now, he was a hollowed-out apparition, emptied of lusts and *joie de vivre*. No way to harken back in his company. He'd mumble not to, out of a face shot dead in the eyes. A strange lost soul he was, a belated puritan. *Must never fuck a married woman.* So on, so forth. The Doctor was off cases. He'd become one himself.

Those years were full of odd ones, grand players and hangers-on forever labeled dumb, a word Rodney hit with an anvil tongue. He made it an eloquence. DUMB! a detonation and damnation. *Oh man, is he dumb!* He liked to toy with the type. Always had.

Back in the '40s, he was in Bridgeport one day with Hackett and Schultz, a city they strolled through in the afternoon, looking for a caper. They found it in a sign in a shop window—BOY WANTED.

First Dangerfield—he was Jack Roy then—asked about the job, inquiring in a way designed to offend the woman shopkeeper. Schultz—Georgie Starr then —followed, and came on refined. It pleased the lady. She told him the job was his—just as Hackett burst through the door, wild-eyed and panting.

Hackett said he was from upstate. He'd heard about the job and needed it bad. *Look fella, she said I have the job,* Starr said, snidely. Hackett carried on. He pleaded, cajoled. Shouting ensued. And back came Dangerfield. *Say, what about the job?* he wondered. It was like a bad movie comedy.

When he was a siding salesman, Dangerfield's travels took him to Nashville, Birmingham, New Orleans, all over. Wherever he went, there were suckers. It meant money to be had, the thought of which worked Rodney into a lather. He'd be sweating minutes after moving through a doorway. Out came the hanky and the bullshit too, words he ran together so fast customers often nodded with no notion of what he was saying. He'd say anything. He'd tell them the material was the finest that money could buy, 100 percent— and he'd drop in a Yiddish phrase to make it sound good. It was always just plain asbestos. But it didn't hurt to load the pitch.

Sometimes canvassers were with him. They set up the customers for him to get on contracts. Jack Roy, closer. When he'd near that moment, his eyes bulged. He'd be in a sweat that required towels after. It even soaked the contract. Yadda yadda. *It's made of 100 percent halvah.* Sign here. And they did. Rodney knew the number.

Nothing changed him. He still liked to tinker with the nitwits. Once, he put two of them in a room and provided a synthetic subject to get them talking. It left him to monitor the conversation for his own amusement.

On another occasion, an out-of-town agent wrote and asked if he was available for a particular room, a place clearly beneath his stardom. The man was an obvious amateur—and so a perfect foil for Rodney. He answered in a way that encouraged further correspondence. A series of letters followed, the mere dictation of which tickled him.

It was the strut of hip, hauteur of the clubby vision, here a midnight doctrine. To beggar existence implied a custodial sense of its grim secrets, and led Rodney to sport with the dunces. *So dumb, man. DUMB.*

With it came a knee-jerk negativism, glimpses of which were in the act. He joked that when his partner rang up the register, it always sounded like beat-the-Jew, beat-the-Jew, beat-the-Jew to him.

Rodney had had hard times. The comeback brought ordeals. He'd suffered a manager whose idea of tact was to upbraid "The Tonight Show" in a letter for declining to have Rodney on. It took Dangerfield time to curry favor on his own. At William Morris, agents told him to invest in a new suit, unaware that the rumpled one he wore was part of the image. DUMB!

He'd made it anyway—and without slighting personal affairs that included a son in a wheelchair. But if Rodney carried on, he was not dissuaded from the foreboding vision. He waged his life as a nose-thumbing gesture against the void. A doctor, detecting a lung problem, advised him to cut down smoking. He increased the habit.

With Rodney, words were what he used against the void. He jammed them into time. The language jumped when he occupied it. And usually he did—with the common cant. *Oh, man, it's all . . .*

On he rattled. In company, he was a wisdom of the waste, talking with the closer's dit dit, not trifling with dialogue when Dangerfield would do. Always he took the contrary view. At a gas station he frequented, the attendant was a simple man who'd answer how-you? with the same unvarying response. *Can't complain, Rodney. Can't complain*—a phrase whose slack utterance maddened him and offended his exquisite rage. *He can't complain. Makes ninety dollars a week. Gets the crap kicked out of him. And he can't complain.*

Rodney could/did/and would—and if form held, he'd be at it when he hit heaven's gate, putting the knock on the place as—what else?—DUMB!

Oh, man . . . you kiddin' me with Elysian Fields. It's Prospect Park. Oh, man . . .

If it was strange times up top, it was no fun coming down.

A comic on the skids was up against forces he often hadn't a clue to. And while it took no sleuth to dope it out after—some flaw of the comic's to blame—it was pain and hurt while it lasted. Comics came out of it with pieces blown.

Will Jordan's case was like that. Once he was a comic prince, a kid with infinite twists in a time of bad jokes and plenty of gumption. At Hanson's, he was an original. *We all used to look for Will*, said Keefe. *See what he's got today. Just for the sheer enjoyment of it. Not for the idea of getting things that we could use. Most of it was "sick" anyway. By those days' standards at least.*

A "sick" comic he was before the term was coined. On Broadway street corners and at the back tables of Hanson's, he was an attraction. The feeling was Will was destined to be very big.

In the early '50s, he was building a name as a mimic, working regularly in Montreal, parts of Pennsylvania, Florida, pushing his wages to five hundred dollars a week. It was good money for a comic who had no name on TV. Jordan was a regular on the screen, but in nondescript shows. He'd made nearly two hundred appearances on TV before he did the one that clicked for him, the Ed Sullivan show.

In 1954, he hit with the Ed Sullivan impression that is now standard comedic vocabulary. His career was on the upswing. Will worked the major rooms. One night out West, he was doing *Me Tarzan, you . . .* and in walked Johnny Weissmuller to say *No, me Tarzan.* Remarks were exchanged. It ended with

WEISS-
MULLER: I'd like to get you in six feet of water.

JORDAN: I'd like to get you in six feet of cement.

Jordan earned up to sixty thousand dollars for a few years. "I went from sixty thousand a year to six thousand. This is after having played Las Vegas and all this. And I suffered through four horrible years with William Morris. In 1959, I made a little bit of a comeback by doing a record of Sullivan, and on the other side Sabu. My salary jumped up to thirty, forty thousand again. And it looked as though I was going to do well in spite of William Morris."

In his mind, he'd suffered some cruel turns, too many for the comic spirit safely to withstand. The narration of it had a practiced and perfervid sound.

JORDAN: Jack Carter's the one that took away the Ed Sullivan bit. That was my entree to stardom. That was the big hit. He knew the value of it. And that's why I'll never forgive him. He did it on the show first and he stole it word for word and later on he got top writers to add and make it . . . better than mine in a sense that it was longer and . . . But I mean . . . the basis of the bit was the shoulder shakes, the eye rolls, the belches, the knuckle cracks, the "rrreally big shoooo." That's the basis of the bit and that's mine. And then, of course, the whole idea of doing Sullivan was mine. He [Carter] was hanging around me in Hollywood. . . . I actually got him in free to see my act at the Mocambo in Hollywood. This bastard who was probably making ten thousand a week then . . . I got him in free. I was getting a big five hundred a week or six hundred a week or something. I got him in free to see my act so that he could steal it. I don't think . . . I've never met anyone that's been that cruel to me.

Q: Well, what was the—

JORDAN: Well, we had a confrontation and I said—

Q: Where? When?

JORDAN: I said, how could you do this to me? He just screamed at me. He just said, "You're small-time and you'll always be small-time." That was his answer. That was his direct answer to a direct question.

Q: Where and when was that?

JORDAN: That was at a big benefit.

Q: In New York or . . .

JORDAN: In New York about a few months after I saw it . . . And then—

Q: Roughly what year is that?

JORDAN: Fifty-five. And then on top of that, seeing Jerry Lewis do it on "The Colgate Comedy Hour." Where did he get it? From Jack Carter. He saw Carter do it. I told Sullivan about it. And Sullivan said, "I'll never hire him on my show." Sullivan had no loyalty. He hired everybody that stole it. Sammy Davis copied it from Jerry Lewis and after that it gets blurred . . . And then you know, I had the humiliation of being booked in a club and somebody calling to say: "We had Jack Carter here last week and he did Sullivan. So we can't use you." I said, "But I'm the original."

Q: What club was that?

JORDAN: It was a Catskill. Somewhere between fifty-five and sixty. I don't remember when exactly.

Q: And Lenny Bruce?

JORDAN: Lenny stealing—that came later. About fifty-nine, I found out Lenny was stealing from me. I didn't know that. Fifty-seven he saw the bit . . . the end of fifty-seven, the beginning of fifty-eight . . .

Q: Saw what bit?

JORDAN: The Hitler bit. In fifty-seven I wrote the Hitler bit. So I was still creating pretty good. I think that's one of the best things I ever wrote in my life. Incidentally, I told that bit to Mel Brooks and that's also in *The Producers*. That's the subplot of *The Producers*. Told that to Mel Brooks on the corner of Fifty-eighth and Sixth. In fact, I told him that Lenny Bruce had stolen it from me and he sat there listening and screaming at this bit. He doesn't . . . . I'm sure, he doesn't even realize he stole it from me. He sat there listening to it, screaming at it.

Q: This is the bit where Hitler is painting and they—

JORDAN: Well, yeah . . . painting. But it's the concept that's the most important thing. It's Hitler's life as a musical. How the agents got Hitler's act together, that kind of thing. That concept is mine. I'm very proud of it. Anyway, that's the subplot of *The Producers,* which Mel Brooks also took.

Q: It's only a couple of bits, no?

JORDAN: Well, Adam Keefe—he and I were very friendly. We worked so closely together. Adam lifted an enormous amount of material from me. In his thirteen appearances on "The Tonight Show" he managed to steal everything I've ever written in my life. And I threatened to kill him. [*Laughs.*] And then I called up the show and I said, "I cannot have this happen. I'm going to have to call lawyers or something. You can't do this to me." So the guy on the show says, "I won't have you upsetting Adam like this before he goes on." I said "Really?"

Anyway, Adam and I didn't speak for years. That's been one of the great problems of my life. I've lost friends galore . . . It's just been endless, endless. And what the final result has been, I'm sorry to say, is I've just frozen up. And I can't write any more. 'Cause I know it's going to be stolen. I know that's foolish. It's hurt me more than anyone else.

If it did not go well with Will, the fault was too simply put to others. It sloughed the inordinate confusions he had, costliest of which was the view he held of mimicry. To Will it was nil, a stunt, a form far inferior to monology, theory that suffered most in his elaboration on it. For it got to where he squandered the gift and came to cross purposes with his audience.

Keefe saw Jordan "kill" a crowd in a Broadway club. *Absolutely destroying the audience. People were like crying. Tears with laughter, banging the tables and like holding themselves together trying to keep from peeing on the chairs.*

Then a strange thing happened. Jordan began to insult the people.

> If you ever get a chance to become an audience, don't take it

or,

> If there's a bus outside, be under it,

lines that left Keefe shaking his head in disbelief. He made a beeline for the dressing room after to ask Jordan what in hell happened. A bunch of squares, Will said, insisting he was "bombing." Keefe argued that the crowd was in his corner. Jordan said no, no.

"I said, 'Couldn't you hear the laughs?' " Keefe recalled. "He said, 'What laughs?' He couldn't hear the laughs. Something in his mind shut off and he couldn't hear the laughing. The people were holding themselves, and banging their heads on the tables. He couldn't hear the laughs."

To people in the business, Jordan was a puzzle, likened by one man to the character Michael Redgrave played in *Dead of Night,* a ventriloquist whose dummy is his undoing, leading him to the trouble the voice of destruct insists on. In Jordan say-nay was, it seemed, all too loud and clear. On the club floor, he'd let a flash of mimicry go awry, the promise capitulated to the siren whisper. He'd discard impressions with a disdain audiences felt, rushing on to jokes he thought were in his "real" voice.

As an ex-manager recalled: "He could have made it work if he revered and respected his gift. He considered mimicry so easy, so unimportant . . . such a small offering that he did the Sullivan only under absolute duress, only if they were screaming and yelling."

Ideas too soon turned to mania that misused the comic machinery. He got dotty about being stolen from, and ended hearing Will where it wasn't. Echoes everywhere. He'd see a rhythm co-opted in a phrase of Lenny's or a grander obligation in the case of Mel Brooks. One night at the Gaslight in the Village, he saw David Frye do Sabu and afterward exclaimed, "That's my 'oooo,' you took my 'ooo.' I don't want you to do it again. Never do it *again.*"

Comedy writer Gary Belkin recalled: "I used to write for *Mad* magazine. And I did Will in an article. *Will Jordan doing Ed Sullivan.* And Will said, 'You stole that from me.' 'No, Will. I *said* it was you.' 'Sullivan never said *shooo* before I did. Sullivan never did it.' 'Will, I *said* it was you. I said it was Will Jordan doing that.' He couldn't hear it. But he was terribly creative and funny."

No question comics took from him. Bruce borrowed. So did others. But it was Will who made it an epitaph. By the early '60s, his career was sinking, and Jordan with it. His hair was falling out. He was party to a paternity suit. A hoped-for marriage missed. It led him to an analyst, the same one, it turned out, Jackie Mason was seeing, tenure that give him to advise Will he was "sick" when still another squabble over rights to material arose.

It was about the time he threatened Adam Keefe.

KEEFE: A very weird thing happened with me and Will. 'Cause Will and I were best friends for a long time . . . uh . . . and I was just getting started. And he reached a point where he decided that he didn't want to do impressions at all. He just wanted to be a comedian.

Q: Before he did the Sullivan imitation?

KEEFE: Oh no, no. He was already swinging. But he decided he wanted to be a comic, just jokes, stories. And he didn't want to do any impressions. And so he kept saying to me, "Anything I do in impressions, you can do. You can use any of my material." So he came down to see me a lot of times and I kept asking him, "Is it all right? I did this bit or that bit. You sure it's all right?" "Yeah, yeah. Anything at all I do with impressions, you can have." Then it got to the point where I was working down in the Village and my own head was going. So whatever things of his I was using, I elaborated on.

Q: Transformed?

KEEFE: Transformed them. And after a point, I didn't know any more what was his and what was my own. I didn't know any more. Completely lost track. And after I had done . . . oh, maybe about fifteen "Tonight Shows" . . . things were really jumping. . . . All of a sudden, one day I come down from NBC and there's Will Jordan. I don't even know how he knew I was going to be there. There's Will Jordan waiting for me and he had tears in his eyes. And he was angry and he says, like "I'm gonna kill you. I'm gonna knock your head off. You've done all my material and I can't get on 'The Tonight Show' because they said that everything I've got, you've already done on the show." And I said to him, "Look, you told me I could do any of this material. You were down to see me. I asked you is it all right. You said it's all right. And by now I've lost track. I don't know what's yours and I don't know what's mine. You know?" He laid a whole number on me. Really made me feel terrible. But I didn't know what to say to him.

Q: He literally had tears in his eyes?

KEEFE: Yeah, I mean but like he wanted to hit me. And he didn't know what he wanted to do. He was just like beside himself.

Q: Was his career going sour at that point?

KEEFE: Yeah, I guess he was having a lot of trouble at that time. Not in getting work. Will was always working, but—

Q: Getting the big—

KEEFE: Yeah, getting anything that meant anything.

By the mid-'60s, he was an ex-name, a comic trading on his past. He became his own agent, working
through the mail. He still does—4,200 cards sent out
every three months to assorted buyers, listing the kinds
of work he has done of late.

ON RADIO

Bogart Type Voice
Radio Advertising Bureau
6 Commercials

VOICE OVER

Straight Narration
Alice Cooper
"Billion Dollar Babies"
TV Commercial

ON CAMERA

Groucho-Ed Sullivan types
Westbroad Lincoln-Mercury
TV Commercials
Columbus, Ohio

wages of the journeyman comic.

In his time, Will earned big money and stretched it
with astute handling. He was not pinched for the buck.
What he missed was the action. When he did work as
a pure comic, it was in scattered one-nighters and benefits and maybe a week in Puerto Rico. It was not up
to the itineraries of the '50s. For that matter, neither
was he.

In his apartment on West 57th Street, he had a
notebook, talk of which put the sorry look in his eyes.
Will Jordan, who'd captivated comics with impromptu

licks decades before, was unable to think funny anymore—and the notebook was a reminder.

Q: Have you tried to write anything new?

JORDAN: Yeah. This book is all full of . . . I'm embarrassed to say it's only full of bitterness.
I'm trying not to . . . the bitterness is
something I don't want the public to know
about. It's there, but I don't want to project it.

Q: Are those bits? [Nodding to notebook.]

JORDAN: It's just rambling. Trying, you know, to
latch on to something. It's just rambling.
It's really like regurgitation more than
anything else.

Q: Is there—

JORDAN: In all fairness, I should say that I'm not
trying to write bits because I don't want
to write material which is done in extreme characterizations as I did before.
All the material written before were wild
characters, screaming Nazis, loud rocket
ships, hunchbacks, Paul Muni switching
eyeballs with Sammy Davis . . . really
very bizarre characters and sometimes
sick. Physical things—stuff like that. I'm
not at all interested in writing in that
form any more. I want to write in the
first person like Alan King or a Jackie
Mason.

Q: Is any of that in your notebook?

JORDAN: Just me talking bitter. That's all, 'cause
. . . there are some funny parts in it.
There's one idea here that I thought was
pretty good. It started to . . .

I'm so sexless, when I invite a girl out, she shows up with another guy for the date.

Uh, you ever notice that most girls today have flabby bottoms. Years ago, girls used to have such firm behinds. Now everybody's bottom just jiggles loosely like boiled chicken. Whatever happened to hard behinds?

Blondes like to touch up their hair. The black roots don't bother 'em. The hair style's what's so important. Their fingernails can be chewed away. Their feet can be absolutely filthy, but hairstyle is all they really care about. The makeup and the hairstyle. The bodies can be rotting away. And they are often. They never wash themselves internally. They're just, you know, filthy. But they care about a certain outward look.

Why is it that every girl that bites her fingernails always smokes a lot of grass and has a black boyfriend.

One of those strange observations.

But I was saying that I think honesty is causing more trouble. Now that people talk about honesty, people are more unhappy than ever. I think it was better when we were all phony. Maybe it's better for all of us. I think—

Q: I missed that last phrase.

JORDAN: I think it was better. And I said . . . and then the gag was

309

Everyone's yelling, "Let it all hang out." Ever since that expression has started, people have been more miserable than ever. Ever since they started to say let it all hang out. I say in order to be happy, put it back in.

And that's really about all I did. The rest of the stuff is just . . . it doesn't sound like comedy material.

Q: So the stuff you've been performing for the last ten years is basically—

JORDAN: Old jokes. Old jokes and the impressions which I know people like.

Q: Old jokes you once created? Or are they just—

JORDAN: They're jokes that I read from the . . . I send away to humor publications, things like that. Or else what we call stock jokes.

Q: Such as?

JORDAN: It's hard to think of one right now.

She asked me if I was a bird fancier. I said, "Yes I'm a bird fancier." "Well, *thpph* . . . fancy that."

Stupid old jokes like that . . .

If he'd lost his magic, he'd kept his interest in show lore. Comics phoning him would find him cataloging movie sound tracks he kept on cassettes, or toying with a book idea—a snapshot and text treatment of performers before and after nose jobs. Jordan owned a collection of photos of stars—Dean Martin, Milton Berle, Jan Murray—with their original beaks.

It was as if he were back in a time when *Variety*

was the paper of record with his bunch and he was its weird eye. The eye had lost its powers. *I mean, I always wondered what happened to him,* said Keefe. *What cut that off? 'Cause, wow! He was like . . . like you talk about Jonathan Winters . . . he had the same kind of mind. He could go extemporaneously . . . I always wondered. For that matter, I'm wondering what happened to mine.*

Keefe had had it in San Francisco the night Shecky Greene came backstage, raving, "You're great! You're fantastic!" *And he says, "You ought to be the biggest star in the world! I'm gonna do something for you! I'm gonna do something for you! I mean it!" And he walks away. That was the last I ever saw of him.*

For Keefe, it was, in retrospect, a wry summation of just-missed glory, elusive piece in the master jigsaw. With comics, stardom always seemed thatclose.

In Keefe's case, it was. In the early '60s, he went from the top clubs to a twenty-thousand-dollar contract * as an NBC property, one of a number of newcomers signed on the Coast at the time. The idea was to have him on tap for a star-primed situation.

Keefe's turned out to be a situation comedy that buckled under the weight of its own preposterous notion. It succumbed as a pilot, leaving Keefe grounded for the rest of the year at the network. Each week, he got a paycheck and the sinking feeling his chance was slipping away. Just the year before, he'd been a nightclub headliner. A commercial he did for a throat lozenge as a Dracula-type pitchman— *When sore throat strikes, vhat do you do? Take citrus juice? Ah ha. Nutin' vil help you? Trrry Isodettes—* netted him twenty thousand dollars and five offers for Broadway shows, including a lead in *Hello Dolly.* He'd opted for NBC instead. Thatclose.

Out as a TV contract player, he drifted through severals years in California. He was just another name there. No star. That much was clear. And it had been since he left the Village. On one TV show, the comic who ran it invited him by his dressing room to chat. Short time after Keefe arrived, there came a knock

---

* With escalating annual options.

at the door. A woman walked in, unzipped the other comic's fly and performed fellatio on him. She took his hundred-dollar bill and left. "Then," said Keefe, "the conversation ended. 'Cause he had nothing else to show me after that."

Keefe was co-host of the Pat Boone show, daytime TV fare that ran thirty-seven weeks and disappeared. He played the Sahara and Aladdin in Las Vegas. He appeared on "The Steve Allen Show" and "Hollywood Palace." It got him nowhere.

Back to New York he came, a bummer return. *A lot of things had happened and I guess I had a real sense of having failed, you know. A real sense of like, Jesus, I thought I was really becoming a star and instead I bombed out.*

Managers and agents stalled him. Keefe read between the lines. *It was like—"Well, if you were gonna make it, you would've made it by now." I expected to come back like I had never left. 'Cause when I left here, I had agents and managers running after me down the street. Then come back and find . . .*

The Village was changed too. Bleecker Street had lost its charm. Demon pizza tonk was moved in. Dopers and assorted street dunces were the apocalypse of the Kerouac romance. For comics, only a few showcases were left.

Keefe was booked for Merv Griffin when it was still in New York, and suffered jitters unlike any he'd had before. Nights he'd lie in bed, worrying over the piece he was to do. The same dream recurred. It was the one the old clown Calvera had in Chaplin's *Limelight*. He goes out and does the routine and nothing happens. No applause.

It was what Keefe dreamed. It didn't occur, though. He did OK, was even invited back. No matter. He was coming apart. The comic mechanism had gone haywire. Tangled hopes/faded dreams. Shortly after he did a follow-up shot on Griffin, he was in the hospital with an ulcer.

Q: Do you still get a kick from working?

KEEFE: Yeah. I always enjoy working.

Q: How much do you work these days?

KEEFE: A few weekend jobs, a few club dates.

Q: How about the material? How does it go over?

KEEFE: Well, you know I'm almost back where I started. 'Cause most of these club dates, you've got to do a club-date act. So I'm doing a lot of stories.

Q: Strange circle?

KEEFE: Yeah, it is in a way.

Q: You get angry?

KEEFE: No. It doesn't make me angry. I still enjoy performing.

Mimics were the odd end of comedy, fellows who lit up in guise of geezers other than them. It was their ready shazam, voice(s)—the supposition went—for lack of their own. Will Jordan's strange turns appeared to have that cognition back of them. Yet when he and David Frye were together, they'd talk in mimicry, the *parlez-vous* of their trade.

Keefe's ulcer was in the tradition. It was to mimicry what the pug nose was to the prize fights. He carried on, his income in recent years drawn mostly from commercials. One of his was commended in a newspaper account of the Cleo awards given the best TV commercials. The lady from *The New York Times* rued its absence among the winners.

> *I would prefer 30 minutes of nothing but Dr. Pepper commercials, especially the one of the ersatz Jimmy Cagney being persuaded by his Mom to leave a police barricaded warehouse and try Dr. Pepper, to anything that Lear and Yorkin have to offer,*

she remarked.

The Cagney in reference was Keefe. Adam wrote *The Times* for not mentioning his name—*Maybe it'll help*—but the letter was never printed. No longer thatclose, he was still trying.

A comic always had a shot. Dangerfield was the example, great gray hope. The wheel turned. Oh, Lord, did it. Bobby Baxter remembered back to the '40s when Rodney was Jack Roy. Baxter was working smart rooms then—Le Ruban Bleu, the Blue Angel, the Hotel Pierre—and Roy was in the toilets. Years passed, and Baxter now worked in *Dangerfield's* on nights the mongol hordes descended, prom time.

BAXTER: I was there in June [1973] when they had the proms and Rodney would do ten minutes or eight minutes. 'Cause he hated them. They're murder, the prom kids are. Yeah, he'd do a few jokes. Says, "Well, I want you to meet a friend of mine here. I want you to treat him as nice as you treated me. Uh, Bob. Come on out here."

And I come out there. And I'd sweat like a madman 'cause you gotta have the time. I'm doing twenty-five, thirty minutes for these wild animals, right? Who are throwing up at your feet and everything, right? I mean what they don't steal, they throw up on you. They take everything. They steal everything. They run out of the club without paying their bills. As a matter of fact Rodney says to me, he says, "I don't know what they teach these kids at these Catholic schools, but they sure can steal. . . ." They stole my props. I got props stolen all the time when they're there. Little magic props or a funny hat. Anything you're gonna use, it's gone.

Baxter had been a comic since the late '30s when he'd busked for coins in Lord Buckley's haunts. *Been making a living since I was sixteen in this business. Not many guys can say that.*

He was an amiable fellow with the boy bounce and rat-a-tat words, hype he made habitable. A smooth chipper guy with fast velvet for patter. Words like "elfin" and "mischievous" cropped up in his reviews. *I make friends when I work. I get them to like me. This toupee—I use it. Make fun of it. Guys can't help liking a comic that does. I'll tell 'em*

> Look, I'm no Communist. I don't believe in sharing. A fellow needs something. I give it to him

and WHOMP, I'll whip off the toupee and throw it on a really bald guy. It always breaks them up. Then I'll point to two bald fellows,

> You two guys put your heads together, you make an ass of yourself.

At one time, he was in chichi rooms. No more. He worked around now. He could juggle, do magic, mime and jokes. He went a number of ways. He had a flyer:

KIDS LOVE "MASTER" MAGICIAN
Uncle 'Bob'
(and he loves them)
He's more fun than a Three Ring Circus

And there was a photo of him—cane in one hand, white gloves in the other. He worked stags too.

Bangkok World (May 1965): "Night club entertainer Bob Baxter, above, seen amusing customers and employees in the Thai Daimaru Department Store the other day when he dropped in unannounced and began a series of sleight of hand tricks. He is presently appearing at the Sani Chateau Night Club."

USO, Playboys, the Mint in Vegas, Eden Roc in Miami, Paris, Manila, Rome, London—he'd been all over the world. *Bobby Baxter? Oh yeah,* said Frankie

315

Ray. *I thought he'd make it. He had a nice manner up there.*

Now Baxter sometimes went for short money. The jobs were often the kind left off résumés, price of which was worked out over the phone. Baxter did it with grace. *Abe, you're a nice fella. We'll see what we can work out. See you Monday.* Hang up the phone. Wink.

In the '40s/'50s, he was less concerned for diplomacy. A weight lifter then, he packed a wallop. *Lotta times, I decked guys then. No more. Too old, I guess.* Back then, he was wild with the women too. In the Show Bar in Boston, to get to dressing quarters, comics had to go through the powder room portion of the women's facilities. Baxter used to walk in without a shirt on, to exploit the Charles Atlas physique. He'd spy a lady he liked and whisk her away.

In the Gypsy Room in Atlanta, he had a drink with a couple. Later the girl came alone to his dressing room. "The room," he said, "was so small, we couldn't lay down. We had to do it standing up. I'm kissing her, got the girdle off. Do it. I'm upstairs, back at the table where she left her boyfriend. She comes up. Boyfriend asks where she was. "Oh, I was downstairs balling the comic here.' He thought it was the funniest thing in the world."

At a hotel in Louisville, the pretty elevator operator kidded him about the women he'd had to his room. At the time Baxter had his bags with him, and was on the way down to check out. He told her none of them was as lovely as she was, and wished he'd had time with her. She told him it was never too late. And it wasn't. She stopped the elevator between floors. He sat on the stool. She lifted her skirt.

If he'd made good on his chances with the ladies, he'd blown a few in the business, memories that made him flinch. "I'm going to make myself sick," he said. " 'Cause you start reliving the past it makes you sick."

In the late '40s, Baxter did the Sullivan show, scared out of his wits. And while he was on, he got the "stretch" sign: he stayed on camera for double what he planned to because another act was not ready.

"So I was a big hit. And I got very small money—a hundred and fifty dollars or something. This is the early days of TV."

Baxter was offered the show several times after but turned it down. He was shy of material. And when Sullivan saw him months later and told him he wanted him back on, Baxter's wisecrack—"Yeah, but you gotta pay me more than a dollar and a quarter"—made the star of the shooo angry. It finished him for good with Sullivan.

Not the last time he'd regret what he said. A few years later, Baxter was in Florida when the MCA agency asked him to take a date for five hundred dollars in New York. He played hard to get with an agent who was only a gofer when he knew him last. A serious error. The man was Freddie Fields, and he'd come up in the world—a vice-president at MCA and later head man at CMA. They'd been pals in earlier days but when Baxter, in his words, "jerked him around," Fields was cool to him after. "It was," Baxter said, "one of the biggest mistakes in my career."

That was in his past. For the present, he lived in a Broadway hotel, the kind of place Fred Allen used to say had rooms so small they made the mice hump-backed. Baxter was not crimped by it. He cooked Oriental dishes in the tiny kitchen and made jokes about the place with a journalist. *Yeah, I know why you come back. You want to get some good adjectives like "squalid," "seamy," words like that.* When he left his room on the seventh floor, he was always dapper.

He was a comic still. He kept at it—to a point. The hard hours he shirked. Some days, he'd make a note —*WORK ON JOKES*—that he'd crumple up at the end of the day without having heeded. It was easier to flick on the TV, tape Carson's monologue and/or Cavett's, maybe play the switch game with jokes. It was how Woody Allen had started. He was once known in the trade as Allen Woody. The line on him was, "He'd rather switch than write." But it taught Allen to think funny. Hard work and kinky genius did the rest.

At one time, Baxter had put in the hours on jokes.

It was when he still had a shot, as he put it, "to make a run for it." *An act can get punchy. Lose his confidence. Am I good? This and that.*

Years ago he lived in hotel suites. Now it was this place with one elevator for its occupants, a lift that suffered its inches up. The hotel before was worse, a regular entry on the precinct sheet. Many of the residents were on welfare. More than gags were stolen there. Baxter, leaving his room, put a spare toupee on a manikan head and propped it under the covers so it'd look like a sleeping figure when he opened the door.

On his return he'd carry on a conversation with a fictitious lady—*I'm back, dear*—until he was inside. Then he'd fabricate a dog—*Thatta boy, thatta boy*—right down to, he swore, its barking response. He was not so wary in his Broadway retreat. He made do, a man with a knack for tomorrows. *That's the thing in comedy. You always got a chance to get lucky.*

It sustained. Bernie Travis remembered an odd minstrel figure from Village days who'd tell him, "I will make it, Mr. Travis. I will make it," an opinion he held unto himself. It was Tiny Tim, the falsetto song man, who eventually did catch on.

Travis too was around for years, looking for a break. A small man with dark barbered hair, he caught only hard times. One night at the Fat Black Pussycat in the Village, he was on the stage when a man in a raincoat approached. *He walked up with his hand in his pocket and says, "Excuse me, I'm going to kill you." To me. Complete silence.*

> Isn't that going too far for not liking the jokes? Could you settle for something else?

I asked. I looked him right in the eye and I didn't show fear. I felt fear. But for some reason . . . He smiled and he said, "Maybe you're right." And just backed away and ran out the back. A man about forty-two with like steel-gray hair. But those eyes. There are certain eyes . . . Travis never actually saw a gun.

"Death" onstage, the comic kind, was infinitely

easier, though not without a toll. *An act can get punchy.* And tetchy too—from words that had tricky spin on them. *Uh, Bernie, it just may not be your room.* Phantom phrases that were YOU STINK in Sunday finery. Against them were nights when the laughs came and Travis locked in, nights to stand up to be-damns, too few unfortunately to matter. He was still a stranger to the public. It cost him in those years.

"I did a show in the mountains," he said. "Think I got seventy-five dollars for the show. No. Sixty dollars. Swan Lake, New York. Place like a haunted house. And I did the show. I said can I get paid? The owner said, 'You come back during the veek and I'll pay you.' He starts walking away. He goes into the kitchen. I said, 'Please. I did my work. Can I get paid?' 'Vat you worry? You're a nice fellow. Have a cup of coffee, have some tea, a cookies. You come back in a veek, you'll get the money.' I said, 'I'm not leaving.'

"He went to where they keep the milk and the cookies in the freezer. It was a big freezer where you walk in. Like a meat freezer. And you have the milk and the bakery goods so they stay fresh. 'Mr. Cohen, I'd like my money.' 'Vat you want money, you're a young fella. You don't need money.' I said, 'I'm not leaving until you give me the money, now I want my money. I want my money.' I'm in there with my tuxedo."

Travis got it every which way. "One time," he said, "I was leaving soon for the mountains to work as an emcee for the summer. And I was out of my apartment. My lease was finished. I called a comic I knew. 'Come with me. Stay in the apartment,' he says. So I get over there. He says it's five dollars a night. I said, hey, a friend. He said, 'You are a friend. Usually I charge ten dollars.'

"I was stuck. So I paid him the money. Meantime, I left my trunk with all my clothing—to pick up at the end of the summer. He said OK. I come back. It was out on the window ledge. And it had been rained on. And the black paint had been removed from the trunk. It was like rusted. I opened the trunk and all the clothes I owned for the winter—I had taken my summer clothes—all the clothes I owned were completely ruined, waterlogged, mildewed, spoors. 'You animal.' "

In 1965, Travis signed on with the USO, wound up in Europe for a year. *I was broke. I needed money. I had to work.* He came back to the Village and went into the Cafe Au Go Go. The Bitter End in 1967— a good review by *The New York Times*. TV debut on Merv Griffin's show. William Morris signed him. He was on his way.

So it seemed. He had a man at Morris behind him, a "heavy" in the trade. But at-last came to alas! The man had coronary problems and retired. Without him, Travis was just another guy there.

It was then he got involved in Lenny lag, post-humous cock-a-doodle over Bruce, poor bastard whose gravestone bore the temporary marker

LEONARD SCHEIDER [sic]
August 1966

the name wronged the way the man was.

Before he became a comic, Travis had worked at the General Artists Corporation when Lenny was signed to the agency. They knew each other. *Fifty-nine/sixty: he was very angular. Staccato movement. Energy. Quick answers, did-dit. Sixty-four: had coffee with him. Burned out. Like a man twice his age. Quiet. Lethargic.*

In 1968, the first stage production of Bruce's life was done. Travis was in it as the former Mr. Schnei-der. It was a multimedia show. Two previews played to sell-out audiences. Then the show was closed. A deal was made. Myth was money.

A man named Herb Altman saw Travis in the show. Altman was back of *Dirtymouth*, a film on Bruce's life. Travis signed to play Lenny, a dandy shot.

The filming started. Altman became suspect as a movie man. He claimed to be a former WWII bomber pilot who'd flown stunt shots in Howard Hughes films. Later, he was

TRAVIS: . . . not his valet, but he was in a certain group of guys.

Q: He told it to you?

TRAVIS: Yeah. Herb did. And one day, Howard Hughes said, "Would you mind, my behind is sore, would you put some starch on it?" Medicated powder. What's the . . . Desenex is for the feet. Anyway, Herb said to him, "Powder your own." And Howard Hughes said, "You're fired."

As his own man, Altman qualified. As his own auteur (*Dirtymouth*. Written, produced and directed by Herbert S. Altman)—no way. Mr. Canby of *The New York Times* said, "*Dirtymouth* has so little on its mind, so little to offer, that while I was watching it yesterday morning at the Penthouse, I wondered if, perhaps, it wasn't watching me. Bad movies prompt paranoid fantasies."

Indeed what was most compelling was not on screen. "One scene," Travis said, "where Lenny's busted in a Philadelphia hotel. Two cops punch me around. Without me knowing it, Herb tells 'em to give it to me good. One of them belts me, the other hits me in the balls. *Get it! Get it! Cut! Wrap it!* I'm on the floor writhing. Nobody's doing anything. I can't talk. I'm holding myself. They forget about me.

"Scene in the New Yorker Hotel. It's supposed to be Lenny's pad. Camera in a wheelchair. Hand-held camera. Am I killing myself or is it an overdose? Leave that open. We had the New Yorker booked four days. It's the last day there. To do the scene, I had to prepare something in my mind—that I never felt worse in my life. Crying is easy. It's the feeling that I felt useless as a human being. I put mood music on. A Sinatra record about unrequited love. Just as we're ready to roll, guy comes in with a wheelbarrow. 'Where do the bricks go? Where do the bricks go?' See, down the hall, they were breaking through a room, making it a suite. 'Get out of here! This is a film!' Little man with a stogie. It was like the Three Stooges.

"Another scene at the end, where I come out of court. And I'm depressed. And I'm walking down Central Park West, and suddenly the Macy's parade comes by. We needed a minute and a half of it for the film. Now to get into the parade, you need a license. We didn't have a license. We had a cameraman there. Herb told me, 'Go lead in the parade.' I said, 'What are you talking about? It's television. It's the Thanksgiving Day parade. You've got Shriners here, you've got the Mummers. Are you kidding? You've got these cats who've waited a whole year to be at the head of the parade.' He says, 'I want it.' Always I want it. So I go in and I march in the parade. Screaming. Cops grab me. He's filming it. So we march from 72nd Street and Central Park West down to 42nd Street, Times Square. Eight different spots, filming me.

"So one of the Mummers—you know the Mummers from Philadelphia? So I'm doing their little steps. Guy very fey, says, 'Who are you?' I said, 'Um, hey Gordon told me to do it.' He says, 'Get the fuck out of here. You're ruining my thing. You're ruining my thing.' And he was screaming, 'He's not in the parade. He's not in the parade.' Cops come. 'What are you doing here?' Grabbed me, and schlepped me away. Altman's going, 'Film it, film it.' "

No matter. Lenny was a pop personage. The film figured to be a boon to Travis on that alone. Another edge—the return of the stage production, this time booked into the Village Gate, with Travis as Bruce again. *Look how I feel. I'm in the Off-Broadway show. I've got the film coming out. So I'm Lenny Bruce in both. I said something's got to happen.*

It did. In litigation. The Off-Broadway play was bumped by the uptown *Lenny* that made Cliff Gorman a star. The *threat* of a suit cut the film to its New York run. And Travis was out in the cold.

TRAVIS: If the film got out of New York, at least it would have gotten some national exposure. I could have cashed in on it.

'Cause an agent said to me, "Sign, and I'll get you seven hundred and fifty a week, a thousand a week. Wherever the film is played, whatever city, we'll book you piggyback."

Q: So what happened? What did you feel?

TRAVIS: Crushed. I was in Central Park and I cried for about an hour and a half. I just kept walking. I started on Fifty-seventh Street and I ended up—

Q: East or West?

TRAVIS: Fifth Avenue. I was just walking in a daze. Through the park. I don't know where. I just kept walking and crying.

Q: Just after the film was in New York?

TRAVIS: Yes. This was the end of May [1971]. And I'm walking and walking. And before I know it, I'm on 110th Street, no, 96th Street. How far does the park go? Toward the end of the park. And I was crying. And I said, "My god. The film. No manager. No colleges. No television."

Q: You cried from Fifty-seventh right up?

TRAVIS: I cried continually. I just was sobbing and weeping. You ever feel . . . what's the word . . . you're weeping inside?

Q: Welling up?

TRAVIS: No. There's just a feeling. I couldn't do anything. I was like a vegetable.

Some time after, Altman phoned Travis to invite him to dinner. Bernie's wife warned him Altman was up to no good. Travis went anyway. Altman arrived with the editor of a sex tabloid. The proposal was simple. If Travis agreed to star in a porno movie for them, they'd see about *Dirtymouth's* re-release.

For Travis, up was where down commenced sure as night followed day. Another story it was with Shelley Berman. At one time, he made $15,400 for a one-night stand, an estimated $500,000 a year. In the early '60s, reams of copy appeared on him, the single most interesting sentence in the *Christian Science Monitor:* "Mr. Berman's voice," it said, "has the battered elegance and mock rhetorical cadences of an elocution teacher, hair tonic salesman and prize fight announcer."

Shelley's decline inspired far fewer words but was no less intriguing, a crazy quilt of allegations and repudiations and contradictory claims all around, most of them uttered with doctrinal surety. At issue was whether he was the source or not of his demise.

If he was, it was not out of evil intent but an overly fastidious sense of what suited him. Simply put, Berman took himself too seriously. "He believed . . . the same as Jack Benny being a penny pincher . . . Shelley Berman was trying to be a perfectionist temperamental star," said Marty Kummer, who once managed him. "He would kid himself on being temperamental. He tried to get that image. But the truth was, he was temperamental and went out of his way, unknowingly, making himself a bad guy."

Indeed the voice that compelled whole freights of prose was, in certain registers, a drear whine, a sound like a novice violin. It came up through the nose, a bilious chalk that uncorked an impeccable anger and made a common beef sound like oratory.

He did it even with the facts of his life. Fifteen years after his early struggles, he recalled the details with the knotted impatience his stage figure worked up to. The treacheries of synthetic fibers for instance— plague of first days on the road: *Someone invented these shirts that you could wash and they'll hang out without any wrinkles. That's what they said. They didn't tell you they were going to turn a rotten sour-cream color and that not all of the threads were nylon. Some of those threads are going to shrink and pucker up your collar. They never told you that.*

Onstage, he coined comedy out of it. Offstage, it was no laughs. Avant Garde's Maynard Sloate called him "a mean and miserable man," but seemed to mean it less severely than it sounded. There was the begrudging twinkle in his recollection of meeting Shelley a few years after having employed him.

"I saw Shelley," said Sloate, "when he was a major star at the Sahara. I saw him in the casino. He said, 'Maynard, by god, how are you?' Hugging and kissing and did-you-see-the-show? I said, 'See your show, Shelley? I've seen enough of you to last me for a lifetime.' And he looked at me and put his hands up in the air, and said, 'Maynard, you're a breath of fresh air.' "

KUMMER: He destroyed himself. He didn't mean to. He's troubled.

Q: ?

KUMMER: He couldn't stop thinking about . . . stop imagining things and stop second-guessing the world. Just do your job and get the hell home. Stop finding fault. For example, it got to a point where he could find fault that a glass wasn't in his dressing room for him to have a glass of water.

Q: What made him—

KUMMER: It's all the things he probably envisioned a star in show biz [should be] when . . . when he was a young man.

Q: Is there—

KUMMER: You've got to understand this is the same fellow who would take an hour of his time to talk to you because he knew that your mother wasn't feeling well. Or go out of his way because he knew every-

thing personally was going wrong. A
very concerned human being.

Q: But?

KUMMER: Self-destructive.

What started his fall was *Comedian Backstage*, a
TV documentary on him that aired in 1963. It was
a close-up of Shelley on an engagement at a major
Florida hotel.

The camera tracked him in his room, in elevators,
in lobbies, backstage. It was with him in casual
moments and on the job. It caught a nervous compulsive quality. Here Berman apologized to a hotel
employee for his room. *It's a little messy. I'm sorry.*
There he strained for the common touch with an
elevator girl. *That's a funny last name you have,
Donna. Donna 176.* A portent was offered in Berman's
warning: *I like extreme quiet back here, George, when
I'm working, because I have an ear on me.*

The scene that proved his undoing was one in which
a phone rang at a poignant moment in his favorite
routine—the immigrant father talking to his son, the
actor. Berman finished the piece and the show. Then
he came backstage.

He ignored the applause out front and fumed. *In
the middle of an act! To ring a friggin' phone!* The
mouth was slack, the eyes stricken. He was close to
tears. *Where did that come from?* In ex-manager
Kummer's memory, Shelley next "ripped" the phone
off the wall. Not so. He removed it from the hook,
though Berman's *I let it drop to the end of the cord,
I didn't throw it* placed him nearer the side of the
angels than strict accuracy allowed. With the phone
still jiggling on its line, he kept on about it. *Have to
ruin the act.* And so on. "That was," said Maynard
Sloate, "perfect Shelley. Ideal Shelley. Shelley at his
best."

Years later, it was the scene the public remembered.
Back then, a critic in the New York *Herald-Tribune*
wrote:

According to the program's evidence, he is extremely nervous, a chronic worrier, full of self-pity, self-deception and colossal ego, a spoiled child with a nasty temper, a petty disposition and a taste for tyranny and a blind insensitivity to others. That is quite a catalog of faults to be airing willingly as if it were splendid public relations.

Berman traced his decline from the program. And yet he had the clapsticks from it on the walls of his Beverly Hills home a decade later. Kummer claimed two versions of the program were taped—one with the phone ringing and one without—and Shelley elected to include the pivotal scene. Berman said he had control of what went into the show.

BERMAN: I did not think that this made me look bad. I thought it made me look like I cared. And I thought that everybody would understand and would empathize and would sympathize . . . No. I was wrong. I was more wrong than I ever dreamed.

Because the disease was a slow disease. From that point on, I'd suddenly been deprived of every single privilege, or annoyance, disagreement. I had suddenly been deprived of even anger because from that moment on, from that time on, no matter what I did that seemed slightly unpleasant it became amplified. Or it was anticipated. I went to Mr. Kelly's. So help me god, this is true. I went to Mr. Kelly's that same year, late that same year. And I had worked Mr. Kelly's every year since I began in 1957. I'd worked Mr. Kelly's six years. And I came in that afternoon to bring in a few of my things. And I saw all of the help, people that I knew when I began, 'cause they didn't have a big turnover in that room, the same maître d's, the same captains, the same waitresses, the same waiters, the same bartender. They were all sitting in the club and there was a maître d' who knew me when I didn't know how to tolerate a moment of silence when I thought there should have been laughter. He knew me when I was disconsolate when there was a bad show. He was saying, "If anyone serves a drink during Mr. Berman's show, I will personally . . ." And I said, "What are you saying?" They didn't even see me standing in the room. "What are you saying? I've never done this to you. You know me." They'd forgotten. They had learned a new me. And they all believed it now. They all believed what they had seen. Even though they knew better.

Q: You never had a no-service . . .

BERMAN: I had had controlled service. I don't want the Waring blender at the bar, please. Makes too much noise. Such and such. But I never insisted on no service in that room, never. I never said . . . I'm hearing a guy say, "Now when Berman's on, don't breathe." Don't breathe? Well, I tell you, it grew. Everywhere I went, things grew. Things got out of proportion. I never . . . just a minute . . I wonder if there's . . . [Gets up to search a desk.] I wish to hell I knew where . . . there's a certain letter I would like you to see. Godammit. Well, it's a shame. There's a letter I wanted you to see. It's too bad, too bad. These things always get filed. Here is a letter I received today, I'll read it for your tape here. It's from the North Shore Music Theatre in

328

Beverly, Massachusetts, in response to my letter written about a week ago.

Dear Shelley,

Thank you for your letter. As far as I am concerned, there is no need to discuss the matter any further. For a number of years, I have heard "things" about you. If they are not true, I would think you should know about it. If they are true and you want to do something about correcting it, I also think you should know about it. I made a decision several weeks ago.

That was to hire me for his summer stock theater.

I have no reason to regret it as yet, and am looking forward to the production with very positive good thoughts. The proof of the pudding is in the eating. I have just received the rehearsal material and I will be sending you a script and score within the next couple of days. We are looking forward to meeting you here in Beverly.

> *Cordially yours,*
> *Stephan Slane*

I can't find the letter that was sent in which he was informed of some of my transgressions.

Q: He got a letter saying that—

BERMAN: No, he did not get a letter. He made a phone call to my previous employer with a road show that I just finished. I was on tour with *Two By Two*, a musical comedy about Noah's Ark. I was on that tour for six months. He had heard that I was difficult. He wanted me to do *The Rothschilds* for him, whch I will be doing this season [summer 1973]. But he called my producers to find out, 'cause he heard so many things about me and how difficult I can be. And he was given by somebody in that office a lot of information about me. It was such a disgusting litany of crimes. It was so untrue and so undeserved that he had . . . that he had second thoughts about whether he wanted to hire me. I had to appeal to this producer to call this man and straighten it out. I was accused of refusing to go on stage for minor, silly things. I was accused of saying I am Shelley Berman, the star. I was accused of insulting the management in curtain speeches and using obscene gestures. None of it was true. But somebody in that office does honestly feel that I did this. He's sure I did it.

Q: Was he around in the flesh or was he just sitting . . .

BERMAN: He was in an office. I'm not talking about the producer himself, but his assistant who really believes it. But even the producer believes it. Even the producer believes it. He believes it. They believe these things. Life has become pretty hellish. There are many, many people who would not hire me and will not hire me because of this. So my . . . the pressures you're asking about are not normal pressures. They're not . . . You're not talking to, say, *any* comedian with pressures. You're talking about a unique set of circumstances now. I'm a man who exposed my anger to the public and am now reaping the harvest of what I sowed. I . . . wow . . . So you find that in an

330

ordinary conversation with a fellow employee, say at a nightclub or when you're
talking to a lighting man, there is a surfeit of pleases and thank yous. There is
an abundance of apologies. There's a
very carefully structured smile and reply
to a person who has called out from the
audience and hurt your act. There's a
good sportsmanlike way that you accept
the fact that you have been handed a
drink for use during your show and have
been charged full price for it each time.
A drink that you use as a prop in the
show. And that they don't charge you
"cost" or they don't give it to you. You're
charged.

Q: Against your salary?

BERMAN: Yah.

Q: And this is since 1963?

BERMAN: All of these things are in accumulation.
I am, in fact, legendary. If this sounds
grossly egotistical to you, I am sorry
about that, but it is true. I'm in the midst
of my own legend. And the legend is
nothing more than an amalgam of facts
with a tendency to fat. I know there are
certain truths about misbehaviors, but I
also know that they are no more than
any other performer's and conceivably
they are less. But I can't get away with
them.

Q: Because you're labeled?

BERMAN: Oh, it's quite well established. And not
only that, it builds. It doesn't melt . . .
it doesn't thaw and resolve itself into a
dew. It stays around. It even gathers you
in your sleep like some evil succubus. It

331

really . . . it haunts you. I worked with a piano that was out of tune. I worked with lights that don't work. And with a bad sound system—because to request or to annoy by the requesting of a sound system or a lighting system is to invite reprisal, either from the press or by that management. And sometimes by your own agent. I went . . . did a concert . . . oh, I don't know, a few years back. This is after this 1963. Everything is predicated upon that. In Hartford, Connecticut, they hired me and they found a theater and they had no spotlight for me. It was a theater. They were selling tickets for seven dollars, ten dollars. Those poor guys didn't know anything. I didn't have a light. But you gotta have a light, man. They said, "We can see you." I said, "No, it's not like that. I know you can see me. I know you can even read in bad light. But no, it's not . . . there's more to perception than that, than just being able to see me. There's far more. I know you need a light. Trust me." There was only one light that was available. It could be rented for seventy-five dollars from another city. I said, "Get it. I'll pay for it." I paid for the light. They had it brought in. The report given to the head of the Variety Department at William Morris, Lee Salomon, who is one of my agents, the report given him by the agent who covered this particular job for me and who, incidentally, wasn't there to help, the report was I was uncooperative. I know what was uncooperative about me. I offered to let those men off their five-thousand-dollar hook. They were paying me five grand for the night. I said, "I can't go on and cheat your people this way. I won't. I'll let you have your five grand back. I won't take money for this. You must have a light. You must get one." It was a theater, a movie theater. And they had a little flickering candlelight back there. I said you need a trooper. And I know the kind they needed. They needed a super trooper for that house. And I paid for it. Now, in order to cooperate, in order to be categorized as cooperative, it would have required that I go on and do my show in almost darkness. Not give the audience the laughter they were entitled to . . . but if this is what is expected of me, I must say that many times I have accommodated them in the last few years.

Q: You mean, tailed off on performance to satisfy management?

BERMAN: Correct. Correct.

Q: Do you resent it?

BERMAN: YOU'RE FUCKING WELL RIGHT I DO! These aren't ordinary pressures. These are extraordinary because you know when you're selling out. You know it. You know when you've let your own fear take over. You look at your wife and your children and your home and you want to hang on to a little bit of that if you can. Well, you have to make a choice. Do you want your self-respect by quitting the business? Or are you willing to compromise just a little bit more in the way you whore? Well, I had decided a little bit more compromising in the way I whore is the only . . . Either decision you can't win.

Q: Where do you . . . what clubs do you—

BERMAN: There are lots of clubs around the country. And I work some of the Playboy clubs and I work other little clubs. I make a reasonable living.

Q: Do you see any way to recoup your gains or are you—

BERMAN: I don't know.

Q: You're rarely on television. How come?

BERMAN: Eventually I lost my heat. But that isn't the most important thing. There's a lot of performers who aren't very hot. I can still draw. And I can still bring a few numbers onto their charts . . . I mean their listings. But if it was a toss-up between two similar talents, let's say, or two talents of a similar quality and a similar status and you know for certain that one is a headache but one isn't, you will take the one who isn't the headache.

Q: The sweetheart?

BERMAN: That's correct. Well, I am the headache. And even after I tried not to be a headache, I found that there was no way around that. Even when I pleaded and I pleaded . . . oh boy, did I plead. I mean I *pleaded.* There are ways of surviving. I will still work. And I will still earn a living. And I still have achievement. I have achievement behind me that people have yet to make. And I'll have more. I have lots. I mean, my life isn't over, but goddammit, it's hard.*

---

* Emmet Thompson, a waiter at Mr. Kelly's since 1955, was there when Berman first appeared—with, as he recalled, shoes that had holes in them. There was, he said, controlled service whenever Berman worked.

Producer Thomas Mallow of American Theater Productions,

Of Berman it was once stated in jest:

> [He] worries about everything in "his
> theater," from the hospital plan for the
> backstage employees to the off-street
> parking for the audience.

Mort Sahl said it at a time when both he and Shelley could afford to be chuckly about their foibles.

The day was past. They were no longer in favor. Sahl's fix on the JFK assassination was a subject whose limits as comedy he soon exhausted. He ended belaboring the point and listeners as well. And he ceased as a leading comic voice.

Inc., did not find Berman blameless in his company's tour of *Two by Two*. He said that he received a report from a Dayton, Ohio, promoter that Berman made an obscene gesture (pertaining to the show's producers) in a curtain speech after the final night on the road. "I was quite livid," Mallow said. "I wrote him a seven-page letter. Then he happened to call me. I told him I'd sent him a letter on it and that I was very livid. And he said, 'If it's that kind of letter, I don't want to read it.' And he sent it back to me unopened. But he profusely denied that he would ever do such a thing."

Mallow's assistant, Jim Janek, conceded he was not present for all the incidents he reported to Stephan Slane. But, he said, his account was based on reports to him from the show's stage manager and other sources. He claimed there were nights Berman threatened not to go on stage unless his beard was trimmed or his boots repaired. "However," he said, "I told Stephan Slane the good and bad both." Added Mallow: "He was giving everybody a bad time . . . on minor things. But by the same token, he made the show happen. . . . He proved to the industry that Shelley Berman was a much finer actor than most of the people in the industry realized."

Stephan Slane, who hired Berman for *The Rothschilds* in spite of his notoriety, said, "Shelley was a hard-working guy and very responsible . . . Uh, I think he got a little uptight during rehearsals. But I had . . . uh . . . great admiration for him because he takes his work very seriously and wants to work hard." Slane said a good number of "stories" about Berman were, he guessed, true. "I would think that Shelley Berman could be a very difficult person under certain circumstances."

Of the incident in Hartford, Connecticut, Lee Salomon of William Morris said that the agency does not "cover" every job its clients have. Asked if the bad report was justified, he said, "Half and half. He [Berman] exaggerates. You're never a hit or a flop based on just the lights."

335

So did Berman. He worked, but without fanfare. Indeed, there was an incident at a Playboy club when a bunny didn't recognize him as the comic, and asked to see his key.

Vegas, which used Berman when he was a national phenomenon, got along without him when he was just another act. Had he forty fast minutes of one-liners it might have found a spot for him.

Las Vegas remained the gauge of conventional tastes. Comedy was more old-timey than not. Its only concession to change was that the jokes were see-through. Sex was not tabu any more, though it was hardly used subtly.

Hackett and Greene, come east to Westbury, Long Island, got laughs in the opening seconds of their act with the same shtick. They grabbed their balls. In their hands, so to speak, it was funny. For they were immensely likable.

> They told me to clean up my act. I did.
> I threw out all the dirty words. All I had
> left was "Hello,"

said Greene, kidding the act again, an agreeable tactic. With his cherubic looks, Hackett could say anything and it sounded out of the mouths of babes.

The both of them and Rickles were the Doctor Feelgoods of the comic trade. They knew about jacking an audience up, the basic lounge technique. It made the act seem spontaneous. In part, it was. The rest was rote, tricked up. Greene, clutching his pianist by the lapels, would shout: *I made that up! Tell 'em! I made that up!* for a line he'd done before. With Hackett, the names and knockers changed. Rickles too was a superior switchboard act.

They all did god-bless as well. It was apparently what their audiences wanted. Not that it was confined to just Vegas. The coffeehouses had their own shibboleths. Klein, ridiculing establishment figures, often thrust forked fingers at their imagined persons, a gesture he found crowds relished. *Jesus, they really go for it.* He began doing it more for a while, curbed it out of the dictates of his own comic.

Sometimes, laughs were stoked by politics in the coffeehouses. Klein had a bit on the Raid insecticide commercial that inveighed against its "kill mentality." He decried its depicting them as amiable critters, in his words, "doing the be-bop in the kitchen," a step whose animation he made a Carmen Miranda number. Against that came the sudden cry of terror —"Jiggers, Raids!"—at the entry of (here was the phrase) *this big fascist bottle.*

The term always brought a walloping roar from his crowd. Klein helped it with the imagery he offered— he stood, arms akimbo, head cocked regally, like the Captain Marvel of insecticides. But the response went beyond mere comedy dynamics. The image touched a nerve in the under-thirty group. Had he performed it before the Rotary Club, he'd have gotten laughs too —but not the belly-up ones he got at the Bijou/Bitter End.

It raised the laugh level so that when Klein took his index finger, placed it atop his head and, with dainty precision, pressed down *CHHHH* to spray, the coffeehouse crowd laughed at the fey form of the so-called fascist container.

> CHHHH. And they go poof! Bam! Dead! Dead! Dead! I wouldn't mind the crap if the product worked. Did you ever know a roach that could care?
>
> Jiggers, RAAIID!
>
> Cockroach: Eh! (*Flashing the middle finger.*)
>
> On a direct hit, you get 'em. Otherwise, they go to apartment Six-H for four weeks. They come back later.

Bluestone, returning from a week at Passim's, just off Harvard Square, noted the place of partisan politics with devilish glee. "You tell 'em something like you don't eat lettuce, they go crazy for you."

Larry Brezner, who'd run the Focus in an activist Upper West Side neighborhood, remembered comic nights that came grounding to a halt on semantic nuances. "We occasionally got into battles," he said, "with some women who were really heavy into women's lib. For a comic, that's deadly, ya know. Comic name of Carl Waxman—guy that emcees down at Folk City and has been a Village comic for nine thousand years—he got into a half-hour debate because of the word 'chicks.'

"And that's the funny thing about new comics, they have to be in some ways more sensitive to their audience and offending people. Young kids would criticize the old comics. . . . But like Lenny Bruce, man, he didn't care who he offended. That was beautiful.

"But let a comic go out and joke with women's lib people, joke racially, and that's not funny because it's politics. And there's a real lack of humor that way. It's—watch-it! Anyway, Waxman said, 'chicks.' And it started a debate that virtually ended the evening. You know, he wound up by saying, 'I'll kick you in the tits,' just to get a laugh. Like, 'Screw the Irish!' Anything. To get the audience on his side. Well, that really did it. Half the audience walked out and that was it.

"And he didn't say it out of anger. He said it because he meant to be funny. He wanted *out* any way he could. And couldn't do it. He was in trouble. And from the audience would come, 'Why are you using that word, *chicks?* And how do you explain it?' Deadly, man, deadly.

"Now, I saw Chris Rush get into the same kind of thing. But he pulled himself out of it by saying,

> I think your demands are outrageous . . . like that demand that you build a hole next to the Washington Monument equally as deep. Now, that's outrageous.

And to me it was a beautiful out."

Peter Anthony, the Vegas lounge comic: "Like one of my opening lines—

You know what true happiness is? True happiness is looking Jewish and being Italian.

"Boom. So right away I got the Jews on my side, and the Italians on my side. And the Polish wondering where I'm at. Then I do some Irish humor. And I got a whole hunk where I bring all nationalities in. Including blacks and Germans and what have you. I really leave it wide open, man. So no matter what I say, nobody is gonna be uptight. I bring in junkies, weirdos, perverts, roller derby queens, fruits, everybody's got a shot. And everybody can somehow relate."

It was a way, man. Comedy as octopi sly, dervish strokes that left the comic a disembodied grin and fevered brow. Black comics knew the number, too. Slappy White wrapped his act up with a black glove on one hand, a white glove on the other and did mumbo jumbo Kennedy/King bup bup brothers under the skin. God-bless was the ticket for some of the soul sound too. It paid, in $pades. Money was their magic. They wanted it for interviews too. Some of them came on coy. *Now your publisher paying you, right? . . . Git what I'm saying?* Foxx's manager, Bardu Ali, was more direct. *What's in it for us, man?* No talk with the cauc without money.

Money was not everything with Dick Gregory. Those who knew him talked of his "strange spiny ethic." Autobiographical collaborator Lipsyte recalled what Gregory did when the book was optioned as a movie: "Greg tore up the old contract so I'd be cut into the movie rights. He said, 'Well, man, it was your words.'"

Gregory was phasing out comedy to get serious. At colleges, he worked preferred rates when hired as a lecturer. (He got up to three thousand dollars for comedy, up to fifteen hundred for a lecture.) His last year working in clubs was 1973. Gregory said it forced him to keep late hours, which bedded him down in the daylight hours when a fellow could be of "service." It was his word. *I can give more service,* he said.

What he had in mind was suspect by the parapolice in the land.

Q: How so?

GREGORY: My phone was tapped, you know. Government agents follow you around.

Q: People were following you?

GREGORY: Yeah. I knew that way before this mess [Watergate] started coming out. I mean, this documented evidence now of the files they got on me.

Q: Have you seen files on you?

GREGORY: I've been able to get hold of some, yeah.

Q: Whose?

GREGORY: Oh, various agencies. The one I got hold of was Air Force Intelligence prepared it.

Q: You remember the gist of it?

GREGORY: I remember the files was that thick. [Indicates.]

Q: About four or five inches thick?

GREGORY: It's about ten inches thick. The interesting thing is how the military views a fast and pure ethics. They said I had . . . They ended the files by saying I had a messiah complex with suicidal tendencies. That's beautiful, man. To know the military is still the military.

Q: Well, ten inches of stuff. What were they getting into?

GREGORY: Where I move. What I did. Who I talked

to. What time I went to bed. What time
I went out. All kinds of things.

Q: How did you get hold of it?

GREGORY: You can get hold of anything you want to
get hold to, man. That ain't no big thing.
You can get hold of anything you want.
And there's a lot of people that give you
things, you see, there's a lot of people
that when they follow you for as long as
some of them been following me, I win
them over. 'Cause when they follow me,
they ain't following nothin' but pure
ethics, man. And that has tremendous
effect.

Q: You say there was some kind of contact . . .

GREGORY: Oh yeah. Sure.

Q: With them? In other words, the thing became humanized?

GREGORY: Right. Yeah.

Q: Did they ever come to see you work in
clubs?

GREGORY: They always come to clubs. I mean, that's
an assignment. You get two types of cats.
You get the cat that sits in the club at
every engagement. Never laughs. So you
know he's The Man. And you get another
cat that little by little he starts breaking,
he starts breaking, he starts breaking.
You start talking to him. Or you throw
something out, you know, about "six
slimy degenerate FBI, CIA agents." And
you see 'em flinch. You see the whole
scene.

Q: When you—

GREGORY: Some of them . . . sometimes their wives or their girl friends come up. Say, "I love you and I'm so disgusted 'bout so and so, so and so . . ."

Q: So and so following?

GREGORY: Yeah.

Q: How do you know your phone's tapped.

GREGORY: Well, you can tell when your phone is tapped. You can hear them talking. See, if I tapped your phone for a few minutes, I might could do it. But when I got to tap it year round, the burden's on me. Somewhere I got to make a mistake. It's like if you run through a stop sign 'cause you're in a hurry, that's one thing. But if you run through a stop sign 'cause that's the way you drive, it's gonna catch up with you. Law of average is gonna catch up with you in the long run. And I can hear them on the phone, pick up the phone. I can call you and hang up and my line won't get released for maybe an hour.

Q: That's happened, literally happened?

GREGORY: Yeah. I've had—when was it? About six weeks ago, I called home. My wife said, "You'll never believe this. The phone ring. I pick up the phone. I said, 'Hello.' I hear something at the other end say, 'Hello, FBI.' So I said, 'Hello.' And they say 'Hello, FBI.'" She said, "I'm answering my phone." And he said, "I'm answering my phone." Somewhere the electronic device cross wired and we got all the FBI's calls that night. I got friends

that you can call my friend's house and
my phone will answer. . . .And then the
one time that I really knew was when I refused to pay my phone bill. And they
wouldn't cut it off. They would not cut
my phone off till I held a press conference. See, as much money as I'm making
in course of a year . . . and I had not
paid my phone bill. And they refused to
cut it off. And then that day, *pshew*, it
goes off.*

Gregory's rap was without the crash idioms some
comics favored. It was a line with the wire-rimmed
specs of the ideologist on it. It was unblinkingly as-
sertive, gospel that never took a step back. *You can
alienate him fast if you disagree,* said Dick Davy,
who was there nights when a doubting word was
spoken.

Gregory's associates used to claim that phone lines
went dead when they shouted into them that J. Edgar
Hoover was a faggot. If the FBI/CIA were Gregory's
bugbears, it was CMA other comics worried over.

Career politics: It was the burning issue—and there
was no need to apologize. The crusaders were few.
Many of the new comics dealt with the issues—not to
was considered a default in the coffeehouses and on
campuses—but resisted the soapbox impulse—and
wisely so. The moment a comic thought he was bigger
than his last laugh, he was in trouble. Or he was
Ralph Nader.

Either way, it made material matter more than
political bravura. Sahl found out. And Lenny would
have too had he lived to do the didactic bushwah he
was into at the end. Free of court snafus, he'd have
lost the outlaw aura that gave him license with crowds.
The lessons were there. The money was in the laughs.
And, in the end, so was the impact a comic could
make with whatever "statement" he had.

---

* In spring '72, investigative columnist Jack Anderson wrote
that the FBI kept a file on Gregory and that his name was also
on the Secret Service's list of potential assassins. (Groucho
Marx's was too.)

No question: it was a political climate in 1973–74 —one that the thinking man's comic was able to use to his advantage. Watergate begged to be lampooned. Out on the streets was the proof—on buttons and bumper stickers. Free the Watergate 5,000/Don't blame me—I voted for McGovern/Impeach the Coxsacker. Campaign buttons that Republicans distributed in 1968 now had a ghoulish ring to them— Nixon's the One.

For some comics, Watergate proved a boon. It gave Steinberg the new act he'd been unable to find before.

> Gerald Ford is the Dale Evans of Washington.

> And John Connally is the rare instance of a rat swimming toward a sinking ship.

Dit-dit: the lines came. Watergate was his mother lode.

Klein spoofed Spiro Agnew's sentence—golf in Palm Springs with Sinatra—and wondered when the hooligan who held up the A&P was going to say to the judge, "Uh . . . I'll take the Agnew punishment, please." When Robert did his Agnew material on "The Tonight Show," censors held a two-hour discussion after.

Watergate suited David Frye too, and proved again that politics made for strange bedfellows. For if Frye's act was politically concerned, he was not. He'd made a reputation on political impressions (LBJ, Hubert Humphrey, Nelson Rockefeller, George Wallace), the success of which relied on the vital functions of those men. When Robert Kennedy's ceased, Frye was aggrieved. With tears in his eyes, booze in his hand, he told comics at the Improvisation that it blew one of his key bits.

Frye was best when he had another man to be. On his own, he was in trouble, a dark brooding figure whose moods capsized in a shot glass. In August 1973, it happened while he was on the job at San Francisco's Fairmont Hotel. He was fired for being, as that city's *Chronicle* said, "drunk as a skunk." The paper's entertainment reporter, John Wasserman, wrote:

> *In 10 years of skulking around this beat, I have never seen anything like it, at least not from a professional. It wasn't even a bad show, in the normal usage of that word, but rather a painfully embarrassing montage of a man falling apart in front of one's own eyes. . . .*
>
> *He was often unintelligible, forgot his routines, repeated lines, was alternately insulting and obsequious toward the audience, garbled his impersonations and generally made a shambles of the entire affair. . . .*

If it gave Gray Line tourists there a jolt, it was ho-hum to New York comics. Frye had been into the gin before, and with bad results. *We've had our ups and down,* said Budd Friedman, who'd given him the heave-ho one night for conduct unbecoming a comic.

Curious: the nuances Frye found in others, he himself lacked. In casual conversation, eye contact was negligible, which was rare among comics. His inability to converse was a sore point with Carson. Frye was booked for "The Tonight Show" on nights Johnny was off. On one such occasion, guest host David Steinberg asked him a simple question about apartments in New York and Frye said he was not prepared to talk about it.

Peter Anthony again: "One time I'm doing shtick on the band. Now there's a guy in the band who I happen to know. I mean, I know the guy socially, right? And while I'm doing shtick on the band—*Hey, this band behbehbeh*—I say,

Boy, that's a bad rug, man

and I look at this guy and just go on with my act. And what do you think happened? The guy got *livid*. After the break, he finally gets me aside, says, 'Peter.' You could feel breathing. 'I don't like the remark about my hair.' And do you know the guy was wearing a rug. And I didn't know. It looked like he combed it like a rug. And he went on. And I tell you, I talked to him for twenty minutes. 'I know you, right? We got mutual friends, right? Would I . . .' 'I had a couple chicks in the audience. And they didn't know.' And . . . so actually, he was uptight because the chicks found out he had the rug on."

It was why acts covered their flanks. *God-bless/ my wife/ my kids/ America*—a rat-a-tat and reminder it was of what a sterling fellow was up there.

It could get silly. At the Friars' roast for Youngman were lines like,

> To this day, gentlemen, it says here Henny's never changed his act. Not one line. If a broad bit his lob, he couldn't ad lib "Ouch."

> But he is the king of the one-liners. We all know that. And he's had some famous one-liners. "He's a cheap motherfucker, but I'll take the date."

> Famous one-liners. "Honey, can I put it in your ass?"

> In West Berlin, he saw a crack in the wall, and he sucked it. In Holland, he stuck his finger in a dike and she kicked him in the balls.

Back of the dais were (count 'em) four American flags, one of them artificially wind-blown for the anthem.

There were no women at Henny's fete, though Totie Fields and Hermione Gingold were mentioned. The references were ribald.

So it went.

The weight of the word was against them in comedy. In gags, women traditionally pivoted on the proverbial nine inches.

Onstage, the ones that made it were of a "type," some species of dizzy dame, bizarre femmes who did screaming meemie acts, a menagerie of distorted femininity.

These days, if ladies were in men's saloons and NASA programs and in cop cruisers too, not many were doing jokes. The Improvisation and now its crosstown rival, Catch a Rising Star, were equal opportunity employers, but in 1973 few new comediennes were around. The Comedy Store in LA too was where the boys were.

Clearly, the gig had no allure for the performing Ms. Too tacky. Lily Tomlin once was in a revue with a girl she thought had a comic flair. "She did an impression," Tomlin recalled. "I said, 'Oh, you're fabulous. You've gotta do that on the stage.' 'Oh, I'd never do anything like that onstage. I don't want anyone to think I'm unattractive.'"

A dearth of example. Too many grotesques had gone by, savaging magic. A hag legacy. It'd be a weird little jill who got off on screech sisters Fields/Raye/Diller and Barth. Somewhere well below Eleanor Roosevelt they ranked for inspiration.

To be warm, funny and a lady was a feat worthy of a Carnegie Medal. It took courage for an attractive woman to do the jokes. The problems were immense. Jessica James found out. As the song lead of "Jessie and the James Boys," she was the sexy dynamo of a music and toomle lounge act in Vegas. A breeze for her. On her own, doing a comedy single, it was trickier.

For her, women often were more a problem than men.

> I'm not on Main Street, interrupting your your business, lady,

she'd say, when they'd booze and then heckle her.

JAMES: Some things with men. In the Thunderbird Lounge once. At a time I was doing singing and comedy both. I'm onstage and I feel a hand come up my leg. And I look down——I'm singing with the microphone in my hand. I didn't have one of those around my neck in that place. And this guy is not looking at me. Looking the other way. But he's like got his hand up my dress like he's making a right turn. Do you follow me?

So I figure I'll solve this problem. I'll move. So I move my leg. I twisted in my chair to go to another angle. And he leaned back and did it again. Now really. I don't know what he thought he was doing but it was almost like he had an arm that had another life. Because he looked like Mr. Peepers. He had like real thick little glasses on. Round ones. Baldheaded. Very simple-looking. Kind of like a minister type, I guess. And he's got his hand up my leg. It's like if I didn't know that his hand was attached to him, I would swear it wasn't him.

Q: And as strictly a comic?

JAMES: I mean a comedienne is a kind of sex by itself. You're not really a girl, you know. Being very very feminine, like Phyllis Diller is now, doesn't make it because it's such an aggressive thing to do. So most of the men in the business . . . agents . . . they'd feel threatened. Very hostile.

Q: How so?

JAMES: Be in competition. Even if they liked me. They would challenge me with a sense of humor. You'd have to be funny with them. They wanted me to laugh at them. What happened to me was that I felt like I was getting more masculine.

Q: How do you mean?

JAMES: With the comics. If you were a girl, they would kind of be cooler about their language. About expressions and their stories. But if you're a comedienne . . . you've got to tell those kind of stories. Am I making myself clear at all?

Q: Can you specify?

JAMES: I'm thinking of one night in the Thunderbird that I was sitting at the table with all these guys. Jack Carter and John Byner. Some others. And it was really a rough conversation. Throwing jokes back and forth. That was all right. That was fun. I would kind of keep out of that because I didn't like to get run over. But then there was a kind of filthiness that started, kind of boys' thing, you know. That's the moment I felt I graduated, that I was one of them. I was a stand-up comic. And I'll tell you, that night I realized that I wasn't a girl anymore with these guys. It hurt me. And I thought, "Oh no, this is terrible. I'm going to end up doing this forever." I kept doing it for quite a while because I enjoyed it. But I decided that I'd just as soon have somebody else's script and be in a show and not have that whole thing.

Q: How'd you mean—a sex by itself?

JAMES: You know, the stance of the thing, the physical thing is very masculine. I mean, you just don't stand up there with your knockers hanging out, especially if they're large like mine. My thing was I would stand up onstage like this kind of thing.

Q: Hands on hips?

JAMES: Yeah. Very aggressive kind of a thing. And my physical posture changed because I was like doing this constantly.

Q: In so-called everyday life?

JAMES: Ya, ya . . . I got very aggressive. Like even in the supermarket.

Q: Less ladylike?

JAMES: You better believe it. I would be like that in the supermarket. I'd be making jokes in the supermarket. I felt like I was getting to be a taxicab driver. Talking out of the side of my mouth. And it sounds terrible, but actually that's what does happen.

Q: All at once?

JAMES: No, it sort of crept up on me.

Q: Any crowning moment?

JAMES: Well, that night I told you with Jack Carter, John Byner and the others. Like it started in the afternoon for brunch with those guys. And then we all went to work. And then the lounge at the Tropicana went on later than any other. They had the latest show. Everyone would catch that show. It went on something like 4:30 in the morning. So that night, those guys were telling these stories, slapping each other around, being very physical. And a couple of them slapped me on the back, almost gave me whiplash, you know. And I said, "Oh, my god, this is it." That was it for me. That night. I found myself heckling John Byner when he went on-stage. All these guys would sit and heckle John from the back of the room. And

350

I was doing the same thing. I mean, I was not being very much of a lady. I was drinking too.

Q: So you changed?

JAMES: Oh my god, yes. You see what happens is that when you are a stand-up comedienne, you feel compelled to be funny all the time. The whole thing. You start to look like one of those hood things on a 'sixty-eight Chevy. You've got your chin out like this, you know, and it's like you're ready anywhere. People are only something to bounce your jokes off. It's a very inhuman kind of thing. Very unfeminine. And the owners out here. Treat you really like you were a man. Oh, they talk to you like you're one of the guys. "Get your ass out on the stage."

Q: Literally?

JAMES: Yes. Literally. Oh god almighty. All the time. Perhaps that's one of the things . . . now that you bring that up . . . that's one of the things that hurt me. "Get your ass out on the stage, baby." Baby nothing. "Get your ass out on the stage now. Go on, bitch." They talk to you like . . . when you were a singer, they didn't talk to you that way.

And once you're onstage, you put on a high-neck thing that does not fit you correctly. It's too big on you, so that nobody can get any sexual ideas toward you because sex and comedy don't make it except in burlesque. So it's like you're sexless out on the stage. You try to be as sexless as possible. I didn't want to look too bizarre. I wanted to look just kind of cool, you know. Like a human being. But I understand what Phyllis Diller did by frizzing up her hair and all this, that and the other. Because when she took completely took her femininity away from her, then she could go out on the stage. The women knew that she wasn't in competition with them. And the men couldn't think of her as a sex object.

If women turned up as comics in the '70s, Lily Tomlin was going to be a reason. She restated a tradition that had borrowed wholesale from the hyped gestalt of the men. She ditched two-fisted mannerisms for a silkier kinetic, a grace that allowed for its paradox.

Onstage, Tomlin stepped lightly, ladylike ease she'd tinker with as she talked. For no apparent reason she'd bend from the waist, touch palms to the floor raise up and go on with the act as if nothing had happened.

It was a squirrelly note in keeping with the blithe and lively intelligence that ran her comic. Tomlin on stage had the impertinence of a J. D. Salinger juvenile. By Lily's recall, she was an unorthodox child.

Growing up, she once saw a comedienne on Sullivan's show whose material she memorized and later performed in backyard vaudeville. To this day, she remembered some of the lines:

> Not that my husband is stingy. It's just that he has short arms and low pockets.

> I'll never forget the first time I saw my husband standing on a hill, his hair blowing in the breeze and he too proud to run after it.

"I used those jokes," she said. "I don't know why I remembered those. I must have been about nine ten. And those jokes apparently struck me as very funny . . . 'cause I remembered 'em and always told 'em."

As a wise child will, she fell in with odd company.

delighted by their grandiose ways, pieces of which cropped up in her characters later. A memorable one from her childhood was Mrs. Rupert, the botanist. "The kind of lady who wore hats and furs and gloves to empty the garbage," she said. "And she took a liking to me. So I spent evenings with Mrs. Rupert. It was a status thing. And she was going to teach me to be a lady. She was going to teach me to 'marry well.' I used to have to wear a little hat 'n' gloves. And I can remember even then . . . really being amused by her and relating what we'd do to other people . . . you know . . . not being suckered in. I just really dug it. I thought she was great.

"The thing I loved most of all that we used to do . . . when we'd go shopping every Saturday. 'Cause she was teaching me to buy linens and fabrics and I had my little purse . . . a lady should be able to get anything without 'rummaging.' The best thing was in wintertime if you're outside walking in the street and you go into a warm place to have cocoa, your nose will start to run if you don't blow your nose first. So we used to go up a side street. And she wasn't very big. She was like a little tiny woman. And I was always rangy. And so she wasn't much bigger than I was. And I loved that too. 'Cause she's like my friend sort of and, uh, I remember we used to go in the doorway and blow our noses. And I thought that was so fabulous . . . and then we'd go in to the restaurant and sure enough there'd be some old person trying to get napkins out of the holder to blow his nose. And we'd be sitting there real cool with our purses."

With her five-year-old character, Edith Ann,

> I do not think I will go to college. I seen pictures where they shoot you in college

and Ernestine the switchboard operator,

> A gracious good afternoon, General, and how is Mrs. Motors. I know you're doing your very best to reduce smog, General. I'm all choked up over it (*snort*),

she kept the cheeky view Mary Jane (her given name)
Tomlin had back then, one that insisted on seeing
things plain. It was her way on stage too. *If I come
out and somebody says, "Hubba hubba," I just throw
'em the finger.* Sweet insouciance.

She was natural too. In her act, she'd put circular
pieces of tape on a stool that she'd arch her body over
rising with the adhesive rings newly emplaced.

> On TV, you're not supposed to know
> there are nipples,

she'd say, hardly impassioned about it, all the better
for making a point. It had the matter-of-fact feel to
it, as if her act came but a step behind her real
thoughts. And so was a proximate truth.

Early on, she worked that way. At the Gaslight
in the Village in the mid-'60s, she was very shy when
she started. So she'd say in a deadpan voice,

> Well, here I am doing the work I love.
> I guess the art of entertaining is just in
> my blood,

spoofing her jitters.

As the show wore on, she succeeded with her monologues. *I'd get a little more confident, a little more
confident. I'd try to relate to somebody. I'd start telling personal things about myself so they'd like me as
a person. And then finally by the end of the show I'm
so confident, you know, I'd say,*

> I'm so elated. And you made me feel so
> much better. And now that I'm going on
> to bigger and better things, I don't need
> you anymore.

Tomlin first came to New York in 1962, staying
at a friend's apartment in the East Village. The friend
was living with a painter who, as Lily put it, was
carrying on the work of Franz Kline. The painter and
mistress did not get on well. They wrote obscene
messages on the walls to each other. *You let your*

arina boil over on the fucking stove. *Goddamn you. I hate you*. Like that. Tomlin slept on a footlocker.

Shortly after, she left New York but was back by 1965, this time to try comedy in the Village and wait tables·on the side. The city's agents got their first real look at Lily one night in 1966. If she was not yet big-time, she did not let on. Out of her '30s wardobe she took an old gown and a white fox wrap. *Really ratty but at night it looked beautiful*. And in that extravagant outfit, she appeared at the door of the Improvisation in a chauffeur-driven limousine.

In, on and out she went, a pack of agents calling her name. Lily stepped back into the limousine and disappeared. A short time before, the limousine had been idling in the theater district, waiting for final curtain. For a fast five dollars, its driver agreed to take her over to 358 West 44th Street and away.

For Lily, a star was borne.

Good as Tomlin was, her example had not yet brought other women out in numbers.

It'd likely take an embattled figure to do that, a woman who'd work with the full white heat of her battered psyche and convert it into laughs spiked all down the line. A Lenny in skirts, a comedienne not afraid to examine the men comics.

Bruce did it in his time with his bit on the comic at the Palladium, a surgical job on the no-taste, no-talent acts doing business then. Any comedienne in it for keeps was bound to start by frisking the comics for their Freudian parcels, and chance outrage doing it. For it'd come to sex with some, and comediennes had yet to take their shots there.

In the end, whatever was good about the lady's material risked reappearing in another act. The switch was no harder here than anywhere else—he/she inversions any hack could do. TV was helpful that way. *If you're going to use any of my material in the book*, said Steve Landesberg, *mention it was on TV*. The "tube" made most comics think twice.

Not all of them, though. A strange tale was told of a comic who stole another's jokes on the subject of prunes and later did them on "The Tonight Show."

The fellow was never invited back. It turned out th gags he'd lifted were stolen property to begin with They'd come from the monologues of Johnny Carson

The electronic age put gadgetry at the service c rogue comics. Out in Las Vegas, Peter Anthony re called: "When I was working in the Bonanza, gu came in who had a rep for stealing material. I'd neve met him but the name was in my head for years. H come back after, says, 'Hey, I'm so and so.' Said 'Hey, glad to meet you.' As I said it, fellow drops small cassette player from under his sleeve. He' gone so far as to get what I said during the show So I guess he also wanted what I was going to sa when I said hello, how are you? He wasn't going t leave nothin' to chance."

If Vegas was promised land for comics, the nev boys looked to Burbank for their immediate future It was there "The Tonight Show" aired. Every half funny kid in the showcases had in mind to make it a midnight on the peacock network.

Some did. For Brenner it was hocus-pocus, th memory of it loosing a gusher of adjectives—amazing incredible, etcetera. And it was: Top money he go doing the jokes up front of Sonny and Cher a shor time after his first shot on "Tonight."

For others, it was no big deal. Mike Preminger, on a number of times, was still not signed to an agency *Just a small thing of impact in the business.* H worked Playboys around the country. But the time o his time was flying by. Just past thirty ("put dow I'm twenty-eight"), he was not where a star shoul be in the comedy game plan. He did not want t end up a journeyman comic. "I can't see myself th rest of my life, 'Ladies and gentlemen, the comed of Mike Preminger.' Getting up on a Thursday evenin in Milwaukee."

At that, he was better off in some ways than he ha been. He had a career—and a social life. There wer women now. "I'm making up," Preminger said, "fo a lot of years when nothing happened. Being a *chozer* I enjoy the hell out of it. I'd be quite content to d just that. Occasionally come up for air, open th windows and do a couple of lines and hop right back in bed."

The ex-Morty Gunty gagman, Richard Lewis, was on "The Tonight Show" in March 1974. For Lewis, it was every wiseacre's sweet returns. In junior high school in Hasbrouck Heights, New Jersey, Lewis remembered, "The principal dismissed the assembly by sections. I was sitting in the center section and he said, the right section—go. Left section—go. The center section, he dismissed by homerooms. Until mine was the only one left. Meanwhile, there was a whole . . . like crowd . . . around the auditorium, waiting to see what's going on. We got to our homeroom. He started dismissing them by rows. And our row was left. And it was sort of ironic. I was sitting right in the fuckin' middle of the auditorium. And he started dismissing people on the side of me. I was the only person left in the auditorium. And over the microphone he boomed out. He said, 'Lewis, you are the troublemaker of this junior high school.' And I cracked up. It was almost like I was in the spotlight at the Copa."

The night Lewis appeared on "The Tonight Show," the Copa was no longer in business, shuttered since the death of Jules Podell months before. For Lewis, midnight was the perfect hour to come back and spook the authorities that had fingered him for this role years ago.

In fact, Lewis recalled those days. Miss LaFuma, the hyperglandular teacher with

> . . . sweat rings under her arms. Like each ring—five years,

and Coach Moose Breckus, who never let a student out class.

> Student: Coach, I have measles.
> Breckus: Walk it off.

It was while Lewis was recollecting Moose Breckus that a strange thing happened. Lewis was telling what a potbellied misfit that coach was, incapable of even blowing a whistle properly. From the audience, clearly audible to listeners, came the screech of a real whistle. Lewis, nervous at the start of his monologue, was quick to react now:

> Couldn't even blow the whistle. "All right, line up." *Thpp* [sound of weak whistle] Never let you—
>
> WHHHHIIIIII [real whistle].
>
> And there he is now, right? He followed me here. Take this, Coach,

and he threw windmill punches, nice enough retort for the pressure he was under.*

Pressure, the kind TV brought, was what Jimmie Walker wanted. With TV, he insisted, his ebony splendor would rocket. Trouble was he couldn't get on the "tube." He was always a shade away.

Then Jack Paar put him on. Steve Landesberg was with Walker when Paar came backstage to reassure him. Jack told Walker not to worry, he'd do OK. "If he doesn't," said Landesberg, "he can always give you a shine."

That night, Walker got big laughs, and a rave from Paar. A few days later, brother Jim ran into an old chum from the South Bronx, who was surprised to see him on 8th Avenue. "What you doin' in the streets, man?" he asked. "You a stah."

He must have known something. For a man from the Lear-Yorkin TV tandem ("All in the Family"/ "Maude"/"Sanford and Son") was looking to cast the loosey-goosey eldest son in a black family sitcom due for early 1974. Walker, in his Paar shot, caught the man's eye—and his fancy. Jimmie was—as he predicted—whisked away to a starring role. "Good Times" was the name of the show. And good times they were. On a night in March 1974, Walker ap-

---

* Though not for "The Tonight Show." Lewis was advised he would not be asked back on—his style was too frenetic. He took it hard, and was not seen for a while. Then one night, he returned to the Improvisation, apparently undaunted.

peared on prime-time CBS. Switch the dial seconds after "Good Times" ended, and he was on Merv Griffin's program, introduced as a new stah.

It was not Lear-Yorkin who saw Bluestone. A policeman did—at Catch a Rising Star. The officer thought he was funny and invited him to perform at a policemen's banquet. It was progress. Twelve months before, Bluestone wouldn't have been asked to a pauper's ball.

In fact, he'd dropped out to work for the satirical magazine *National Lampoon*. His macabre touch was just right for a periodical whose avowed goal was, in Bluestone's words, "to combine intellectual pretention with raw sewage."

For the eight months he was there, he met standards. Word around the office was that his story on the sexual propensities of former President William Howard Taft ("The Oral Passions of . . .") had moved the Ohio Tafts to see if they could limit the issue's newsstand distribution.

Bluestone's anti-Christ "sermonettes" provoked a Catholic journal to call them "blasphemous":

> *The National Lampoon, a self-styled "humor" magazine, is currently printing a series of comic strips depicting such humorous scenes as a miniature Christ vomiting up a sacred host forced into His mouth by a priest of the "Archdiocese of Greater New York" as part of a TV-show miracle demonstration.*

The January 1973 *Lampoon* cover that depicted a dog with a gun up against its head and this notation —*If You Don't Buy This Magazine, We'll Kill This Dog*—was a Bluestone concept too. It drew the magazine's largest mail pull, much of it unamused. The issue was the *Lampoon's* best seller in 1973.

When he returned to the stage, he began to work looser. Soon he was doing paid dates. Passim's in Cambridge. The Great Southeast Music Hall in Atlanta. A policemen's bash hardly seemed a spot for a sacrilegious longhair comic. He went anyway.

It was held in the basement of a Manhattan church. Blue and gold streamers. Balloons. A buffet feed. Bluestone got up and looked the lawmen over and said,

> I don't believe I'm here and my wallet
> just got stolen,

cracking the cops up.

Months before, he did his jokes in apology. He had the croaker's pall about him, an eye that foresaw imminent doom. No more. The scaredy-cat look was almost gone.

> You mounted police have it knocked.
> No problem with traffic. Car gives you
> trouble, you have the horse shit on it.
> Guy mouths off, you send for a horse
> with diarrhea.

He gave them strokes, and they took to him. When he spoke of the educational influence in law enforcement, namely "chiropractic criminology—which is the science of rehabilitating criminals by damaging their backs," a cop quipped, "We've been doing that for years."

> Feel sorry for this guy's horse,

said Bluestone.

They roared at his regular material too. It remained to X-rated sentiment what Edgar Guest was to puppy-dog prose. His economy funeral plan, for instance, came with a eulogy from the sound track of *Death of A Salesman*.

> No matter who dies, you hear, "A lotta
> people liked Willy Loman."

> You go to the cemetery in chauffeured
> Toyotas.

> Get there, ya see the grave being dug by
> three German Shepherds.

> No inscription on the tombstone. They
> cut the deceased's name out of the phone
> book and paste it on.

> My brother was the highlight of the fu-
> neral. Comes wrecked. Tried to pass out
> joints with the deceased's name on it.

He was fast losing his inhibitions. When TV producer Greg Garrison, casting about for new comics to
introduce on a summer replacement show on NBC,
came by the Improvisation, Bluestone and others got
up to do their acts. A nerve-riddled night—big chance
for comic unknowns. On the floor, Bluestone was
working when a heckler interrupted. He knew what
to do now. A few swift lines and he put the cat away.
Then, rather than ignore the occasion and what was
at stake, he monkeyed with it. He turned to Garrison,
who was sitting with Nipsey Russell, and remarked,
"You know, Mr. Garrison. Most comics would have
become hostile. But not me. I thought I handled the
cocksucker rather well."

Years back it was Garrison who thought Klein was
not good enough for TV. Now Robert was past need-
ing the tube. The album sold just under thirty-nine
thousand copies in 1973—far fewer than expected.
But it gained a Grammy nomination and the recogni-
tion he wanted. On the college circuit, he was bona
fide, booked in concert at up to thirty-five hundred
dollars a night. His itinerary appeared in *Rolling
Stone*. In New York, he sold out Carnegie Hall. In
LA, he made a convert of the Troubadour's Weston.
At Buddah's urging, Weston let Klein open for singer
Leo Kottke. Business was good—and Kottke was not
the only reason. Afterwards, Weston mailed a two-
hundred-and-fifty-dollar bonus to the Rollins and
Joffe office, with a covering letter that gave Klein his
belated due.

Manager Morra got offers he couldn't refuse. One
afternoon, a call came from a young lady in Chicago.
She wanted Klein to perform at a private party she
was throwing. As she later wrote,

> *[It]* *will honor my boyfriend, who at 27*
> *years old, is graduating from college after*
> *dropping in and out of academia for sev-*
> *eral years.*

It sounded odd to Morra, who asked two thousand dollars, a sum he figured was out of her range. Price, it turned out, was no obstacle. Klein went to Chicago. He was flying high now—*loopdeloop-luderts* in the old Decatur Avenue idiom. He even had an offer of a teaching fellowship in comedy from Robert Brustein of the Yale Drama School.

In the early '50s, he'd stood on the sidewalks outside of the Paramount Theater in Times Square to wait for Martin and Lewis to appear at their dressing-room window. Dean and Jerry, after each show, stuck their heads out, scattered confetti and kibitzed with the crowds.

Twenty years later, he was in the dressing room of the Bijou in Philadelphia, between shows. He stood at a window, looking down on the street at lines forming to see him. He watched for a while, then slid the window up its runner and, ducking his head out, asked the crowd below who was at the Bijou.

Out of faces creased with smiles came his name.

Names were fugitive in the comic trade.

Hailed today, gone tomorrow.

In Dick Davy's apartment was a scrapbook in black leather with gilt borders. *presenting dick davy . . .* , it said in one corner.

Inside was a prints pastiche of a career. Newspaper features that ranged from the *Village Voice* to the LA *Times* to the scandalous *National Insider* ("I Make Negroes Laugh at Anti-Negro Jokes Says White Comedian"). There were album promos. A *Variety* review. Club advertisements (Slate Bros./NOW! That "Old Black Magic" Man BILLY DANIELS/plus: new comic DICK DAVY). Fan letters. A one-liner attributed to Davy in Earl Wilson's column. A post-card from Nat Hentoff who reviewed his album in *Hi-Fi/Stereo Review*.

The dates ran from 1965 to 1967. The stories were

part fiction. No mention of Davy's city roots or rabbinical father. Here he was an Arkansas rhubarb farmer. There he was from Evening Shade, Arkansas. In still another story, this sentence appeared: "At 18, he made an adventuresome leap to Arkansas State Teachers, then got into some trouble and had to leave the state."

And then the stories ceased save for one New York *Post* advertisement for the Schaefer Music Festival in Central Park in July 1970. *Frankie Valli and The Four Seasons/Dick Davy . . . SCHAEFER BEER . . . when you're having more than one.* It was on the final page of the scrapbook.

Like a damn warm bath the laughs were. But with the racially changed times, they'd stopped. It was not the whole story. A career was a calculus of comedic factors. Wit was not its only wisdom.

Davy remembered being heckled in Vancouver, British Columbia, for antiwar material. Most of the crowd got on him, shouted he was a traitor and a Commie. (One exception: an ex-truck driver/roofer named Tommy Chong, who came by after to shake hands with him.)

"And," Davy said, "I wasn't very good when somebody was very vicious. Don Rickles I ain't. . . . Somebody calls out something vicious that I don't feel is true but obviously is full of hatred, I get scared. Because that's a whole psychological thing with me. Whenever anybody accuses me of something, I always think I'm guilty, or at least I'm afraid of 'em anyway. I'm guilty about so many things, I figure that anybody lashes out at me, it must have been ones I missed out on. So it's almost . . . like I must be guilty."

In part, it was fear that kept him from trying to rally his career. Davy conceded he didn't stick to it. "I guess," he said, "I don't like to have to fight. I don't like to have to sell myself. I don't like to have to meet people and tell them how good I am and be told to wait around. I never got over the fear of rejection and the pain that comes from it. So I don't dare very greatly anymore. I don't have a thick skin enough for that."

He was back to teaching in the city school system

—in economically deprived neighborhoods. He talked out of the drawl sometimes.

Q: Do you run into any comics from Village days?

DAVY: No. I've been hibernating for four or five years. Living in East Harlem and going to the school and getting my kicks getting kids to laugh in class. I do stuff off the top of mah head or *they* funny sometimes. The kids are funny back with me. Funnier than I am with them.

Q: Do they know that you were a comic once?

DAVY: Not very often. Once in a while I find a kid that has my album. But that doesn't happen much. No, they just figure that I'm a little bit strange and I like it that way. "You sure you're a teacher?" I get that line. "Where'd you go to school?" They can't believe I went to college. Because I murder the language. And I go along with it. I tell 'em, "Well, they just let anybody teach in New York. I was walking along the street and they needed a teacher. I happened to be passing by and they say, 'Come on in, you're a big feller, we'll put you in the room with the kids.' " I mean I do some material, but then . . . they're much better than the Improvisation cause I can relax with them and . . . even if I ain't funny . . . whether I win or I lose, I still win because I'm putting in my time. And they're going to pay me the money at the end of the month. But it hurts to pay carfare, cab or something, to go down to a joint. You hang around forever. Like it's a big deal just to get on a damned stage to try out in front of a microphone and some people that's sitting in this club boozing. And you get up there and it's life or death for about, five or ten minutes to see if you can get them to laugh. And when it's all over, whether they laughed or they didn't laugh—ain't nothing to show for it. You gonna still ride home, in the middle of the night. And you're just going to be one of a whole lots out of a sad crop of hopefuls trying to get somewhere in show business. And you don't feel like you're worth shit.

Whereas in a school, I'm somebody. I'm a teacher. I'm putting in the time. Maybe I take the easy way out, but I like the kids and they're a much better audience than . . . They especially good audience because they hate school. I mean most of the school's a waste of time. The teacher's laying a whole lot of stuff on them that ain't going to do them any good even if they do learn it. Memorizing . . . regurgitate it back on some test. So here comes somebody like me along who don't give a damn whether they cut the class or whether they don't belong there. They say sometimes, "He don't belong in the class." I say, "Well, let him come in if he wants to come in. He must want to be here better than he be in the hall. Messing with some girl. Or writing on the wall. Let him come in." So I lose some that's supposed to be there and I get a whole lot that ain't supposed to be there. But they delighted, see, because how much humor do they run across during their math class. Teachers are a dull lot, right? So I got a sort of an audience that's ready for me. Much more so than one of 'em jaded crowds in some club that's boozing with some girls.

Q: Do you literally do routines?

DAVY: Yeah, well, I tell 'em how New York's a bad scene

> . . . with the FBI tapping your phones and the junkies breaking your bones. You stay in the house, get bugged. Go outside, get mugged. Ain't safe nowhere.
>
> 'at's why you see all them ladies— even the young girls got protection in their purses. They got hatpins and spray guns and si-reens for fellows they don't want grabbing them. And then for the fellow they do want, they got other kinds of protection, right? Any way you mess with them, they ready.

And you can do that with these kids. I'll try that out if they're listening or I'll do a whole thing called "The Cremation of Sam McGee" . . . a long poem I like. By Robert Service. I do a little poem . . . like I learned once from Sam Levenson. I make out like some kid wrote it. Try to encourage the kids to write poetry. "Anything you feel, you write it down. You become a poet."

Q: How do the kids react?

DAVY: Mostly they like it. They think I'm a natural from the South. . . . Funny, but like a girl from like say one of those islands . . . like Trinidad . . . they're very serious. Those black girls . . . and boys. So they don't think it's right to fool around in a class. They came to school to learn, right? So they just dismiss me as irrelevant to their career, or their future, or whatever supposed to be going on in school. We-eelll, you take whatever comes

. . . but I do what I need to and so far I've been getting away with it.

Months later, Davy asked a fellow he knew had he ever tried a hand at the jokes. He was looking for material. Thinking of a comeback, he reckoned.

Anything was possible in comedic crapshoot.

Remember Alan Bursky?

was the line on that once-upon teen sensation.

In a short season, the former Achilles Sambursky went from parking-lot attendant to TV hotshot to suspect goods.

Bursky never worked a paid date before he did "The Tonight Show," his first appearance of consequence. He'd gone in as a novelty and come out a talent.

So it seemed.

It turned out otherwise. Bursky took success too seriously. He got to posturing at it. He fired gag writer Monaghan and hired another act, paying several thousand dollars for it to a fellow comic (ret.) he used to steal from back when Bursky was a dirty word.

It still was. That hadn't changed. What had was Alan's luck. It went bad. He bungled the second shot on "The Tonight Show." The routine went like a hat down a windy street, just out of his reach. A case of bum timing.

His star fell. He was not ready. It showed when he hit the road. Right down the plumbing he went in Chicago, San Juan and Miami. Later, visiting New York, some nights he was shut out at the Improvisation. *Sorry. Tight tonight.*

On the heels of the fast-sinking Bursky came another prodigy, Freddie Prinze, a New Yorker whose parentage he referred to as Hunga-rican (Hungarian-Puerto Rican), a coupling he said came by chance.

They met in the subway. Picking each other's pocket.

Prinze was purported to be "nineteen." He had what Bursky did not: a point of view and material he had acquired in the approved way. He'd put in the hours on it, a regular at the Improvisation and Catch a Rising Star.

Prinze was a hit on the Paar Show and then on Carson's, successes that won him a TV pilot, "Chico and the Man." * Nobody minded. He had gone the route. No shortcuts. His act was the comic extension of him and not hand-me-down. Whether he could keep coming up with the lines remained to be seen.

As for Bursky: If he appeared to be a footnote in comic history, no one was saying it out loud.

The wheel turned.

. . . and turned.

The place used to be called Duke's Dilemma.

It drew a bad crowd. There were fistfights out front. Drug incidents. The landlord closed it up.

He gave it to Richie Havens to run, who revived the name it had had in the days when he'd performed on Macdougal. Cafe Wha?

Havens put rock acts in, and underbilled them with comics. Not all of them were new either. One night a pro who was at the Wha? a decade before heard his introduction with its big-time credits, came out and

> Thank you for announcing I've been to the heights and am now back to the depths.

And with the laughs starting to come, Adam Keefe went back to work.

---

* An irony: When Prinze relocated in LA for the pilot, he met another young comic looking to split rent. Kid name of Bursky. Prinze moved in awhile.

Index

369